MIGRATION, MINORITIES AND CITIZENSHIP

General Editors: Zig Layton-Henry, *Professor of Politics, University of Warwick*; and Danièle Joly, *Director, Centre for Research in Ethnic Relations, University of Warwick*

This series has been developed to promote books on a wide range of topics concerned with migration and settlement, immigration policy, refugees, the integration and engagement of minorities, dimensions of social exclusion, racism and xenophobia, ethnic mobilization, ethnicity and nationalism. The focus of the series is multidisciplinary and international. The series publishes both theoretical and empirical works based on original research. Priority is given to single-authored books but edited books of high quality are considered.

Titles include:

Naomi Carmon (*editor*)
IMMIGRATION AND INTEGRATION IN POST-INDUSTRIAL SOCIETIES
Theoretical Analysis and Policy-Related Research

Adrian Favell
PHILOSOPHIES OF INTEGRATION
Immigration and the Idea of Citizenship in France and Britain

Danièle Joly
HAVEN OR HELL?
Asylum Policies and Refugees in Europe

SCAPEGOATS AND SOCIAL ACTORS
The Exclusion and Integration of Minorities in Western and Eastern Europe

Simon Holdaway and Anne-Marie Barron
RESIGNERS? THE EXPERIENCE OF BLACK AND ASIAN POLICE OFFICERS

Jørgen S. Nielsen
TOWARDS A EUROPEAN ISLAM

John Rex
ETHNIC MINORITIES IN THE MODERN NATION STATE
Working Papers in the Theory of Multiculturalism and Political
Integration

Carl-Ulrik Schierup (*editor*)
SCRAMBLE FOR THE BALKANS
Nationalism, Globalism and the Political Economy of Reconstruction

Steven Vertovec and Ceri Peach (*editors*)
ISLAM IN EUROPE
The Politics of Religion and Community

Östen Wahlbeck
KURDISH DIASPORAS
A Comparative Study of Kurdish Refugee Communities

Migration, Minorities and Citizenship
Series Standing Order ISBN 0–333–71047–9
(*outside North America only*)

You can receive future titles in this series as they are published by placing a standing order.
Please contact your bookseller or, in case of difficulty, write to us at the address below with
your name and address, the title of the series and the ISBN quoted above.

Customer Services Department, Macmillan Distribution Ltd
Houndmills, Basingstoke, Hampshire RG21 6XS, England

Kurdish Diasporas

A Comparative Study of Kurdish Refugee Communities

Östen Wahlbeck
Åbo Akademi University and
Institute of Migration
Turku, Finland

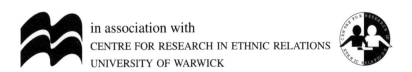

in association with
CENTRE FOR RESEARCH IN ETHNIC RELATIONS
UNIVERSITY OF WARWICK

First published in Great Britain 1999 by
MACMILLAN PRESS LTD
Houndmills, Basingstoke, Hampshire RG21 6XS and London
Companies and representatives throughout the world

A catalogue record for this book is available from the British Library.

ISBN 0–333–75011–X

First published in the United States of America 1999 by
ST. MARTIN'S PRESS, INC.,
Scholarly and Reference Division,
175 Fifth Avenue, New York, N.Y. 10010

ISBN 0–312–22067–7

Library of Congress Cataloging-in-Publication Data
Wahlbeck, Östen, 1965–
Kurdish diasporas : a comparative study of Kurdish refugee
communities / Östen Wahlbeck.
      p.   cm. — (Migration, minorities, and citizenship)
Includes bibliographical references (p.   ) and index.
ISBN 0–312–22067–7 (cloth)
1. Kurds—Relocation—Great Britain.   2. Kurds—Relocation–
–Finland.   3. Refugees, Kurdish.   4. Kurds—Politics and government.
I. Title.   II. Series.
DS59.K86W34   1999
305.891'597041—dc21   98–44644
                                                              CIP

This book is printed on paper suitable for recycling and made from fully managed and sustained forest sources.

10   9   8   7   6   5   4   3   2   1
08   07   06   05   04   03   02   01   00   99

Printed and bound in Great Britain by
Antony Rowe Ltd, Chippenham, Wiltshire

For Ella

Contents

List of Figures and Tables

Figure

Table

Acknowledgements

First of all, I would like to express my gratitude to all the Kurdish refugees and organizations who helped me and gave me information during this study. I want to thank you for your friendship, hospitality and patience during the fieldwork. Unfortunately, because of the situation in Kurdistan today, you all have to remain anonymous.

This book is based on research made for a PhD dissertation at the University of Warwick in the UK. I am grateful to my supervisors, Dr Danièle Joly at the Centre for Research in Ethnic Relations and Professor Robin Cohen at the Department of Sociology, whose expertise in this area of study was invaluable. The Institute of Migration in Turku, Finland, provided me with the space and time needed to finish this book. Inspiration and support was given by both staff and students at these two institutions.

Many other persons have been helpful in many different ways and at different stages of the research process. I especially want to thank Professor Robert Burgess, Professor Emeritus Elizabeth Colson, Dr Peter Fairbrother, Dr Clive Harris, Professor Amir Hassanpour, Dr Mark Johnson, Dr Ronald Kaye, Professor Zig Layton-Henry, Dr Mike McDaid, Dr Philip Muus, Professor Emeritus John Rex, Professor Tom Sandlund, Professor Carl-Ulrik Schierup, Mr Omar Sheikhmous and Professor Matti Similä.

The valuable collections in the libraries at the School of Oriental and African Studies in London and at the Refugee Studies Programme at Oxford University were of great help during this project. Support for the completion of this study was provided by the Academy of Finland and the KONE Foundation. I am also grateful for the support given from Agneta och Carl-Erik Olins stipendiefond, Svenska Kulturfonden, Oskar Öflunds Stiftelse and the Overseas Research Student Award.

Abbreviations and Glossary

DSS	Department of Social Security
ELR	Exceptional Leave to Remain
ERNK	Enîya Rizgarîya Netewa Kurdistan, National Liberation Front of Kurdistan
KCC	Kurdish Cultural Centre
KDP	Kurdish Democratic Party (Iraq)
KDP-Iran	Kurdish Democratic Party of Iran
KWA	Kurdistan Workers' Association
PKK	Partîya Karkerên Kurdistan, Kurdistan Workers' Party
PUK	Patriotic Union of Kurdistan
[t]	Translation
UNHCR	United Nations High Commissioner for Refugees
Newroz:	Kurdish New Year (21 March)
Peshmerga:	Kurdish guerrilla soldier. The term is used mainly in southern Kurdistan (i.e. Iraq and Iran)

Introduction

According to the United Nations (UNHCR, 1997), there were 14 million refugees world-wide in 1995. In addition, a further 30 million persons were displaced within the borders of their own countries. Most refugees stay in neighbouring countries, but a small number are forced to seek safety far away from their countries of origin. This book is about Kurdish refugees from Turkey, Iraq and Iran. Since the 1970s increasing numbers of Kurds have been forced to flee the various conflicts in Kurdistan. Today, some of these refugees are present in European countries. Contemporary changes in population movements have led to a situation where countries previously unaffected by immigration have received increased numbers of refugees and migrants. These global changes have also altered migration and refugee flows to countries with a long history of immigration (Castles and Miller, 1993). These new population movements and the consequent establishment of new migrant and refugee communities are relatively little studied phenomena.

The arguments presented in this book are based on a study of Kurdish refugee communities in Britain and Finland. Britain, which for a long time experienced immigration and emigration within the British Commonwealth, has received increased numbers of refugees in recent years from countries with which Britain has very few historical ties. Finland, which traditionally has been a country of emigration, turned into one of immigration during the 1980s. The two countries of settlement are in significant respects different and this study aims, from a sociological and comparative point of view, to analyse the process of 'integration' of newly arrived refugees into these two different societies. The refugees' relation to the countries of origin from which they were forced to flee is also of interest here. Hence, this book describes the social organization of the Kurdish refugee communities and how this is influenced by the refugees' relation to the country of origin on the one hand and to the country of settlement on the other. The concept of diaspora is utilized here as an analytical framework, which also has a wider theoretical significance within the area of international migration and ethnic relations.

My interest in questions relating to refugee resettlement and

1

'integration' first emerged during the work on my MA thesis (Wahlbeck, 1992) which discusses Finnish opinions towards refugees. Following the completion of my MA degree I worked for a year as a social worker with responsibility for the resettlement of Iranian Kurdish refugees in a small Finnish municipality. During these two periods of my life I frequently had to confront the question of how refugees 'adapt to life in Finland'. This question often seemed to assume that the integration of refugees into the wider society is dependent on the refugees' own cultural and social resources, or even their own choices about whether or not to 'adapt'. I also noticed a tendency to emphasize the importance of assumed cultural differences in the process of 'refugee integration'. It was commonly assumed that refugees had a fundamentally different culture which could not easily be combined with Finnish cultural values and it was believed that this would inevitably lead to various cultural conflicts.

However, during my job as a refugee resettlement worker I found that the refugees in the municipality were generally eager to become integrated into the wider society. It soon became clear to me that the biggest obstacles to the integration of the refugees were by no means associated with their own cultural 'luggage' or with the exercise of 'free choice' on their part in respect of adaptation. Instead, the obstacles seemed to be related to the receiving society itself. Factors like unemployment, social isolation, discrimination and racism seemed to play a far bigger role in the process of integration than was usually understood to be the case by the wider Finnish population. At the same time the importance of cultural differences and conflicts seemed to be widely exaggerated.

Another issue to draw my attention was that of the retention of pre-migration social networks among refugee communities. When it comes to the issue of resettlement, it is commonly assumed that refugees have lost everything they have had and that, in a way, they have to start their lives all over again. This approach, so dominant in refugee resettlement discourse, does not acknowledge that refugees may have resources and social networks of their own. My own experiences as a social worker suggested to me that, right from the beginning, refugees are able to set up well-functioning social networks through which advice and information can be obtained. Almost immediately upon arrival in Finland the refugees were able to get in touch with compatriots, friends and relatives in Finland, Europe and Kurdistan. Rather than being individuals totally torn away from their social settings, refugees are able, at least to some extent, to retain pre-migration social organizations and networks. These contradictions between my own experiences with refugees, on the one hand, and the discourse dominating refugee resettlement, on the other, provided the starting point for this research. As a result, I decided to study how refugees themselves experience the process of integration into their new countries of settlement. My aim in doing so was to study, from a sociological point of view, the relationships which newly arrived refugees have, both with their countries of settlement and with their countries of origin.

An initial aim of the study has been to develop a theoretical framework that would make it possible to avoid some of the common misunderstandings and dangers in refugee research and political discourses. In particular, the study aims to avoid three common pitfalls in refugee research. The first is the danger that the exoticism or cultural distinctiveness of refugee groups is excessively emphasized. This approach can reinforce racist and culturalist discourses which define refugees as the 'other' and can support various exclusionary policies. The second danger is to see refugees as a 'problem'. This is often the case in studies dealing with assimilation and integration from the point of view of the receiving society. Refugees are seen as individuals who can choose, more or less freely, whether or not to 'adapt', and to the extent that they resist integration they are defined as a 'problem'. This approach fails to recognize the profound influence of social structures on social relations. The third and opposite danger is to overemphasize the importance of social structures. Refugees are regarded as powerless victims of racism and as totally ruled by social structures. This view overlooks the refugees' own resources and the fact that social relations consist of both structure and agency. The challenge for refugee research is to strike a balance among these three extreme positions.

My initial assumption was that theories of ethnic relations could be used to highlight these issues. However, during my fieldwork it soon became clear that refugee issues could not be fully understood with what might loosely be called an 'ethnic relations' approach. Rather, as I will attempt to show in this book, an understanding of refugee issues needs a more sophisticated conceptual framework. Thus, the aim of this book is to present a conceptual framework which besides explaining the empirical findings in this study also has a wider relevance for refugee studies. In this respect it is argued that the concept of diaspora is a useful tool for an understanding of the social organization of refugee communities.

The aim is to describe from a sociological point of view the processes which influence the social organization and integration of the Kurdish refugee communities. However, this book seeks not only to be a descriptive study, but also to develop the concept of diaspora as a theoretical tool. The theories employed serve as interpretative frameworks which can further a sociological understanding of the social organization of refugee communities in the countries of settlement. In terms of Burgess's (1984) classification of presentations of field data, this study is neither a descriptive account of the Kurdish refugee communities nor a substantive theoretical account of refugee integration and diasporas. Instead this book will furnish what Burgess calls an analytic description whereby the conceptual scheme used (in this case the concept of diaspora) is developed on the basis of the data that are obtained.

The methods used in the study were traditional ethnographic field research methods as outlined by Burgess (1984) and Schatzman and Strauss (1973). The fieldwork was guided by the aim to understand the refugees' own perspective on the issues under study. Semi-structured interviews and field research methods were utilized in order to achieve this objective. This choice of methods also supported the aim of avoiding some of the earlier mentioned common pitfalls in refugee research. Since I became acquainted with many Kurds during my previous job as a social worker I wanted to concentrate the study on Kurdish refugees and their experiences. (However, the empirical material was collected almost two years after I finished my job as a social worker.) The research was planned and carried out in close cooperation with Kurdish refugees and their associations. I also made a deliberate decision to avoid contacts with the authorities in the two countries of settlement.

The comparative perspective in this research required the collection of a good deal of empirical material. The social organization of the Kurdish refugee communities was studied in relation to both the refugees' society of origin and society of settlement. In order to be able to investigate these relations from a comparative point of view it was necessary to have at least two countries of origin and two countries of settlement. The two countries of settlement chosen for this study were England and Finland. These two locations were regarded as sufficiently different in order to study the influence of the society of settlement on the refugee communities. As described in Chapter 3, these countries can provide examples of two different models of refugee resettlement. The fieldwork in the receiving countries was carried out between August and December 1994 in Finland and between January and September 1995 in England. In the end, rather than looking at only two countries of origin, Kurdish refugees from three countries of origin were studied: Turkey, Iraq and Iran. This selection was influenced by some of the Kurds themselves who wanted to emphasize that all Kurds should be seen as one single entity. However, as described in this book, Kurdish refugees actually constitute a very heterogeneous group. This diversity of the empirical material provided a good opportunity to study the general social processes connected to the integration of refugees. Thus, the book is able to present a conceptual framework which, besides describing these specific cases, also has a wider significance for refugee studies in general.

The fieldwork consisted of different types of interviews and participant observation in a wide variety of settings. Roughly described, the fieldwork had two focuses. The first focus has been on 50 semi-structured interviews which were carried out among a sample of refugees from Turkey, Iraq and Iran (28 in England and 22 in Finland). In order to study the experiences of Kurdish refugees in the country of settlement the interviewees were adult refugees who had lived in the country of settlement between two and ten years (the terms 'interviewee' and 'respondent' refer to persons who took part in the semi-structured interviews, while the term 'informant' is used for all other persons who gave information during the course of the fieldwork). The second focus has been on Kurdish associations and the importance of these for the Kurdish refugees. All Kurdish associations in the two countries have been studied. Several different languages were used during the fieldwork. In this book a translation of an interview statement, made by me or by an interpreter, is indicated with '[t]' after the quotation. The fieldwork and methods are described in more detail in a separate appendix.

Chapter 1 discusses concepts and theories which are of relevance in this area of study. The chapter concludes with a suggestion for a conceptual framework for understanding how the social organization of refugee communities is related to both the country of origin and the country of settlement. The societies of origin and the political developments in Kurdistan are described in Chapter 2. Chapter 3 offers brief descriptions of the two receiving societies and analyses the different refugee resettlement policies in Finland and England. The following three chapters present the results from the fieldwork. In Chapter 4 the refugees' experiences in their new

country of settlement are described, while Chapter 5 concentrates
on describing the process of integration. The refugee associations
and the transnational Kurdish diaspora are discussed in Chapter 6.
These three main chapters discuss the relation to the country of
origin on the one hand and the country of exile on the other, as
well as the influence these have on the refugees and their communities. The chapters relate the results to the previously presented
theoretical and conceptual issues. A final summary of the results
and arguments is presented in Chapter 7.

Some issues which this book is not able to address have to be
mentioned. First of all, the aim is not to describe Kurdish society,
history or politics. During the fieldwork it was repeatedly suggested
to me that I should concentrate on the problems in Kurdistan rather
than on the Kurds in exile, since 'Kurdistan is where the real problems
are'. However, within the scope of this study it was not possible to
focus on the situation in Kurdistan. In fact, there are already a
number of books about Kurdish history, nationalism and politics,
as well as numerous reports on the human rights situation in
Kurdistan. On the other hand, an understanding of the refugees'
situation in exile does require familiarity with the reasons for their
flight. Therefore, Chapter 2 contains a brief description of Kurdish
history and the political situation in the three countries of origin.
(For those who wish to gain a more thorough knowledge of these
issues this chapter also includes plenty of references to the literature available on the subject.)

Secondly, this book does not deal with refugees' psychological
adaptation to life in exile. Rather, the aim is to study the processes of integration and the social organization of the refugee
communities from a *sociological* point of view. Social and psychological processes are of course related to one another. However, a
study of adaptation, identity formation and other psychological and
social-psychological processes related to refugee resettlement would
have required a totally different approach and different methods
to those used in this research. Thus, this book is focused upon the
wider sociological and 'macro' perspectives, rather than on the
psychological processes related to refugee integration.

Before concluding this introduction, it is necessary to explain
some terminological issues pertaining to this study. Generally, this
book uses the terms and definitions used by the Kurdish informants and interviewees themselves, rather than using any 'objective
criteria' or some other externally imposed definitions. The book

aims, as far as possible, to describe the Kurdish refugees' own points of view, since it can be argued that their definition of the situation is the one which is of greatest sociological interest.

The term 'refugee' is a legal term with a clearly defined meaning within international law. However, here the term is used primarily as a sociological term. The legal definition is often too narrow to apply as part of a sociological approach (partly because the implementation of the United Nations Refugee Convention is inconsistent and responds to political shifts in the receiving countries). In this study the term refugee includes all those who feel that they are refugees, which in practice includes persons with full refugee status, quota refugees, asylum seekers, and persons with some of the 'B-statuses' given to asylum seekers. These more specific descriptions are of course also used where appropriate.

Some Kurds prefer to use the expressions 'North Kurdistan' or 'North-West Kurdistan' rather than Turkey, 'South Kurdistan' rather than Iraq and 'East Kurdistan' rather than Iran. For the most part, this book reproduces the expressions used by the informants themselves. In the general parts of the text I have chosen to use the terms 'Turkey', 'Iraq' and 'Iran', since these are more easily understood by the reader. For similar reasons the expressions 'Kurd from Turkey' and 'Kurd from Iraq' are preferred. However, the use of 'Turkish Kurd' and 'Iraqi Kurd' is avoided since these concepts may be considered offensive and contradictory. An exception is the term 'Iranian Kurd', which is generally accepted and widely used by the Kurds from Iran, and for this reason this term is also employed here.

The use of the geographical term 'England' is in this book an intentional choice. The research has been conducted in London and Birmingham and so is located in England. However, the term 'United Kingdom' is used when referring to the state which gives asylum to the refugees. United Kingdom is a shorter name for The United Kingdom of Great Britain and Northern Ireland, while Great Britain includes England, Scotland and Wales, but not Northern Ireland.

1 Inclusion and Exclusion of Refugees: Rethinking Concepts and Theories

A broad perspective is required in order to develop sound theoretical approaches applicable to refugees. Richmond (1988, 1993, 1994) argues that refugee theory should be seen as a part of wider migration theory. However, it is possible to go further than this and argue that general theories of ethnic relations are necessary in order to understand the social processes involved in the integration of refugees into the receiving society. This chapter explains the central concepts and theories utilized in this book. A sociological point of view is adopted in this book in order to study the processes which influence the social organization[1] of the Kurdish refugee communities in exile. The book concerns itself with refugees' specific experiences and social situation. Thus, the chapter concentrates on those discussions within the research area of international migration and ethnic relations which have a relevance for a study of the inclusion and exclusion of refugees in the country of settlement.

REFUGEE THEORY

According to international law, a refugee is a person who 'owing to well-founded fear of being persecuted for reasons of race, religion, nationality, membership of a particular social group or political opinion, is outside the country of his [sic] nationality' (United Nations, 1954: 152). From a sociological point of view it is important to note that such a person belongs to a group of people which has a very distinctive relationship with both the country it has been forced to flee from and the country where it is involuntarily settled. As Kunz argues: 'It is the reluctance to uproot oneself, and the absence of positive original motivations to settle elsewhere, which characterizes all refugee decisions and distinguishes the refugee from the voluntary migrants' (Kunz, 1973: 130). This book attempts to describe the special relationships that refugees have

8

with both the country of origin and the country of settlement.

'Refugee studies' has recently developed into an independent research domain with its own institutions, journals and discourse. As the research overviews by Stein (1981b), Escalona and Black (1995) and Srinivasan (1995) indicate, there is an abundance of literature on refugees, but only a small number of publications are sociological studies and even fewer consider theoretical questions relating to refugees' situation in the receiving countries. One weakness with refugee research is that most research 'has been tactical, *ad hoc*, diffuse and reactive' (Robinson, 1993: 6). In addition, the existing empirical studies have to a great extent been uninformed by general sociological theory and the experiences of refugees are rarely distinguished from those of other migrants (Richmond, 1988). Similar arguments are presented by Gold (1992) who finds that studies in the ethnographic sociological tradition are rare, and that policy-oriented research has dominated the field at the expense of independent, holistic scholarship. Key concepts like 'identity' and 'culture', which are both widely debated and held to be problematic in the social sciences, are too often used in an uninformed and confusing way in refugee research (Steen, 1992; Malkki, 1995).

Many of the few theoretical contributions that exist in the area of forced migration have developed typologies to distinguish between different migration movements. Zolberg, Suhrke and Aguayo (1989) identify refugees as either activists, targets or victims. Kunz (1973) distinguishes free migrants from refugee settlers, and furthermore makes a distinction between anticipatory and acute refugee movements. Richmond (1988, 1993, 1994), however, argues that a distinction between voluntary and involuntary migration is of doubtful validity since all migration movements in various degrees and forms include different constraints. Instead he is, inspired by structuration theory within sociology, suggesting an elaborate typology of several forms of proactive and reactive migrations.

Hein (1993), in an overview of the discussion about the differences between refugees and migrants, argues that from a sociological point of view it is only in their relation to the state, whether in country of origin, during flight, or in the country of asylum, that refugees are distinguished from ordinary migrants. Quite correctly he concludes that 'refugee status is a relationship to the state that takes a number of forms during the process of uprooting, migration and adaptation' (Hein, 1993: 55).

There are authors who specifically discuss refugees' integration into the society of settlement. For example, Stein (1981a) and Vasquez (1989) describe how over time refugees pass through different stages in their psychological relation to life in exile. However, Malkki (1995) argues that there is reason to question the implicit functionalism in refugee studies which has influenced the understanding of the process of integration and adaptation. 'Again and again, one finds in this literature the assumption that to become uprooted and removed from a national community is automatically to lose one's identity, traditions, and culture' (Malkki, 1995: 508). As demonstrated in this book, the process of integration is more complex than is usually understood among researchers and practitioners of refugee resettlement.

Joly (1996) emphasizes that there still is a need for more research in the area of how refugees relate to the country of settlement and how the refugee experience will distinguish them from other migrants. She also argues that refugee adaptation is not just a matter of time; instead 'the refugees' pattern of group formation and social interaction with the receiving society must be examined in relation to their position within and *vis-à-vis* the structure of conflict in the society of origin' (Joly, 1995a: 27). As Joly (1996) points out, Egon Kunz (1971, 1973, 1981) was one of the few authors who made an attempt to present a refugee theory that bridges the gap between country of origin and country of settlement. Kunz argued that different types of refugees show different patterns of integration in the country of exile. Unfortunately, his model is not easily applied to empirical studies since his elaborate classifications are only vaguely defined in a short article (Kunz, 1981).[2]

A problem, connected to all theories developing different descriptive categorizations of refugees, is that a mere description of different cases is not sufficient if one wants to understand the social processes behind the categories. The social processes are better understood by a more qualitative and ethnographic approach. There are a number of interesting ethnographic studies which have described refugee communities in exile from a sociological or anthropological point of view. These studies often investigate refugees within a context taking into account both the country of origin and the country of settlement. Politically active refugees have been studied in the cases of Vietnamese refugees in Paris (Bousquet, 1991), Ukrainian refugees in Canada (Luciuk, 1986), Latin American refugees in Sweden (Lundberg, 1989) and Tamil refugees in Switzerland (McDowell, 1996). A comparative perspective has been used by

Gold (1992) in his study of Vietnamese and Soviet Jewish refugees in California, and by Steen (1992) in her study of Sri Lankan Tamils in Denmark and England. Furthermore, Kay (1987) has added an important gender perspective in her study of Chilean refugees in Scotland. All these studies describe how the refugee communities display a political and social orientation towards the country of origin. In many cases political events and conflicts 'at home' continue to influence and often seriously divide the communities. It can be argued that this pattern is different from the relationship other migrants have with their countries of origin. Paradoxically enough, it looks as if refugee communities are greatly divided, usually along political lines, at the same time as the communities often contain large resources for ethnic or political mobilization because of the refugees' similar backgrounds and life histories. Thus, one of the questions this book discusses is to what extent the politicization of the refugee community is a help or a hindrance for refugees in their new country of settlement.

CONCEPTUALIZING INCLUSION

It can be argued that refugee studies cannot on their own provide sufficient theoretical guidance for a sociological study of refugees in the country of settlement. There is a need for more adequate theories and clearly defined concepts which could describe the specific experiences of refugees. Thus, one also needs to look at theoretical traditions in the wider area of international migration and ethnic relations. Within these research traditions one can find a number of theories and concepts describing the inclusion and exclusion of migrants. The processes and discourses that establish a difference between 'us' and 'them' are common in all societies, but they take very different forms depending on the social circumstances. Nevertheless, a shared feature is that by defining the 'other' we are also defining who we are ourselves. The following sections will discuss some of the concepts and theories which have been used to conceptualize various forms of inclusion and exclusion of refugees and immigrants. The presentation will first concentrate on three key concepts, assimilation, acculturation and integration.

Assimilation

According to the *Collins Dictionary of Sociology,* assimilation is 'the process in which a minority group adopts the values and patterns of behaviour of a majority group or host culture, ultimately becoming absorbed by the majority group' (Jary and Jary, 1991: 31–2). However, a definition of assimilation should also take into account that this is a process which can affect both sides in the relation, the majority may also change its values, patterns of behaviour and culture. This type of process is exemplified in the American debate about the 'melting pot' at the beginning of the century when it was argued that all immigrants in the United States would assimilate into each other and become 'American'. One of the most influential American sociologists advocating an assimilationist theory was Robert E. Park, one of the leading scholars in the so-called Chicago school within sociology. Park developed a model he called the 'race relations cycle'. The final outcome in this cycle is assimilation, where people see each other as individuals and not only as members of different groups (Park, 1950; Park and Burgess, 1930). Hence, assimilation comprises an inclusion of individuals into the society at large. A society based on assimilation does not, however, include diverse cultures or separate ethnic groups in the way a multicultural society does. Today it is obvious that assimilation seldom is established in the way envisaged in Park's race relations cycle. In the USA, for example, this was first described by Glazer and Moynihan (1963). They argued that ethnicity remained important in the United States and that ethnic groups largely become political interest groups.

The assimilationist discourse was also dominant in Britain during the early post-war years. When the post-war migrants started to arrive in the UK it was commonly assumed that they would assimilate and/or integrate into British society if they stayed for a longer time. It was thought that the racism that existed was 'caused by the "strangeness" of the immigrants, and that with the acculturation and eventual assimilation of the immigrants, or their children, the issue of racism would disappear' (Anthias and Yuval-Davis, 1992: 158). The belief in an easy integration into British society was also common among the immigrants themselves. Most immigrants from the so-called New Commonwealth were English-speaking British citizens and there was no reason why they would not be welcome in Britain. Assimilation policies were dominant until the early 1960s. Already in the late 1950s it began to be apparent that the process of assimilation did not work as smoothly as was earlier hoped. The immigrants were met by increased hostility and an apparent and open racism in the early post-war years (Rex and Tomlinson, 1979).

Although it is clear today that complete assimilation rarely occurs, it is still a key concept. In a discussion of Gordon's (1964, 1978) well-known theory of assimilation, Yinger (1985) argues that there are four variables which can be seen as separate but interdependent subprocesses of assimilation: integration (structural aspect), acculturation (cultural aspect), identification (psychological aspect) and amalgamation (biological aspect). Yinger's definitions of these four concepts seem to be logical and useful. However, the use of the concept of assimilation as a general term encompassing these four concepts is not unanimously accepted.

Acculturation

Acculturation can be understood as 'a process in which contacts between different cultural groups lead to the acquisition of new cultural patterns by one, or perhaps both, group(s), with the adoption of all or parts of the other's culture' (Jary and Jary, 1991: 3). As mentioned above, Gordon (1964, 1978) and Yinger (1985) also describe acculturation as the cultural aspect of assimilation.

Another way of using the concept of acculturation can be found within the area of social-psychology in Berry's (1988) often quoted acculturation model. Here acculturation is seen as the process in which 'individuals negotiate their way into life in a plural society' (Berry, 1988: 2). Although I will not use this definition of acculturation, the model still includes a useful distinction between the concepts of assimilation and integration. Berry sees the difference between assimilation and integration in the individual's degree of retention of identity. An integrated person from a minority can keep his/her minority identity but if a person is assimilated he/she will have the same identity as the majority. I find this to be a more useful and precise definition of assimilation than the wider interpretation suggested by Yinger.

Integration

As mentioned earlier, integration should be seen as describing a *structural* process, rather than individual assimilation or cultural acculturation. Integration as a structural aspect means that a person can keep his or her distinct identity and belong to an ethnic minority group, rather than assimilate, and at the same time be a structural part of the wider society. A society in which integration, and not assimilation, is the dominant pattern of inclusion is often a multicultural society, where people are usually regarded as living in different communities.

The concept of community needs clarification before some of the other theoretical issues can be discussed. A community can be described as 'any set of social relationships operating within certain boundaries, locations or territories' (Jary and Jary, 1991: 97). These social relationships do not necessarily have to operate within geographical boundaries but can also exist at a more abstract and ideological level. This concept is often used as a translation of *Gemeinschaft* (Tönnies, 1970). Since community is a term with positive connotations it has been much used and 'it has been suggested that the concept is one of the most difficult and controversial in modern society' (Jary and Jary, 1991: 97–8).

If one talks about the process of integration it has to be clear into what community the integration is supposed to happen. One of the first sociologists who tried to tackle this issue was Raymond Breton (1964) who argued that immigrant integration is possible in at least three different directions: within the majority community, within another ethnic minority group, or within the immigrants' own ethnic group. According to Breton, the integration can happen in one, two or three directions at the same time and finally, it is also possible for the immigrant to be unintegrated. Furthermore, he argues that the ability of the different communities to integrate immigrants largely depends on the institutional completeness of the community. Breton's framework is obviously an oversimplification. The process of integration is not a clear-cut and straight-line process. There are many ways of being integrated into society and in some situations one may be more integrated than in others. The concept presupposes a group of people who are being integrated into another social formation. However, in practice it is often difficult to identify these social groups and formations as well as their boundaries. Actually, if one takes a post-modernist stance one could probably argue that nobody is fully integrated into our so-called post-modern society. Since the whole concept of community is imprecise and ambiguous it is obvious that a unitary and homogenous 'majority community' does not exist. Furthermore, another interesting question is who defines the minority, which is usually supposed to change in order to become more integrated. The concept of integration often represents the point of view of the dominant majority and contributes to the creation of a 'we' who belong and 'the others' who do not belong (Schierup, 1987; Miles, 1993; Ekholm, 1994).

Given the fact that there are no precise definitions of integration or apparent ways in which it could be measured it is not surprising that recent books on the subject avoid defining the concept altogether. None of the contributors in *Avenues to Integration* (Delle Donne, 1995) or *Immigration and Integration in Post-Industrial Societies* (Carmon, 1996) offers an exact definition of integration. Occasionally it is not even clear in these edited books if integration is seen as a structural or psychological process. Because of the problems with the concept of integration this book will not use the concept as if it represented an absolute measurable phenomenon. Instead, the concept of integration used here describes tendencies in the structural aspects of the process by which refugees become part of social groups and institutions in society.

MULTICULTURALISM

In Britain, multiculturalism became an issue from the 1960s onwards and followed the more assimilationist policies that had been predominant since the war. This change in policy was largely an answer to the problems of racism, discrimination and lack of integration among the newly arrived immigrants (Anthias and Yuval-Davis, 1992; Rex and Tomlinson, 1979). The British multicultural political discourse was characterized by notions such as cultural diversity, equality of opportunity and tolerance (Rex, 1994). These notions of liberal and cultural pluralism were also the dominant perspectives in the academic 'race-relations' discourse until the end of the 1970s (Denney, 1983).

Multiculturalism is today a much used, and abused, concept, despite the fact that it is an imprecise concept that raises a number of theoretical questions (cf. Vertovec, 1996; Samad, 1997). Firstly, this concept describes a notion of a society marked by cultural pluralism. This means that the concept implies both inclusion and exclusion at the same time: people belonging to the same society but at the same time forming different cultural groups. When we look at present day societies we soon notice that almost all societies are, to various degrees, multicultural. In all contemporary states we find different ethnic minorities and subcultures. Actually, multiculturalism seems to be more the rule than the exception. A second problem connected with the concept of multiculturalism is that it is a political concept, usually with strong positive connotations. This means that the concept is ambiguous and its meaning shifts depending on the situation, thus one has to be careful when it is used in a scientific discussion. A third problem with the term multiculturalism concerns the concept of culture itself. There seems to be disagreement about what this 'culture', of which furthermore there are supposed to be multiples, really is and what its relation to other social phenomena might be.

The sociologist John Rex has tried to define the multicultural value-standpoint. According to him we first of all have to make a distinction between equality, which is a quite different value-standpoint, and multiculturalism. Logically speaking, the multicultural society must mean a society in which people are not equally but differently treated. Equality is of course a noble goal in itself, but to pretend that it has something to do with multiculturalism can only create fuzziness (Rex, 1996). One way of clarifying this distinction is to look at some of the studies that are made about the 'plural society'. Both the classical studies made by Furnivall (1939) and M. G. Smith (1965) describe colonial or post-colonial societies which are far from equal or harmonious and institutionally divided between different ethnic groups. Rex argues that the ideal multicultural society instead should be a society 'which is unitary in the public domain but which encourages diversity in what are thought of as private or communal matters' (Rex, 1996: 15). By dividing society into these two domains we avoid confusing the ideal multicultural society with the undesirable colonial variants of pluralism.

The institutions of law, politics and economy belong to the public domain of society. In the multicultural society all citizens are equally integrated and have equality in these institutions. In the private domain, on the other hand, one finds matters relating to the family, to morality and to religion. In a multicultural society there is a diversity and cultural pluralism in these matters. There are areas of society, like education, which intrude into both domains and these are areas where conflicts might occur and where some kinds of compromise have to be found. However, even in the absence of different cultures society is by no means unitary. There will always be conflicts in society, but societies are also able to produce institutions to deal with these conflicts (Rex, 1996). The concept of a multicultural society understood in this way also relates to the concept of integration. People might be integrated into society at a structural level (that is, the public domain) and at the same time keep their own culture and identity. The concept of assimilation, on the other hand, would presuppose that people would give up their separate identities and cultures.

The implementation of multicultural policies in immigrant countries has, however, occasionally supported differential integration in the public domain as well. Ålund and Schierup (1991) and Schierup (1992, 1994) demonstrate that the Swedish official multiculturalist policy has indirectly supported a culturalist construction of new discriminatory boundaries. The welfare bureaucracy in Sweden has undertaken to construct an organized multicultural society, and thereby it has created a society divided by artificial cultural boundaries. Consequently, multicultural policies can reinforce divisions and inequalities in society. This analysis is also applicable to British society. The British case is extensively discussed by Anthias and Yuval-Davis (1992), who describe how the racialized boundaries have been created in different contexts.

Multicultural policies presume that there are easily recognizable communities which have clear cultural boundaries and constitute viable ethnic communities. These policies have also played a part in the racialization and culturalization of differences between groups in society. Among refugee communities it becomes even clearer than among other ethnic minorities that there are no clear and simple unitary ethnic communities. For example, the earlier-mentioned political disagreements between refugees seem to be a typical feature of refugee communities. Thus, multicultural policies presuming that easily recognizable communities do exist are not always the most suitable for refugee resettlement programmes. The relation between the British multicultural discourse and refugee resettlement policies is discussed in more detail in Chapter 3.

An easy answer to the dilemmas of multiculturalism would be to abolish notions about common cultures or ethnic groups and only see people as individuals. However, this individualism leads to a neglect of structures. It is a fact that people are divided into different social groups and also see themselves as belonging to different social groups. There might be 'hidden' practices and ideologies in society which lead to discrimination against people on the grounds of their membership of different groups. An individualistic approach is not able to take these kinds of structural disadvantages into account.

Hence, despite the positive features connected with multicultural policies, these policies are not able to solve all the problems connected with tendencies to exclude certain ethnically defined social groups from certain areas of social life. There are a number of exclusionary structures, ideologies and discourses which have a continuous presence in contemporary societies. The following sections deal with three phenomena: racism, ethnicity and nationalism.

RACISM

In Britain the multiculturalist discourse was followed from the late 1970s by another dominant value-standpoint – anti-racism. This standpoint emphasizes that an acceptance of cultural pluralism is not enough when the structures of society still create disadvantages for some groups. Prejudice and a lack of cultural knowledge are not the main causes behind racism, as the multiculturalist discourse often suggests. Instead of creating an understanding of different cultures and counteracting prejudice, the policy should be to fight against racist structures in society. Obviously, it is not the differences in themselves, but the meaning given to these differences which creates the problem.

By the late 1970s, when the anti-racist standpoint became an issue in Britain, it was clear for most social scientists that a multicultural policy would not be able to end the disadvantage of the black population in the UK. The discrimination against the black population could not be explained solely by looking at prejudice or cultural conflicts. Instead, racism and discrimination had to be removed by promoting structural change within society (Denney, 1983). Among the white population the rise of anti-racism can be seen in relation to the socially oriented and radical atmosphere of the 1970s, but more militant and separatist attitudes were also gaining support among the black population (Rex and Tomlinson, 1979). Similar anti-racist arguments have been discussed in the United States, where Omi and Winant (1994) present an important critique of ethnicity theory in the US. According to them, Glazer and Moynihan's (1963, 1975) understanding of ethnic groups as interest groups, by which individuals can freely work for the improvement of their conditions, does not take into account the 'racial formation' in the United States.

Racism and discrimination are clearly obstacles to both assimilation and integration because of the boundaries and structures of exclusion they create. Thus any discussion about integration or assimilation has to take into account racism and other processes of exclusion. In the social sciences the advent of racist ideologies in the nineteenth century is usually related to the historical development of colonialism, capitalism and modernity. Racism is an ideology which is used to legitimize the exclusion and exploitation of certain groups. In addition, the discourse of 'race' is intrinsically connected to the idea that social groups can be regarded as natural ones. However, racism is not only a historical phenomenon. A typical feature of racism is that it seems to take different disguises depending on the social contexts. Racism, and the assumption that social groups can be regarded as natural, has taken new forms in the contemporary world and can still be seen as part of the social construction of reality in western societies (Miles, 1989; Goldberg, 1993; Malik, 1996).

New Racism

One attempt to describe how racist ideology might take new forms and lead to different outcomes in the contemporary world is encapsulated in the term 'new racism'. Broadly speaking, this term refers to contemporary changes in exclusionary discourses and practices where the notion of cultural differences has replaced the idea of biological differences in the process of defining 'the other', and where 'races' largely become conceptualized as nations instead of biological groups (Barker, 1981; Malik, 1996).

Although Miles (1989, 1993) finds that 'new racism' is a vague term,[3] it can be argued that this concept can be useful in order to depict the changing disguises in which exclusionary ideologies can appear. In Britain, for example, the processes of exclusion in contemporary society are no longer simply a question of 'race' or colour of skin; instead exclusionary practices today are taking much more subtle forms (Cohen, 1994). The concept of new racism has been advocated by persons working within the tradition of cultural studies. For example Paul Gilroy (1992) argues that the new racism in Britain has three features. Firstly, it uses a coded language where racial meanings are inferred rather than stated. Secondly, it identifies race with the terms 'culture' and 'identity', and finally:

The new racism has a third important feature . . . This is the close-
ness it suggests between the idea of race and the ideas of nation,
nationality and national belonging. We increasingly face a racism
which avoids being recognized as such because it is able to link
'race' with nationhood, patriotism and nationalism, a racism which
has taken a necessary distance from crude ideas of biological
inferiority and superiority and now seeks to present an imaginary definition of the nation as a unified *cultural* community. It
constructs and defends an image of national culture – homoge-
neous in its whiteness yet precarious and perpetually vulnerable
to attack from enemies within and without. The analogy of war
and invasion is increasingly used to make sense of events. (Gilroy,
1992: 53)

As this quotation indicates, the concept of new racism leads us to
look at the question of nationalism in the receiving society in order
to understand contemporary processes of exclusion of immigrants
and refugees. Most of the discussion on racism in this chapter is
based on the British academic discourse, and one can ask to what
extent these concepts and theories have any significance in Finland.
Obviously, the Finnish context is different, and the public discourse
is based on a different history and uses other concepts. Nevertheless, a general tendency to regard social groups as natural groups,
the emergence of a new racism linked to a culturalist discourse,
and a strong tendency towards an exclusionary perception of the
nation are clearly all present in the Finnish case.

Rethinking Culture, Difference and Racism

The recent discussion in Britain concerning multiculturalism and
racism has revolved around the question of how 'culture' really
should be understood. The notion of multiculturalism has been
criticized recently because it usually involves a static view of culture and a preoccupation with tangible culture (the 'saris, samosas
and steel-bands syndrome'[4]). This notion might also lead to an
overemphasis on cultural differences. Research which only pays
attention to cultural differences and cultural content may result in
the researched group being defined as 'the other'. This easily leads
to an erroneous treatment of social problems, whose origins are
located in social structures, as problems created by cultural differences (Donald and Rattansi, 1992).

This emphasis on cultural differences is clearly evident in the case of refugees. They are often seen as experiencing huge cultural conflicts between their old culture and the culture of the new country of settlement. Sometimes this is described as a culture-shock. This relates to the whole discourse of multiculturalism which emphasizes cultural differences. Some studies of refugees acknowledge the fact that their culture can be used as a resource, but usually the refugees' lack of acculturation is regarded as a problem and one that will lead to conflicts with the culture prevailing in the receiving society. This culturalist discourse often distracts attention from the structural reasons for the problems that refugees experience. In this way the culturalist discourse hides the social inequalities and power relations that are the root causes of exclusion, conflicts and problems. It is possible to argue that culturalist explanations often have far too big an influence on both researchers and practitioners of refugee resettlement.

Donald and Rattansi (1992) suggest a critical rereading of the concept of culture to overcome the problems connected with the notion of multiculturalism. One of the leading British theorists in this 'rereading of culture' is Paul Gilroy. He argues that we should understand 'the cultural not as an intrinsic property of ethnic particularity but as a mediating space between agents and structures' (Gilroy, 1987: 16). Gilroy (1992) has also criticized the limited anti-racist project because it involves too narrow a view of society. A limited anti-racist project is not able to attack the more subtle forms of exclusion in contemporary societies. Furthermore, Gilroy criticizes both the British multiculturalist approach and the anti-racist project because of their preoccupation with ethnic differences. He argues that the key to understanding the problem is to look at how culture itself is understood.

At the end of the day, an absolute commitment to cultural insiderism is as bad as an absolute commitment to biological insiderism. I think we need to be theoretically and politically clear that no single culture is hermetically sealed off from others. There can be no neat and tidy pluralistic separation of racial groups in this country.... Culture, even the culture which defines the groups we know as races, is never fixed, finished or final. It is fluid, it is actively and continually made and re-made. (Gilroy, 1992: 57)

The problem seems to be that the multiculturalist and anti-racist policies are largely based on the same notions of differences that they are trying to attack. 'Thus, establishing a system of identity politics as a form of resistance to Eurocentrism, orientalism and racism, fails exactly because its basic assumptions have been formed within the discourse of difference it most wants to attack' (Anthias and Yuval-Davis, 1992: 194).

Yet, one should not forget that the multicultural and the anti-racist standpoints have led to improvements for, and the empowerment of, the minorities in the UK. However, these policies have not been able to change the systems of thought based on mutually exclusive categories of people divided by cultural differences, which largely lies behind exclusionary policies. Thus the multicultural and anti-racist projects themselves have also contributed to the racialization and culturalization of difference. There is a need for a proper understanding of culture which takes into account its fluid and changing character (Gilroy, 1987, 1992). It can, however, be argued that this discussion concerning the nature of culture is not totally new; similar ideas have previously been presented within anthropology and in some theories about ethnicity.

ETHNICITY AND NATIONALISM

Ethnic groups and ethnicity, which is 'the character or quality of an ethnic group' (Glazer and Moynihan, 1975: 1), are central concepts in any study of the social dimensions of international migration. It has been common to understand an ethnic group as a minority. However, in a widely influential text Glazer and Moynihan use the term to refer 'not only to subgroups, to minorities, but to all the groups of a society characterized by a distinct sense of difference owing to culture and descent' (Glazer and Moynihan, 1975: 4). This broad definition is clearly more logical and has rightly gained a dominant position within present day anthropology (Eriksen, 1993). Hence, it can be argued that all persons belong to ethnic groups.

There has been a major theoretical debate within sociology and anthropology which has focused on the question whether ethnicity is a permanent and essential condition based on common descent, which represents a primordialist point of view, or whether ethnicity is situational and instrumental. For example, Abner Cohen (1969) and Glazer and Moynihan (1975) have convincingly argued that there are instrumental and political reasons why a group asserts and maintains an ethnic identity. Today, few social scientists advocate a pure primordialist point of view.

One of the most influential theories about ethnic groups is the theory first presented by the anthropologist Fredrik Barth (1969). Early writings on ethnicity often stressed the importance of shared cultural values as a basic element in ethnic group membership. Barth's work is a rejection of the view of ethnicity as a shared culture, and can at the same time be seen as a critique of primordial views of ethnicity (Rex, 1986a, 1996). Barth suggests that ethnic groups are socially constructed. 'Ethnic groups are categories of ascription and identification by the actors themselves' (Barth, 1969: 10). He argues that these processes of constructing and maintaining the boundaries should be the object of study. The most important notion is that it is not the cultural content which constitutes the ethnicity of a group but, instead, the boundaries between different groups. The participants own definition of the situation becomes important and the struggle for scarce resources is an important force in the process of ethnicity. Barth's perspective has had a fundamental influence on theories of ethnicity and his article is one of the most frequently cited anthropological texts in this area of research. This perspective emphasizes that ethnicity is a relation and that ethnic groups always need at least one other group upon which to reflect their ethnicity (Wallman, 1986; Eriksen, 1993; Banks, 1996).

Ethnicity also comprises two different sides. According to Eriksen (1993), ethnicity comprises aspects of meaning as well as politics. As Daniel Bell (1975: 169) stated: 'Ethnicity has become more salient because it can combine an interest with an affective tie.' For a long time ethnicity was seen as a factor which would disappear from the social arena due to the processes of modernity in society. This kind of primordial attachment would disappear in the change from *Gemeinschaft* to *Gesellschaft* (Tönnies, 1970) and from 'mechanical solidarity' to 'organic solidarity' (Durkheim, 1938). This has clearly not happened; instead ethnic phenomena are perhaps more salient today than ever. This development can only be understood if we look at the twofold structure of ethnicity. The first factor is that ethnic groups can act as interest groups within society and there can be economic and political advantages connected to group membership. These are, of course, functions that social groups in general, and social classes in particular, are able to provide to their members. However, the second crucial factor is the emotional, symbolic and meaningful side of ethnicity. Ethnicity can give meaning to our lives and a sense of belonging in contemporary impersonal, global and alienating societies. This is the reason why ethnicity is still an important social force today.

Both theories of ethnicity and of nationalism tend to stress that collective identities and communities are socially constructed (Eriksen, 1993). According to Gellner (1983: 1), 'nationalism is a theory of political legitimacy, which requires that ethnic boundaries should not cut across political ones'. The basis for this ideology is the notion that there are groups of people who constitute 'nations', and these nations should have a 'state'. The aim is that the nations should have political control over a specific territory which is regarded as the 'homeland'. Nationalism creates a feeling of a continuing and eternal nation, perceived as a natural *Gemeinschaft*. In this sense the nation can be regarded as an 'imagined community' (Anderson, 1983). Nationalism is historically connected to the emergence of the modern society in eighteenth century Europe. For example, Gellner (1983) argues that the nation-state is a cultural form and political system that is necessary for economic growth.

Anthony Smith has a different focus in his studies of nationalism. He takes issue with those who look at nationalism as simply a consequence of modernity. According to Smith (1986), nations have ethnic origins and ethnicity is an independent element of nationalism not reducible to other economic or social processes. Consequently, nationalism has its roots in older history although it is a modern ideology (A. Smith, 1983, 1986). Although Smith himself disputes it,[5] he is commonly regarded as representing a primordialist view, which is largely at odds with the situational view with its emphasis on the social construction of ethnicity and nationalism. The question is whether Smith's approach is sufficient for a sociological understanding of ethnicity and nationalism. Certainly, political power relations and social changes have a profound effect on ethnic feelings and national identities. It is doubtful whether Smith's approach sufficiently takes into account the relation between nationalism and ethnicity on the one hand and social structures and forces on the other.

Nevertheless, Smith's theories remain important insofar as he highlights the logical connection between nationalism and ethnicity. The theories within these two fields have largely developed independently, but they still have very much in common (Eriksen, 1993; Banks, 1996). One common characteristic is that theories of ethnicity and nationalism have usually assumed that the communities which are identified as ethnic groups or nations only exist within specific, clearly defined, geographical locations.

GLOBALIZATION, TRANSNATIONALISM AND DE-TERRITORIALIZATION

In the contemporary world the process of globalization is challenging the traditional ways in which ethnicity, nationalism and migration have been conceptualized. Globalization may be defined as a 'social process in which the constraints of geography on the social and cultural arrangements recede and in which people become increasingly aware that they are receding' (Waters, 1995: 3). Recent technological developments and international migration have made various new transnational, global and even totally de-territorialized social relations possible. This is obviously not leading to a new uniform world culture (Featherstone, 1990). Instead, the contemporary global world with its drastic expansion of mobility is a place where 'difference is encountered in the adjoining neighbourhood, the familiar turns up at the ends of the earth' (Clifford, 1988: 14). Consequently, the local and the global become increasingly intertwined in a process of 'glocalization' (Robertson, 1995).

The social relations emerging from these developments are not easily confined within the borders of nation-states. Thus they can be regarded as transnational, a term which indicates a relation over and beyond, rather than between or in, the nation-states. The discussion of transnationalism has been especially vibrant within anthropology (Kearney, 1995; Hannerz, 1996) where the strict localization of cultures and social relations has been questioned by many authors (Clifford, 1992; Gupta and Ferguson, 1992). Some of the most interesting contributions to the discussion on transnationalism and international migration were first included in Glick Schiller, Basch and Blanc-Szanton (1992). In a later publication Basch, Glick Schiller and Blanc-Szanton (1994) write in more detail about migrants from the Caribbean and the Philippines living in the USA. The authors describe how the migrants' social, economic, political and cultural networks involve both country of origin and country of settlement. These processes are described using the notion of transnationalism:

We define 'transnationalism' as the processes by which immigrants forge and sustain multi-stranded social relations that link together their societies of origin and settlement. We call these processes transnationalism to emphasize that many immigrants today build social fields that cross geographic, cultural, and political borders. (Basch et al., 1994: 7)

The authors have also later advocated the expression 'transnational processes' rather than 'transnationalism' (Blanc-Szanton, Glick Schiller and Basch, 1995). Linguistically, this has the obvious advantage that it avoids the mistake of regarding transnationalism as a form of nationalism.

Furthermore, although the debate surrounding globalization has mainly occurred during recent years, the process itself is obviously not an entirely new phenomenon. Global migration, for example, is older than recorded human history and transnational social relations also existed before the advent of jet flights and the Internet. Not surprisingly, attempts to conceptualize migrants' transnational and de-territorialized social relations were also made by migration researchers before the 1980s. Schierup (1985) as well as Schierup and Ålund (1986) point out that there are anthropologists who have managed to see migration as a dynamic process. The social processes which constitute and reproduce the total 'social field' of migrants' life experiences can be described using the concept of 'migrancy', which connotes the continuous processual character of migration. Schierup and Ålund refer to the concept's usage by the anthropologist Mayer (1962), who studied the process of urbanization among migrants in South Africa. Mayer shows that the various parts of migration – emigration, immigration, integration, remigration – cannot be isolated from one another. Furthermore, migration is never absolute and an oscillation between town and country may occur for a long time.[6] Thus, migration has never meant a definite end to the old social context in which migrants have lived. Instead, as Schierup (1985) points out, although migrants live in one 'social field', this field consists of a double existential frame of reference in which migrants continue to live for a long time:

For the immigrant this double existential frame of reference is not a socio-psychological aspect alone, but is authentically rooted in social and material realities. Separation from social networks, groupings, material possessions and alternatives of labour and education in the countries of origin takes place only slowly – for some not at all. (Schierup, 1985: 153)

There are, of course, significant differences in this 'double existential frame of reference' between labour migrants and refugees. Furthermore there is also reason for not treating this issue as a duality since this suggests that there is necessarily something contradictory or irrational in the social reality of migrants and refugees. It is more fruitful to understand this issue as something transnational, since the social relations of a refugee are largely unrelated to his or her actual geographical location.

In addition to anthropological studies, there is reason not to forget the classical work of Thomas and Znaniecki (1958). In their study of Polish migrants they examined the social organization of the Polish peasant in Poland *and* in the United States. Although their study was carried out at the beginning of the century, it can still be regarded as a good model for the sociological study of a transnational reality (cf. Lie, 1995). The importance of social networks transcending national borders has also been discussed within more contemporary migration research (Tilly, 1990; Koser, 1997b). As Wahlbeck (1996) points out, the interest in networks is found in many empirical studies of chain-migration. Furthermore, the importance of social networks can also be discerned in studies emphasizing that immigrant and ethnic minority associations, both formal and informal, can have many important functions for their communities (Rex, Joly and Wilpert, 1987; Jenkins, 1988; Carey-Wood et al., 1995; Joly, 1995b, 1996).

Ethnicity and Globalization

The contemporary processes of globalization do not diminish the importance of ethnicity; on the contrary, it is given a new significance in a global world (Featherstone, 1990; Hall, 1991; Waters, 1995). One major change is that the connection between ethnicity and locality becomes blurred. 'Ethnicity, once a genie contained in the bottle of some sort of locality (however large) has now become a global force, forever slipping in and through the cracks between states and borders' (Appadurai, 1990: 306). The processes of globalization have, among other things, led to the emergence of de-territorialized ethnicities.

Since refugees can be distinguished from migrants by the fact that refugees have been forced to leave their country of origin, it is plausible that de-territorialization would be an especially salient feature among refugees. For example, the Tamil refugees in Steen's (1992) study have one obvious thing in common:

> They do not form a 'people' or a 'community', which means that they cannot be represented 'as if' one was anthropologizing in a Jaffna village in the North of Sri Lanka. There is thus no question of writing a monography in the conventional sense of the term, assuming an easy correspondence between a people and a place. 'The setting' (or the equivalent) cannot appear at a crucial point in chapter one. For refugees there is no such fixed setting; this is, indeed, *the whole point about them*, regrettably missed in many refugee studies. Moreover, it is this point which clearly distinguishes migrants from refugees. Migrants 'decide' to leave and to re-create their life in another place; refugees are torn away from their homeland and still cling to it. . . . In the case of refugees *everything* that should normally define them in a socio-cultural context is non-existent, or rather, still back home. (Steen, 1992: 110)

In addition to various transnational social relations, de-territorialization as a lived experience seems to be intrinsically connected to life in exile. This has implications for the adaptation of theories of ethnic relations to refugee groups. In the literature on ethnicity, an ethnic group is often regarded as being defined by its relation to and interaction with other groups (e.g. Barth, 1969). An ethnic minority is thus defined in relation to the ethnic majority within a specific society. However, it is difficult to adapt this relational context to the de-territorialized reality in which refugees live. Gisèle Bousquet (1991) finds that theories of ethnic relations are not easily applied to refugee communities. She disputes Abner Cohen's (1969) idea that ethnicity is used to mobilize the members of an ethnic group within contemporary urban political conflicts, on the ground that the Vietnamese refugees in her study arrived in the host-country as an already distinct culturally and politically self-identified ethnic group. Unfortunately, she does not develop her challenge much further than this, nor does she draw any wider conclusions from her results. It can be suggested that the problem has nothing to do with theories of ethnic relations as such, but with the strict localization of ethnic relations that these theories usually assume. In an increasingly globalized world ethnicity might also be defined in relations which are transnational or even totally de-territorialized. 'Although much of the theoretical writing about ethnicity has been concerned with the attachment of an ethnic group to a territory, in fact ethnic communities are often concerned precisely with their *detachment* from a territory' (Rex, 1996: 103).

The changing and processual character of the process of 'migrancy', as well as the continuous transnational social networks, also constitute challenges for the typologies of refugee movements presented earlier. Is it useful to formulate theories of migration on the basis of strict classifications of migration movements in cases where these are under constant change? In other words, a person who initially leaves his or her country as one type of migrant may, depending on the situation and/or the passing of time, become another type of migrant.

DIASPORAS

Refugee research needs a new conceptual framework in which the refugees' de-territorialized and transnational social relations can be described. In recent years there has been an increased interest in the notion of diasporas. John Lie (1995) argues that there has been a change of focus in recent publications within the sociology of international migration. Instead of studying international migration the focus is often on transnational diasporas. The new diaspora discourse has thus meant that the former interest in immigration and assimilation has largely given way to an interest in transnational networks and communities (Lie, 1995).

Originally, the concept of diaspora referred to the dispersal of the Jews from their historic homeland. Today it is often used to describe various well-established communities which have an experience of 'displacement', like the overseas Chinese, the Armenians in exile, Palestinian refugees, Gypsies or the whole African diaspora (Chaliand and Rageau, 1991; Safran, 1991; Clifford, 1994; Cohen, 1997). The concept of diaspora is clearly associated with transnationalism, as Khachig Tölölyan writes: 'Diasporas are the exemplary communities of the transnational moment' (Tölölyan, 1991: 4). It is common to argue that one criterion of a diaspora is forcible dispersal. Chaliand describes diasporas as 'born from a forced dispersion, they conscientiously strive to keep a memory of the past alive and foster the will to transmit a heritage and to survive as a diaspora' (Chaliand, 1989: xiv). The idea of the 'homeland' can be seen as another criterion; the notion of diaspora thus indicates a nationalism in exile.

Diasporic phenomena have a long history and are not only associated with the modern world (Cohen, 1997). What, however, is new in the contemporary world is the steadily increasing impact of globalization. It is a process which, through the ease of international mobility and the facilitating of transnational social relations, increases the opportunities for diaspora formation. Today the concept of diaspora is used increasingly to describe any community which in one way or another has a history of migration (Marienstras, 1989; Tölölyan, 1996). The concept has been regarded as useful in describing the geographical displacement and/or de-territorialization of identities and cultures in the contemporary world. This approach includes writings on syncretic cultures, 'hybridity' and cultures of resistance among groups of migrant origin (Gilroy, 1987; Hall, 1993; Brah, 1996). Thus, today the concept of diaspora is used to describe the processes of transnationalism, the experience of displacement as well as the salience of pre-migration social networks, cultures, politics and capital, in a wide range of communities (Sheffer, 1986; Safran, 1991; Clifford, 1994; Cohen, 1997).

It can be argued that today an increasing number of communities have a diasporic relation to the society in which they live. The transnational social organization these groups display diverges from the traditional way the nation-state and its citizens are understood. Cohen (1995) argues that these groups represent a challenge to the exclusivist claims of modern nation-states. It may be that these forms of social organization 'have pre-dated the nation-state, lived within it and now may, in significant respects, transcend and succeed it' (Cohen, 1995: 16). A slightly different perspective is given by Basch et al. (1994) who argue that international migration, rather than contesting nation-states, leads to nations and even nation-states themselves becoming de-territorialized as a result of the dispersal of populations.

The concept of diaspora seems to encompass the transnational and de-territorialized social relations of refugees as well as to outline the specific refugee experience. The concept can conceive the political project in the 'homeland' which plays such a fundamental role for many refugees. Seeing refugees as living in a diasporic relation is a way of throwing some more light on the special relationships that refugees have with both the society of origin and society of settlement. Thus, the concept of diaspora can also help to bridge the artificial 'before' and 'after' distinction commonly applied to migration, and hereby it can encompass the refugees' own definition of their situation.

The Ethnic Origins of Diasporas

Sheffer (1986, 1995) argues that diasporas play an increasing role in international politics, an influence which in the USA, for example, has been described by Shain (1995). These new trans-state organizations have largely been neglected by politicians and analysts although clearly their number and significance are growing in the contemporary world. The increase in migration and the new global means of communication and transport all contribute to this process. Sheffer's profile of modern diasporas reflects his interest in the political dimension of diasporas:

> [Diasporas] were created as a result of either forced or voluntary migration . . . ; they consciously maintain their ethno-national identity; they create communal organizations, or are on the way to creating them; equally consciously, they maintain explicit and implicit ties with their homelands; even if only in a rudimentary form, they develop trans-state networks connecting them with their respective homelands and their brethren in other host countries; and they face grave dilemmas concerning dual and divided loyalties to their homelands and host countries. (Sheffer, 1995: 9)

Sheffer (1995) wants to stress the autonomous individual and collective decisions taken by migrants after arrival in the country of settlement. He argues that it is not the migrant's background but their free choice to join existing diasporas, or become new diasporas in the country of settlement, which is the most accurate explanation for the emergence of new diasporas. Furthermore he wants to emphasize the ethnic character of contemporary diasporas. According to Sheffer, the attachment to the homeland can be attributed to the primordial nature of ethnicity. In the conclusion of his article, Sheffer (1995) also argues that diasporas are neither 'imagined' nor 'invented' communities in the sense described by Anderson (1983). However, this critique of Anderson is not fully explained.

Sheffer's (1995) emphasis on migrants' free choice seems to be widely exaggerated. Obviously, it is not in the power of individuals to freely choose their identity and group membership. Furthermore, Sheffer's own emphasis on the primordial dimension of ethnicity is, of course, in conflict with the issue of free choice (which he also acknowledges). Thus, Sheffer's argument is rather confusing since it tries to support both a primordial view on ethnicity and an instrumental view where migrants are able to make free choices. However, it would appear that these different points of view are still connected with each other since Sheffer (1995: 18) declares that his analysis subscribes to a 'synthetic' approach to the meaning of ethnicity. In this approach, largely formulated by Anthony Smith (1981), 'the origins of modern ethnicity lie in an inseparable combination of primordial, instrumental and environmental factors' (Sheffer, 1995: 18). Sheffer's argument on the ethnic nature of diasporas finds strong support in Smith's own writings:

> An *ethnie* need not be in physical possession of 'its' territory; what matters is that it has a symbolic geographical centre, a sacred habitat, a 'homeland' to which it may symbolically return, even when its members are scattered across the globe and have lost their homeland centuries ago. *Ethnie* do not cease to be *ethnie* when they are dispersed and have lost their homeland; for ethnicity is a matter of myths, memories, values and symbols, and not of material possessions or political power. (Smith, 1986: 28)

The main problem with Sheffer's approach to diasporas remains the same as with Smith's more or less primordial view on ethnicity. It is doubtful if these approaches can sufficiently take into account the structural constraints and power relations within social relations. In the case of diasporas, it is clear that policies in the host-society also have a great impact on the diasporas. Exclusionary or inclusionary ideologies, structures and policies within the host-society all influence ethnic diasporas. Neither Smith's notion of ethnicity nor Sheffer's notion of diasporas sufficiently takes into account these structures in society.

Diaspora as an Analytical Tool

The concept of diaspora is currently very popular and there are numerous definitions of the term. The range of phenomena supposedly spanned by the concept is such that it is in danger of losing its explanatory power. In order to be able to use the concept analytically I prefer the precise definition of diaspora presented in the first issue of the journal *Diaspora*, where according to William Safran diasporas are:

> Expatriate minority communities whose members share several of the following characteristics: 1) they, or their ancestors, have been dispersed from a specific original "center" to two or more "peripheral," or foreign, regions; 2) they retain a collective memory, vision, or myth about their original homeland – its physical location, history, and achievements; 3) they believe they are not – and perhaps cannot be – fully accepted by their host society and therefore feel partly alienated and insulated from it; 4) they regard their ancestral homeland as their true, ideal home and as the place to which they or their descendants would (or should) eventually return – when conditions are appropriate; 5) they believe that they should, collectively, be committed to the maintenance or restoration of their original homeland and to its safety and prosperity; and 6) they continue to relate, personally or vicariously, to that homeland in one way or another, and their ethnocommunal consciousness and solidarity are importantly defined by the existence of such a relationship. (Safran, 1991: 83–4)

One of the main themes of this book is to explore to what extent the above-mentioned characteristics of a diaspora can be found in the Kurdish refugee communities. As this definition suggests, dispersal alone is not enough to qualify a group as a diaspora. To live in a diaspora also includes a very specific relationship to both the homeland and the country of settlement. In fact, many of the groups traditionally regarded as diasporas fulfil only a few of Safran's six criteria. Clifford (1994) argues that Safran's normative definition is too strict, and does not take into account all those instances that can be called a diaspora. He argues, for example, that there does not necessarily have to be any centre for the diaspora, nor do all members of the diaspora necessarily want to return 'home'. However, for the purpose of this study there is no point in using Clifford's less precise definition since, as I will argue later, Safran's specific criteria are to a great extent fulfilled by the Kurdish refugee communities. The use of a less precise definition can only add to the confusion surrounding the concept of diaspora. Hence, the definition of a diaspora utilized in this book is a very strict definition which may even exclude some of the groups traditionally referred to as diasporas.

Of wider theoretical importance is Cohen's (1997) discussion of Safran's typology. Firstly, he points out that although Safran's definition is useful, there is some degree of repetition concerning the relationship of the diasporic group to its homeland. Furthermore, he adds that on occasion the goal of a diaspora is not simply a question of the maintenance or restoration of a homeland, but one of its very creation (the case of the Kurds and the Sikhs are here mentioned as examples). Secondly he argues that some issues dealing with the nature of the relationship to the country of exile have to be added in order to include 'trade, labour and imperial diasporas' (Cohen, 1997: 24) as well as the more 'post-modern' cultural diasporas. A third addition mentioned by Cohen (1997) is the question of time. This was first pointed out by Richard Marienstras in his discussion of the notion of diaspora: 'Certainly, the word diaspora is used today to describe any community that has emigrated whose numbers make it visible in the host community. But in order to know whether it is really a diaspora, time has to pass' (Marienstras, 1989: 125). In a study of recently arrived refugees, the influence of time does add some uncertainty to the analysis of the observed phenomena. However, this does not rule out the possibility of using the concept of diaspora as an analytical tool to study contemporary social processes.

Cohen (1997) wants to emphasize the fact that although diasporas are associated with victims and suffering, they also paradoxically involve possibilities and resources. He argues that it is important to supersede the victim-tradition of diasporas. In fact, there are plenty of examples of the creativity and inventiveness of diasporas. The African diaspora's achievements in the arts and popular music, the Jewish diaspora's successes in science and the Chinese diaspora's accomplishments in trade are just a few well known examples. It can be argued that achievements like these have not happened despite the diaspora, but rather because life in the diaspora has been the impetus behind these achievements. Life in a diaspora may both include new possibilities and propel exiles towards new levels of accomplishment and inventiveness (Cohen, 1996, 1997). Some indication of the rationale behind this paradox is found in an article by Edward Said, himself a Palestinian exile:

Exile, unlike nationalism, is fundamentally a discontinuous state of being. Exiles are cut off from their roots, their land, their past. They generally do not have armies or states, although they are often in search of them. Exiles feel, therefore, an urgent need to reconstitute their broken lives, usually by choosing to see themselves as part of a triumphant ideology or a restored people. The crucial thing is that a state of exile free from this triumphant ideology – designed to reassemble an exile's broken history into a new whole – is virtually unbearable, and virtually impossible in today's world. Look at the fate of the Jews, the Palestinians and the Armenians. (Said, 1990: 360)

The exile's search for a new whole history not only takes political forms, it might also evolve into intellectual activities:

Much of the exile's life is taken up with compensating for disorienting loss by creating a new world to rule. It is not surprising that so many exiles seem to be novelists, chess players, political activists, and intellectuals. Each of these occupations requires a minimal investment in objects and places a great premium on mobility and skill. The exile's new world, logically enough, is unnatural and its unreality resembles fiction. (Said, 1990: 363)

One example of an author who gets his inspiration from life in exile is Salman Rushdie whose work largely has been related to the creation of what he calls 'imaginary homelands' (Rushdie, 1991).

Diaspora and Ethnic Relations

In most definitions diasporas are regarded as communities. Despite this, the concept has seldom been used as a well-defined sociological concept. Instead the concept has mainly been used in order to describe feelings and experiences of displacement. However, it is important to note that a diaspora can be seen as a social organization – in fact, Cohen (1995, 1996) explicitly uses the term social organization, although he never develops this idea further. Hence, to live in a diaspora is not only a question of having a diasporic consciousness, culture or identity, but it can also have a profound influence on the social organization of the community.

Obviously, diaspora theories have a lot to gain from previous studies of migration and transnational social networks, a connection which seems to be largely overlooked in much of the literature on diasporas. For example, Safran (1991) identifies a number of open questions and research agendas in the study of the diaspora phenomena, including the following:

> In the relationship between perceptions of discrimination, actual oppression, and diaspora sentiments, which are the independent and which the dependent variables? Is there a reciprocal causality? Is diaspora consciousness a concomitant of a feeling of otherness, of alienation, or of a lack of hospitality on the part of the host society; or, on the contrary, is the lack of hospitality a response by the host society to the exceptionalism that diaspora consciousness signifies? (Safran, 1991: 96)

These are, of course, central questions. However, it is important to remember that these are not new questions for social scientists. The interest in migrant communities and minority–majority relations is as old as social science itself. It is obvious from most studies in this area that the way in which immigrants are integrated is largely dependent upon the existing social structures and the policies adopted by the receiving society. Exclusionary policies, racism, discrimination, and xenophobia all have a great impact on integration. When using the concept of diaspora it is important not to forget this. There is a danger that the concept 'diaspora', with its preoccupation with 'migrant communities' and their relationship to the country of origin, may disregard the host-society and the power structures involved in majority–minority relations. If this happens the introduction of the concept leads back to culturalist and other social and psychological theories in which immigrants are largely seen as choosing to integrate or not, and exclusionary structures and ideologies, like racism, are not seen to play any significant role.

> Theories and discourses that diasporize or internationalize "minorities" can deflect attention from long-standing, structured inequalities of class and race. It is as if the problem were multinationalism – issues of translation, education, and tolerance – rather than of economic exploitation and racism. While clearly necessary, making *cultural* room for Salvadorans, Samoans, Sikhs, Haitians, Khmers, and so forth, does not, of itself, produce a living wage, decent housing, or health care. Moreover, at the level of everyday social practice cultural differences are persist-

ently racialized, classed, and gendered. Diaspora theories need to account for these concrete, cross-cutting structures. (Clifford, 1994: 313)

It is important to remember that there is no reason to see diasporas as a solely positive development. As Clifford suggests: 'Suffice it to say that diasporic consciousness "makes the best of a bad situation". Experience of loss, marginality, and exile . . . are often reinforced by systematic exploitation and blocked advancement' (Clifford, 1994: 312). Although diasporas are often defined in relation to nation-states, it must be remembered that a diaspora cannot provide its members with the same services and opportunities that are provided by a state for its citizens. Thus, it is important not to see diasporas as a positive and sufficient alternative to egalitarian welfare states. Furthermore, there is not necessarily any reason to celebrate the social qualities of diasporas. As Ong and Nonini point out: 'There is nothing intrinsically liberating about diaspora cultures' (Ong and Nonini, 1997: 32). On the contrary, diasporas can revive old forms of oppression in a new setting.

CONCLUSION

The diaspora discourse and the notion of diasporas can provide useful analytical tools for refugee studies. The notion of diaspora can describe the dispersal, as well as feeling of displacement, which is common to all refugees. Furthermore this framework can take into account the transnationalism and de-territorialization of social relations connected to contemporary migration phenomena. This framework conceptualizes the dual orientation towards both the country of origin and country of settlement among migrants and refugees, and can thus bridge the artificial distinction between before migration and after migration which is common in many migration studies. Thus, in this book the social organization of the Kurdish refugee communities in Finland and England is studied within a conceptual scheme based on the concept of diaspora. The definition of a diaspora which is utilized here is the one presented by Safran (1991).

However, it is obvious that the diaspora framework needs some modifications in order to be used as an analytical sociological concept. When using the concept of diaspora, one has to take into account previous research and theories of ethnic relations, international migration and forced migration. Despite the emphasis on transnationalism it has to be understood that diasporas are influenced by exclusionary and inclusionary structures and policies in the country of settlement. For example, racist ideologies and various exclusionary discourses have a profound effect on refugee communities. A diaspora, although it might create a strong transnational community, cannot replace the advantages to be gained from an inclusion into an egalitarian welfare state. This book presents an attempt to use the notion of diaspora in such a way that it takes into account both the inclusionary and exclusionary processes in the society of settlement as well as the diasporic group's continuous transnational relation to the country of origin.

2 Politics and Forced Migration in Kurdistan

In order to understand the experiences of refugees in the country of exile, an understanding of their background and reasons for flight is absolutely necessary. This chapter thus provides a short general introduction to the Kurdish question, and then continues with a brief description of recent political developments and forced migration in each of the three countries of origin.

The area traditionally inhabited by the Kurds, Kurdistan, is divided between Turkey, Syria, Iraq and Iran. There are also indigenous Kurdish populations in Armenia, Azerbaijan, Georgia and Turkmenistan (Kendal, 1993b). This chapter will deal mainly with the situation in Turkey, Iraq and Iran. These three countries account for at least 90 per cent of the Kurdish population, and all the refugees in this study originate in one of these countries. The Kurds, who are estimated to number almost 30 million,[1] are often referred to as the world's biggest nation without a state. The Kurds are commonly portrayed as persecuted minorities in all the states dividing Kurdistan. Although this can be said to be generally true, a more detailed picture is needed in order to understand the Kurdish tragedy.

Kurdish political history and the problems experienced by the Kurdish nationalist projects can only be understood if one takes into account that Kurdistan lies in an area where several empires and regional powers meet. However, the states in the area have always had problems controlling the mountainous Kurdish regions and the numerous Kurdish insurrections. It is only since the advent of modern warfare that the states, often with disastrous consequences, have attempted to gain full control over Kurdistan.

The Kurdish emirates under the Ottoman Empire had a degree of independence and the Mahabad republic declared independence in 1946. Still, these political units only comprised small parts of what today is commonly regarded as Kurdistan and the entire area has never formed a state. Instead, Kurdish society was for a long time a tribal society, where tribal allegiances had a considerable influence on the political and social structure. However, over time the tribal structure has given way to other loyalties, for example loyalties based on nationalist and socialist discourses (Bruinessen, 1992a). Nationalism arrived relatively late in Kurdistan, which is also a reason for the difficulties experienced by Kurdish nationalism. There are a number of recent authoritative publications outlining the history of Kurdistan and the Kurdish national struggle (Bulloch and Morris, 1993; Chaliand, 1993, 1994; Entessar, 1992; Gunter, 1990, 1992, 1997; Kreyenbroek and Sperl, 1992; Laizer, 1996a; McDowall, 1992, 1996; Olson, 1996). Instead of going into great historical detail I will refer my readers to these books.

The Kurdish language is an Indo-European language related to Farsi (Persian), but not related to Arabic or Turkish. The countries in the region today use different alphabets: the Arabic alphabet in Iraq, Syria and Iran, the Roman alphabet in Turkey and the Cyrillic alphabet in the CIS. The Kurdish dialects have developed in widely different directions because of the cultural persecution of the Kurds, the lack of a Kurdish cultural and political centre and the absence of a common written Kurdish language. Many of the dialects are today mutually unintelligible. The two most important dialects are Kurmanji, spoken in northern Kurdistan, and Sorani, spoken in southern Kurdistan (Entessar, 1992; Kreyenbroek, 1992; Nerweyi, 1991). The Kurdish dialects, despite their huge differences, do not have clear borders between each other; nor do the differences in dialects have anything to do with the actual political borders in the region. One also has to remember that many Kurds today use the main language in the state where they are living as their first language. This is especially true in Turkey where the assimilation policy, with its prohibition of the Kurdish language, has forced many Kurds to abandon Kurdish. In Iran the Kurdish language is often used only in private while Farsi is used in public.[2]

When it comes to religion, most Kurds are Sunni Muslims, but there are also significant communities of Shia Muslim, Alevi, Yezidi and Jewish Kurds (Bruinessen, 1992a, 1992b). There are also Christian communities in Kurdistan, but persons belonging to these are not usually regarded as Kurds. Because of the religious diversity, religion cannot be used as an ethnic marker in the case of Kurds.

All the above-mentioned factors would suggest that it is hard to define who is a 'Kurd' and who is not. However, my own experience is that the Kurds themselves are very clear of their own identity and ethnic boundaries. Consequently, in this research the only definition of 'Kurd' that is used is one that is based on self-definition.

Although all the Kurds I have met are proud of their Kurdish identity there might also be some persons of Kurdish ancestry who choose not to identify themselves as Kurds and who avoid using the Kurdish language. This might happen because of the social stigma that is sometimes attached to Kurdishness.

> Because of their unhappy present political condition, the name of Kurd is usually associated with the idea of resistance to national suppression and the sufferings from human rights violations. Our oppressors have described us, unjustly and successively, as a primitive mountain people refractory to civilization, lawless nomadic tribes without any national consciousness, highway robbers, eternal rebels, bloody landlords, red communists, and today as international terrorists. Contrary to historical facts, we are said to have never been organized into a state or states of our own. Our past has been so blurred, our present is so full of struggle that it is often forgotten that we are a people of the Hurrians and the Medes respectively the Kurds' first and second ancestors. (Kurdistan Parliament in Exile, 1995: 3)

The anthropologist Martin van Bruinessen (1990, 1992a, 1992b), points out that while the Kurdish people have ancient historical roots, Kurdish ethnic identity as a clear-cut category uniting all Kurds and separating them from other possible ethnic identities is a rather recent phenomenon. He stresses that Kurdish identity has largely developed as a reaction to cultural and political domination by the Turks, Persians and Arabs.

> What unites them is not any set of objective, economic, political or cultural criteria, but only the awareness among many of them that they constitute one people. This awareness is a result of a series of historical developments, the most important of which was the rise of Kurdish nationalism. To the extent that the Kurds feel one and have an awareness of a common destiny, they are a nation. But for each individual Kurd, the Kurdish nation is not the only entity with which he [*sic*] feels he shares a common destiny. Beside those who have been assimilated to a dominant nation by force, there are also Kurds who have quite willingly chosen to identify themselves primarily as citizens of their state or as followers of a particular religion or sect. (Bruinessen, 1990: 26–7)

The Kurdish nationalist project, like all other nationalisms, is eager to construct a common Kurdish history, identity, culture and language. At the same time the opponents of Kurdish nationalism, especially the Iranian, Iraqi and Turkish states, are trying to prove that the Kurds are not a nation. It must be stressed that the aim of this book is not to take part in the heated dispute between the advocates and opponents of Kurdish nationalism. Furthermore, the theoretical framework of this book largely relies on the assumption that ethnic groups and nations are always social constructions, and thus there cannot be any 'objective' criteria for who constitutes a nation and who does not. Undoubtedly, however, there is today a strong Kurdish nationalism which influences many Kurds from all parts of Kurdistan and which regards all the Kurds as belonging to one nation. Consequently, there is only one Kurdish national project, but in practice there are disagreements among the Kurds about how Kurdish interests can best be defended.

Due to the political divisions a wide range of political parties are found within Kurdistan and in the Kurdish diaspora. In all three countries there are Kurdish parties and organizations, which are mainly various left-wing and/or nationalistic movements.[3] Especially in Iran, and at least until recently in Turkey, Kurds have also been active in all-Iranian and all-Turkish parties. The existing Kurdish parties, despite their appeal to Kurdish nationalism, are largely confined to the present political borders in the region. Furthermore, they usually regard a political solution within the existing political borders as the only realistic aim in the present situation.

The Kurdish political parties have often been forced to depend on support from neighbouring states. Throughout their history the Kurds have also been taken advantage of in conflicts between states in the region. In fact, many of the Kurdish rebellions have been opposed and fought against by other Kurds. To a large extent the divisions and conflicts between Kurdish parties can be explained by their different political alliances to the neighbouring states. The governments of these states have usually oppressed their own Kurdish minorities, and therefore the Kurdish parties have often become involved in complex political relations with both international and domestic repercussions.

Many of my informants pointed out that the democratic tradition in Kurdistan is not very well developed. Most organizations in Kurdistan are associated with some of the political parties. The Kurdish political scientist Omar Sheikhmous (1995) points out that formal organizations without affiliation to a political party have been almost non-existent in Kurdistan (with the possible exception of Iran). According to him, the lack of a tradition of free organizations can partly be understood as a consequence of the overwhelming influence of the communist parties. These were the first 'modern' organizations in Kurdistan, and usually they were also influenced by a political culture in which all other organizations, political as well as non-political, had to be affiliated to the communist party. The Kurdish nationalist parties were established after the communist parties and often used the latter's organizational structure as a model, and consequently all social, cultural, sport and other organizations were affiliated to some of the political parties. According to Sheikhmous (1995), this tradition still has a profound effect on Kurdish organizations in the diaspora, but one can discern some degree of change away from this model and towards a more liberal democratic form of organization since the beginning of the 1980s.

The influence of socialism and communism on the Kurdish political scene can only be understood when taking into account the relative economic underdevelopment of the Kurdish regions and the social, cultural and political persecution of the Kurds. Van Bruinessen calls the economic process in the whole of Kurdistan one 'that deserves the name of underdevelopment rather than that of development' (Bruinessen, 1992a: 20). The underdevelopment of the Kurdish regions in Turkey is described by Kendal (1993a) and Chaliand (1994). Majeed Jafar (1976) uses the term 'under-underdevelopment' for the situation of the Kurdish parts of underdeveloped Turkey. The Turkish sociologist Ismail Besikci (1991) describes Kurdistan as an interstate colony.[4] Similar economic situations can also be found in Iraq, where according to Chaliand (1994) the Iraqi government's policy has long been to economically marginalize the Kurdish regions. The underdevelopment of Iranian Kurdistan in comparison to other parts of Iran is described by Abdul Rahman Ghassemlou (1993). He is also the author of the first comprehensive study published in English about the economic situation of Kurdistan: *Kurdistan and the Kurds* (Ghassemlou, 1965).[5] The underdevelopment of Kurdistan, described in the above-mentioned sources, includes features like high rates of illiteracy, high birthrates and poor health services in the Kurdish areas. There are, however, big differences between urban and rural areas within Kurdistan. For example, illiteracy is especially high among women in the countryside, while more affluent Kurds in the cities have much better opportunities to gain an education.

Given the economic and political situation in Kurdistan, many Kurds have perceived their struggle for independence as an anti-colonial or anti-imperialist struggle. In the literature of the Kurdish parties there are often references to other independence struggles in the third world. The political solutions in Palestine and South Africa are mentioned as possible models for a solution to the Kurdish problems, and during a demonstration I attended in London one of the most popular phrases was 'yesterday Vietnam, today Kurdistan'.

TURKEY/NORTH-WEST KURDISTAN

After the disintegration of the Ottoman Empire the Treaty of Sèvres, signed in 1920, sought to guarantee statehood to 'Armenia, Kurdistan and Arabia' (Vanly, 1993: 145). However, this agreement was re-placed by the Treaty of Lausanne (1924) after the turbulent events in Anatolia ended with Mustafa Kemal gaining the power in Tur-key. The Kemalist programme of Turkish national liberation, unity, secularism and modernization was largely influenced by European nationalist ideology. This was an ideology alien in the Middle East and not easy to implement in the multi-ethnic environment of Anatolia. The most serious ethnic conflicts in the disintegrating Ottoman Empire were between Muslims and the Armenians as well as the Greeks. These conflicts ended with the Armenian genocide[6] and massive population exchanges between Greece and Turkey at the beginning of this century. The Kurds in Anatolia ended up in conflict with the Kemalist ideology after Mustafa Kemal in 1922 declared that the new state was Turkish. In 1924 the Kurdish lan-guage was banned. Several Kurdish rebellions followed, which were violently suppressed by the Turkish state, the last major uprising being in Dersim in 1936–8 (Bruinessen, 1994; Chaliand, 1994).

Even the existence of a Kurdish minority has been in conflict with Turkish nationalism and the Kemalist ideology on which modern Turkey is founded. During Turkey's entire existence the Turkish government has tried to deny that Kurds exist and the minority has been forced to assimilate. The Kurds have been called 'moun-tain Turks' and Kurdish identity has been oppressed through legislation forbidding anything 'Kurdish' or even any mention of the fact that Kurds exist. Consequently, there are no official figures of how many Kurds there are in Turkey. Bruinessen (1992a) estimates that in 1975 the total number was at least 7.5 million, or at least 19 per cent of the population. In the mid-1990s the number of Kurds in Turkey was estimated to be around 14 million (Sheikh-mous, 1994) or 12 million (Chaliand, 1994).

Although there have been some cosmetic changes in legislation in recent years, the cultural oppression of the Kurds continues to this day. There has been a clear policy of forced assimilation of the Kurdish population in Turkey. It is argued that if a Kurd is prepared to accept Turkish identity, the person will be accepted as a Turk, and in fact many assimilated Kurds can be found in important positions in Turkish society. Despite this, there is a clear tendency to regard any expression of Kurdish identity or culture as a dangerous threat to national unity. In Turkey, 'separatism' is a crime that leads to harsh prison sentences.

The Kurds in Turkey have experienced a strong ethnic revival and nationalistic movement since the beginning of the 1980s. Since 1984 there has also been an increase in the activities of Kurdish guerrillas from the Kurdistan Workers Party (Partîya Karkerên Kurdistan, PKK). The PKK was originally a political party with an explicit Marxist-Leninist ideology. The party and its leader Abdullah 'Apo' Öcalan have used a clear Marxist rhetoric (e.g. Öcalan, 1992). However, during the mid-1990s the party distanced itself from Marxism-Leninism. In 1985 another organization working closely with the PKK was founded, The National Liberation Front of Kurdistan (Enîya Rizgarîya Netewa Kurdistan, ERNK).

There are, and have been, several other Kurdish parties and organizations in Turkey, nearly all of which have been declared illegal in Turkey. In London I found that many Kurds from Turkey also supported other left-wing parties besides the PKK. One worth mentioning is the Socialist Party of Kurdistan (PSK, formerly named Turkish Kurdistan Socialist Party), which has advocated a peaceful solution to the Kurdish question but is nevertheless forbidden in Turkey. During the early 1990s the polarization of the conflict in Turkey led to a situation where the PKK and its sister organization the ERNK became clearly the most important Kurdish political organizations (Barkey, 1993).

Although the PKK is usually thought to be committed to an independent Kurdistan and opposed to any solution based on autonomy (in contrast to the Kurdish parties in Iraq and Iran), this is not supported by the literature examined during this research.

Actually, in a recent letter Öcalan writes: 'I would like to emphasize that we are not insistent on the division of Turkey, and that
such propaganda does not reflect our approach to the question'
(ERNK, 1995: 26). In 1984 the PKK started its armed struggle against
the Turkish government and those whom they regarded as collabor-
ators in the Turkish imperialists' oppression of the Kurds in
North-West Kurdistan. The Turkish republic has had a violent and
polarized political history and the Kurdish conflict is a case in point.
The PKK has used extraordinarily violent methods, especially in
the beginning of its campaign (Gunter, 1990; Bruinessen, 1988).
Moreover, the response of the Turkish government to the Kurdish
nationalist movement and the guerrilla war was not only one of
armed force, but in practice it also involved an increase in the
persecution of all Kurds in eastern Turkey.

The PKK is considered a 'terrorist' organization by the Turkish
authorities and the Turkish mass media. The British Parliamentary
Human Rights Group, led by Lord Avebury, who carried out a mission
to Turkish Kurdistan in October 1993 came to the conclusion that:

> In Britain and elsewhere, the question of Turkish Kurdistan is
> often presented as one of a reasonably democratic government
> seeking to cope with an intractable problem of terrorism. We
> believe that the reality is one of military terrorists aiming to ex-
> tinguish the identity of a people. (Parliamentary Human Rights
> Group, 1993: 28)

The discussions I had with Kurdish refugees from Turkey gave me
the impression that a clear majority of the Kurdish population supported the national uprising led by the PKK and the ERNK. As
the above mentioned report observes: 'Whether the majority of the
people in the region actually support the PKK itself, they are widely
opposed to the continuation of Turkish rule in its present form'
(Parliamentary Human Rights Group, 1993: 6). Kurdish informants pointed out that the historical importance of the PKK's struggle
is that the party has managed to continue to fight longer than any
other Kurdish movement. The present movement also has a greater
level of popular support than previous Kurdish uprisings, which
largely served the interests of tribal and feudal leaders. It seems to
be clear that the PKK in the mid-1990s had considerable support
among the Kurds in Turkey, but especially among the most
marginalized parts of the Kurdish population.

The situation during recent years in the Kurdish parts of Turkey can only be described as a civil war between the PKK and the Turkish army. The clashes between the PKK and the Turkish army are even occasionally fought out inside northern Iraq where the PKK has several bases. In the mid-1990s there were also approximately 20 000 Kurdish refugees from Turkey living in northern Iraq (McDowall, 1996). Bruinessen (1988) refers to an account in the Turkish newspaper *Cumhuriyet* (12 February 1986) where a 'fact-finding mission of the parliamentary opposition party, the Social Democrat-Populist Party, reported that all of eastern Turkey had become a sort of concentration camp where every citizen is being treated as a suspect and where oppression, torture and insult by the military are the rule rather than the exception' (Bruinessen, 1988: 46). According to official Turkish sources (*Cumhuriyet*, 9 May 1994, cited by ERNK, 1995), 9595 persons had lost their lives in the conflict, of which 3028 were civilians (that is, neither PKK guerrillas nor government soldiers). Kurdish sources (ERNK, 1995) estimated in August 1994 that 34 000 persons had died during the civil war, of which 5000 were civilians. 2000 villages had been destroyed and 3.5 million people had been forced to move. The human rights situation has clearly deteriorated during the 1990s. Amnesty International (1993b) and the Human Rights Watch (1993c) place most of the blame on the Turkish security forces, but also find PKK guerrillas guilty of gross violations of human rights. During the 1990s the PKK has at least twice unilaterally declared a ceasefire, but this has not stopped the hostilities. The Turkish government has also resolutely refused to negotiate with organizations they regard as 'terrorists'.

The situation is particularly bad for the Kurdish villagers who find themselves in the middle of the conflict. The Turkish authorities have established a system of village guards to fight the PKK. If villagers do not participate in this system they will face repression from the army and their villages might be destroyed; and if they do participate they will find themselves in conflict with the PKK (Amnesty International, 1993b; Rugman and Hutchings, 1996). According to McDowall (1996), several Kurdish tribes have migrated to avoid coming under either the government or PKK pressure. In the mid-1990s the government's policy appeared to be directed towards totally depopulating the rural areas in eastern Turkey, and it seems that villages were systematically burned down by the Turkish security forces (Rugman and Hutchings, 1996).

Whatever the methods of the PKK, the population rapidly
discovered that there was little it did which was not matched by
the ruthlessness of the security forces. A major migration to town
began for those caught in the crossfire of the conflict. (McDowall,
1996: 424)

The political situation in Turkey differs from the situation in Iraq
and Iran, since the Turkish government proclaims its commitment
to a western-style democracy. For example, Gellner (1994) argues
that the idea of a secular democracy (although in a combination
with a strong army) is a profoundly important part of Kemalism.
However, it looks as though Turkish democracy does not include
the Kurdish question and the provinces in the east, 'Following Özal's
death in April 1993, it has become clearer than ever that when it
comes to the Kurdish question, it is not the civilian led elected
government which determines policy but the army dominated
National Security Council' (Kutschera, 1994: 14).

There has also been an increase in the number of extrajudicial
killings and 'disappearances' in eastern Turkey. According to Amnesty International (1993a), people active in the legal opposition
or suspected of having contacts with the PKK have been killed
either directly by, or with the collusion of the Turkish security forces.
Kurdish sources (for example numerous articles in *Kurdistan Report*) also point out that many of the atrocities in eastern Turkey
are carried out by death squads and irregular troops, the so-called
contra-guerrillas.

In the 1990s there seems to have happened a polarization of
Turkish society on the Kurdish question. As McDowall observes:
'From 1990 onwards ... the majority of Turks began to view the
Kurdish minority itself as a profound menace' (McDowall, 1996:
440). At the same time the government's crackdown on the PKK
has also affected moderate Kurdish and Turkish associations, politicians, artists and intellectuals (Barkey, 1993). Even Kurdish members
of Parliament who have opposed the government's policies have
been imprisoned. In the 1990s assimilated Kurds, who cannot speak
Kurdish and have never before strongly identified themselves as
Kurds, have been largely forced to choose sides in an increasingly
polarized conflict.

Alevi Kurds

A majority of the Kurds from Turkey living in London are Kurdish Alevis. In Turkey, 'Alevi' is a term used for a large number of different heterodox communities (Bruinessen, 1996). What they have in common is that they do not belong to either the Sunni or the Shia sects of Islam and they do not follow Islam's traditional religious rituals. There are over three million Alevis in Turkey,[7] of whom one-third are Kurdish. Traditionally Alevis are a socially stigmatized group, and to this day they have been a marginalized underclass in Turkish society (McDowall, 1992). The Alevi community has experienced a large rural–urban migration, which has led them to towns where they often live in their own quarters and are regarded as a threat by the dominant Sunni population (Bruinessen, 1992b). The Alevis have also experienced large-scale forced migration, where the population has been forced to move from areas with high PKK activity (McDowall, 1992). The social situation of the Alevis has traditionally made them incline towards the political left in Turkey (McDowall, 1992). As a couple of my informants told me, this has also made it easy for Alevi Kurds to start to support the PKK during the 1990s, despite the fact that originally the PKK was largely associated with the Sunni Kurdish communities.

To understand the sudden influx of Alevi Kurds in Britain in 1989, one has to go back to 1978 when 'tensions between the rightist and leftists in Marash province culminated in a major massacre of Alevis organized by the fascist Grey Wolves (National Action Party), in which at least one hundred, and probably several hundred, died' (McDowall, 1992: 59). In the local elections in Marash in 1989 Sunni Muslim revivalists and rightists did particularly well, and among the Alevis in Marash there was a fear that the events of 1978 would be repeated (McDowall, 1992). According to Collinson (1990), the Turkish authorities' sharp reaction to the May Day demonstrations in 1989 was also a contributing factor. In May and June 1989 a large number of Turkish citizens arrived in Britain to seek asylum, and according to my informants in London most of these were Alevi Kurds, mainly from Marash and Sivas. There seem to be several reasons why they chose to flee to Britain rather than any other country. During my fieldwork most Kurds described the migration as a chain migration, where people had relatives or friends who had previously arrived in Britain.

Escape from Turkey

Because of the labour migration from Turkey in the 1960s and 1970s, there are established Turkish and Kurdish communities in many European cities. The present refugee migration is therefore often a continuation of previous chain migrations (cf. Hjarnø, 1991). Today, as during earlier migration movements from Turkey, it is not always easy to distinguish between political and economic reasons for the flight. This is especially true since the persecution of the Kurds takes both economic and political forms.

Although the interviewees in this study were not asked about the reasons for their flight from Turkey, many persons volunteered to explain this. Most refugees disclosed that the only thing they had done was publicly to express support for the Kurdish cause, and that they therefore faced imprisonment or feared for their life in Turkey. Actually, none of the persons I met said that they would have been personally active in the PKK or the ERNK in Turkey. This is in contrast to the Iraqi and Iranian refugees who often described how they had actively taken part in the Kurdish resistance movements.

The refugees from Turkey whom I met during the fieldwork often had used their connections in Europe, as well as the resources of their relatives in Turkey, in order to be able to travel to Europe. The refugees in London usually had travelled more or less directly from Turkey to Britain. Often they had planned from the beginning to go to Britain. There were also some persons who had arrived as students but who, because of the developments in eastern Turkey and their political activism in Britain, found that they could not safely return to Turkey. It was difficult to find any clear pattern of migration among the refugees in Finland because of the small sample, but it appears that many persons travelled through the Soviet Union/CIS and ended up in Finland in their attempt to reach Western Europe.

IRAQ/SOUTH KURDISTAN

After the First World War the British established a new state out of the three ancient Ottoman *vilayets* of Basra, Baghdad and Mosul. Largely against their will, the Kurds therefore found themselves living in a state with a predominantly Arab population (Vanly, 1993).

The Kurds in the mid-1990s are estimated to be around 23 per cent of the population of Iraq, numbering approximately four and a half million (Sheikhmous, 1994).

Relations between the Iraqi government and the Kurds have never worked well. The Kurdish areas have occasionally been granted limited autonomy by the government, but usually the (Arab) state's wish for political hegemony has led to conflicts between the Kurdish minority and the government. Kurdish *peshmergas* (guerrilla soldiers) have recurrently been involved in a guerrilla war with the government. The Kurdish *peshmergas* have periodically controlled large parts of northern Iraq. During the 1920s and 1930 the Kurdish uprisings were mostly local conflicts, but from the 1960s the wars between the Kurds and the government were fought on a larger scale (Chaliand, 1994). During the war in 1974 the Kurds were able to get considerable support from Iran and were able successfully to fight government troops until Iran suddenly withdrew its support in 1975. After the defeat in 1975, the Kurdish movement split into two parties which have continued their separate struggles for autonomy.

The two main Kurdish parties in Iraq are the Kurdish Democratic Party (KDP) and the Patriotic Union of Kurdistan (PUK). These two parties gained 45 per cent and 43.6 per cent of the votes respectively in the Kurdish elections in 1992 (McDowall, 1996). The Kurdish nationalist movement in Iraq has been divided by different alliances with foreign countries and by a friction between modern left-wing intellectuals from an urban background and those supporting a more traditional Kurdish leadership (Sherzad, 1992). This friction is also noticeable in the problematic relations between the KDP and the PUK. The KDP's leader Masud Barzani is often regarded as a more traditional leader while the PUK's Jalal Talabani has a background in left-wing intellectual organizations. There is also a geographical difference: most KDP supporters are in the northern Kurmanji-speaking parts of Iraq, while the PUK is more powerful in the Sorani-speaking south (cf. Laizer, 1996a).

The Kurds in Iraq have always had a clear Kurdish identity and have also enjoyed greater cultural rights than their Kurdish neighbours in Iran and Turkey. For example, the Kurdish language has been accepted as an official language in the Kurdish areas (McDowall, 1992; Chaliand, 1994). Although the Kurds in Iraq have had cultural rights, the government has repeatedly fought a war against its Kurdish minority. Saddam Hussein's policy towards the Kurds can be described as genocidal,[8] including forcible deportations, chemical warfare, mass executions and human rights violations on an enormous scale. During the late 1980s the Iraqi government's war with the Kurds entered a new phase. After the war between Iran and Iraq ended in 1988, the Iraqi army was able to concentrate all its resources on the Kurdish rebellion. Saddam Hussein introduced the *Anfal* campaign in 1988, a new extensive programme of Arabization and genocide of the Kurdish population during which at least 50 000, but probably 100 000 Kurds were killed by the government (Human Rights Watch, 1993a). McDowall (1996) puts his estimate even higher and writes that 150 000 – 200 000 persons perished in the *Anfal* operations. More than half of the Kurdish villages in Iraq were destroyed in the campaign (Bruinessen, 1992a; Chaliand, 1994). In many cases Kurdish villagers were transported to concentration camps where the men were executed and women and children deported to another part of Iraq (McDowall, 1996). About 800 000 Kurds were deported from the Kurdish areas to camps in other parts of Iraq (Sherzad, 1992). In addition, between 1969 and 1988 at least 130 000 Faili Kurds were deported from Iraq to Iran, since these were not regarded to be citizens of Iraq (Morad, 1992).

During the *Anfal* campaign Saddam Hussein repeatedly bombed Kurdish villages and towns with chemical weapons. According to Kurdish sources cited in Chaliand (1994), bombardments with chemical weapons against civilians took place repeatedly between 15 April 1987 and 15 May 1988. During this time these bombardments drew surprisingly little attention from the international community. The most tragic case is the bombing of the town of Halabja on 16 March 1988, where 5000 people died.

The Kurdish rebellion collapsed in 1988, and a large number of the *peshmergas* and many civilians fled to Iran and Turkey. Chaliand (1994) estimates that the total number of refugees created by the conflict in Iraq was 400 000 persons of whom 370 000 fled to Iran. McDowall (1996), on the other hand, estimates that the total number of Kurdish refugees from Iraq living in Iran in 1988 was around 250 000 persons. Most of the Iraqi refugees I met during my fieldwork are persons who fled into Iran around 1988 and, as will be explained later, were not able to stay there.

In 1990 the Iraqi invasion of Kuwait created a new situation for the Kurds in Iraq. Despite encouragement from the Allies, the Kurdish parties were reluctant to join the fight against Saddam

Hussein. But in March 1991 a spontaneous uprising in Kurdistan led to the whole of northern Iraq being controlled by the Kurds. After it became clear that Saddam Hussein was not, after all, defeated and that the uprising would not get support from the Allies, it soon became clear that this rebellion would end in disaster. Remembering Saddam Hussein's earlier atrocities against the Kurds, the population fled *en masse* towards the neighbouring countries (Chaliand, 1994). According to the UNHCR (1992), there were 1.4 million Kurdish refugees from Iraq in Iran, and 450 000 refugees on the Turkish border by mid April 1991. For the first time in Kurdish history this humanitarian catastrophe was closely followed by the Western media. In order to alleviate this massive disaster, a humanitarian intervention by troops from the USA was soon started. Largely on the initiative of the British government, a safe haven for the Kurds under the protection of the United Nations was established in northern Iraq (Bulloch and Morris, 1993).

The Kurdish parties soon organized an election for a National Assembly and established control over northern Iraq. Negotiations with Saddam Hussein about autonomy failed, so the Kurdish National Assembly unilaterally declared autonomy for the region. Symptomatic of the Kurds' precarious situation is the fact that the National Assembly did not declare Kurdistan independent. Nor would any of the neighbouring states support an independent Kurdish state. In a seldom seen mutual understanding, the foreign ministers of Turkey, Iran and Syria met in November 1992 and issued a joint statement declaring their commitment to Iraq's territorial integrity (Barkey, 1993).

Many Kurdish refugees in Europe managed to visit northern Iraq after it came under the protection of the UN. For example, many Kurdish male refugees were able to travel back to northern Iraq in order to marry. Many of my informants also told me that they again started to hope that it would be possible to move back. However, the economic situation in the region was extremely vulnerable. All the wars had destroyed much of the infrastructure and a large part of the Kurdish villages. Because northern Iraq is still a part of Iraq, the UN sanctions against Iraq also affect the Kurdish regions. Since also Saddam Hussein stopped all trade with the Kurdish areas, the region has become totally dependent on the trade at the border with Turkey. In this way the Kurds in Iraq became largely reliant on the good will of the Turkish government, a fact that has led to conflicts with the PKK.

The complicated problems in northern Iraq did not help to resolve the old disagreements between the two main parties, the KDP and the PUK. Repeated violent clashes between *peshmergas* from different parties (the KDP, PUK, PKK and the Kurdish Islamic Movement in different constellations) as well as a disagreement over the tax income from the border trade, finally led to open civil war between the two main parties during 1994 and 1995 (Laizer, 1996a). At the time of writing the hostilities between the KDP and the PUK continue. What started as a promising attempt to achieve Kurdish autonomy seems to have ended in economic despair, social breakdown, human rights violations and civil war (Amnesty International, 1995a; Ofteringer and Bäcker, 1994; Laizer, 1996a). Furthermore, Saddam Hussein is still in power in Baghdad and it is not clear for how long the United Nations will be ready to provide protection for the Kurds. Clearly, this is not a situation where any return migration of refugees can take place. On the contrary, the situation in northern Iraq might create new refugees.

Escape from Iraq

The Kurdish refugees from Iraq whom I met during this study were mostly persons who were active in the Kurdish resistance movement and who were forced to flee to Iran in 1988. I did not specifically ask the interviewees about their activities before the flight, but most of the refugees from Iraq told me that they had been *peshmergas* for several years before they fled the country. A few interviewees also arrived in Europe earlier, in two cases as students.

The Kurds who fled from Iraq in 1988 were accepted as refugees by Iran. Iran has acceded to the Geneva Refugee Convention and Protocol (United Nations, 1995) and has, in fact, taken care of a large proportion of the world's refugees. According to the UNHCR (1993), 4.4 million refugees lived in Iran in December 1991, of whom most were from Afghanistan. The Kurdish refugees were accommodated in Iran in camps where 'conditions have been physically deprived and restricted, with strictly limited time allowed outside camp, and inadequate food and health facilities inside' (McDowall, 1992: 111). When the Kurdish refugees from Iraq arrived in 1988 there were already 50 000 Kurds from Iraq living in Iran who had arrived as refugees in 1975, and also an unknown number of Faili Kurds who had been deported from Iraq (McDowall, 1996).

Many of the refugees from Iraq held political opinions clearly in conflict with the dominant ideology in the Iranian Islamic Republic. Many Kurdish refugees did not feel safe in Iran, especially since the conflict between the Iranian Kurds and the Iranian government remained unsolved. Many Kurdish refugees from Iraq have therefore tried to continue their flight from Iran. Since the Kurdish refugees from Iraq (for obvious reasons) do not have any official Iraqi passports or travel documents, these have to be obtained in Iran. All the persons I interviewed in Britain had been forced to buy expensive false travel documents in order to get out of Iran. As Koser (1997a) writes, refugees who travel directly from Iran largely have to rely on intermediaries or 'travel agents'. Few of the refugees I interviewed had any clear plan of where they wanted to travel. Most interviewees seemed to have had a very poor knowledge of possible destinations. A woman from Suleimanya in Iraq described her knowledge of Europe:

> It is incredible when I think of it now, but I had never heard about visas or anything and was not aware of Europe or did know about the countries and way of life here. I knew of capitalism and that Europe was highly industrialized but that was it. Although I lived in a town, I was from a poorer part of the town and I had never met a European and did not know or had not met anybody who had been to Europe.

Some Kurds from Iran and Iraq told me that Sweden had a reputation as a country where human rights were respected, and consequently many persons tried to get to Sweden. In practice it was often those who sold the travel documents and flight tickets who decided where the refugees would fly. One refugee explained that she had bought a visa for the United Kingdom, since this was the cheapest one available, which was probably because the UK was regarded as the country where it would be most difficult to get asylum. Two other persons told me that they had been on their way to Sweden, but because of problems with their travel documents during the change of flight at Heathrow Airport they had to apply for asylum in Britain.

After 1988 many of the refugees from Iraq also continued their flight from Iran to Turkey, where the Turkish authorities have kept Kurdish refugees from Iraq strictly isolated from the local Kurdish population in elementary camps near the Iraqi border (Laizer, 1991), or in some cases under the protection of the UNHCR in towns in the western part of the country. The UNHCR in Turkey has been able to organize resettlement for some of the refugees in a third country (this will be discussed in more detail in the section about Iran). The creation of the safe haven in northern Iraq in 1991 slightly changed the situation, but because of the circumstances described earlier, refugees still come to Turkey from Iraq. However, according to Amnesty International (1994), the policy of the Turkish authorities in 1993 was that there were no longer any genuine refugees coming from Iraq. Therefore the authorities endorsed a forced return and even denied the refugees from Iraq the right to leave Turkey for another country.

Beginning in 1990, Finland has invited a number of Iraqi refugees from UNHCR camps in Turkey and Pakistan as part of the Finnish annual refugee quota. Most of the Iraqi refugees in Finland have therefore arrived as quota refugees, although there are also many who have travelled through the CIS and the Baltic states to arrive in the country as asylum seekers. In my sample in Finland all refugees from Iraq had arrived as quota refugees. None of those I interviewed had planned to go to Finland, and many told me that they had never heard about the country before they were given the opportunity to be resettled there.

IRAN/EAST KURDISTAN

The part of Kurdistan that today lies within the borders of Iran consists of areas that in 1514 were incorporated into the Safavid (Persian) empire. The Kurds usually have a sense of closer affinity with the Persian language and culture than with Turkish or Arabic. The Iranian state is also a multicultural state with several minorities (Azeri, Arabs, Baluchi, and so on) and it has a far longer history as a state than Turkey and Iraq. The Kurds comprise between 10 per cent (Bruinessen, 1992a; McDowall, 1992) and 15 per cent (Chaliand, 1994; Sheikhmous, 1994) of the Iranian population, or between 5.5 million and 8 million persons in the mid-1990s. As McDowall (1992) points out, the sense of affinity with Iran impels today's Kurds towards autonomy rather than independence from Iran. This sense of an identity as Iranians, although not identification with the present government, has also been evident in most of my interviews with Iranian Kurdish refugees.

Despite this, one of the most important events in the history of Kurdish nationalism took place in this part of Kurdistan. The Mahabad Republic declared itself independent in 1946. The republic was instigated by, but failed to get support from, the Soviet Union, and was crushed within a year by the Iranian army. Although the Iranian state has not denied the Kurds their cultural identity, the persecution and assimilation policy has been 'more cunning' (Vanly, 1993, 139). The Kurdish aspirations for greater autonomy have always been received with hostility from the government and the Kurdish language is not used as a language of instruction in schools. Especially since the revolution in 1979, one difference that might be of importance is that the Iranian Kurds are mostly Sunni Muslims, while most other Iranians are Shia Muslims.

The Iranian Kurds' relations with the government deteriorated badly after the Iranian revolution in 1979. Many Kurds participated in the revolution in the belief that this would lead to a better situation for the Kurds. The Kurds acquired de facto autonomy over the Kurdish parts of the country and started negotiations with the new government over the future role of the region. It soon became clear that the new government under Ayatollah Khomeini would not allow autonomy since it would be contrary to Islamic principles and would divide the Muslims (Koohi-Kamali, 1992). In 1979 Khomeini issued a *fatwa* declaring a holy war 'against the atheist people of Kurdistan' (Chaliand, 1994: 78).

There have been two Kurdish political parties of importance in Iran. The most influential and popular is the Kurdistan Democratic Party of Iran (KDP-Iran). In March 1980 the KDP-Iran received 80 per cent of the votes in Kurdistan in the Iranian parliamentary elections (Chaliand, 1994). The second important party is the more radical Marxist party, the Revolutionary Organization of Toilers, known as *Komala* (The Organization). This party has worked as the Kurdish section of the Iranian Communist Party, although demanding autonomy for the Kurdish regions in Iran (Komala, 1984).

After the negotiations with the government broke down, Khomeini sent revolutionary guards to take control of Kurdistan. Despite this, the Kurdish parties and other Iranian opposition parties were able to control the mountains in Iranian Kurdistan for several years. Fights between Kurdish *peshmergas* and government troops continued until 1983 inside Iran, but since then the Iranian opposition has largely been forced to operate from inside Iraq (Chaliand, 1994).

Political disagreements and violent clashes between the two Kurdish parties during the late 1980s also hampered their efforts. Furthermore, there have also been divisions inside the parties. The relations between the Iranian and Iraqi Kurdish parties have always been problematic because of the different alliances the parties have had with the two states. After the outbreak of the Iran–Iraq war in 1980, relations between the Kurdish parties in the two countries became even more complicated (Koohi-Kamali, 1992).

According to my informants, Kurdish sources indicate that about 55 000 Iranian Kurds died in the armed conflicts with the government in 1979–92, of whom only 5000 were *peshmergas*. Similar figures are mentioned by Laizer (1996a), who adds that approximately 300 Iranian Kurdish villages have been destroyed. At the beginning of the 1990s Iranian Kurdistan was under tight military control and foreigners were not allowed to visit the area. The Iranian government's human rights abuses against Kurds and other Iranian citizens have continued until recent years, including political arrests, unfair trials and summary executions (Amnesty International, 1995b).

In recent years, the future of the Iranian Kurdish opposition movements has not looked very bright. Bruinessen suggests that Komala 'gradually became weaker and more isolated, it turned increasingly radical, and came to see itself as the vanguard of world revolution. The Party split in the late 1980s, and many of its leaders sought refuge in European countries' (Bruinessen, 1992a: 42). The assassination of Iranian opposition party leaders in exile also seriously affected the activities of the parties. It is commonly assumed that agents working for the Iranian government lie behind these assassinations. These suspicions were confirmed in April 1997 when a German court held Iranian authorities responsible for the assassination in 1992 of three Kurds at the 'Mykonos' restaurant in Berlin. In 1988 the KDP-Iran was split into two branches. According to Bruinessen, 'Both branches of the party still had headquarters in Iraqi Kurdistan by the beginning of 1991 but their position was very delicate, and they seemed not to have any clear strategies' (Bruinessen, 1992a: 42). This disunity continued until 1997, when it was reported that the two branches were reunited.

The Escape from Iran

During my fieldwork I mostly met Kurdish refugees from Iran who had been active in Kurdish opposition movements. These refugees had often lived for a long time – up to ten years – in the liberated areas in the Kurdish mountains where they had been active as *peshmergas* in one or other of the Kurdish parties. Many of the interviewees had continued their flight from the liberated areas in the mountains to Turkey, or in some cases to Iraq. Other refugees had travelled straight from Iran over the border to Turkey. According to Amnesty International (1994), every year hundreds of Iranian refugees arrive in Turkey, and the International Organization for Migration estimates that nearly 1.5 million Iranians have entered Turkey since the late 1970s (IOM, 1996).

It seems that the earlier mentioned disintegration of the parties and their infrastructure has forced many refugees to leave the mountains. Some persons have been wounded or have suffered from other physical weaknesses, and are more a burden than an asset for the Kurdish parties, thus having to seek asylum elsewhere. Several of the Iranian Kurds who participated in this research said that the disunity and decline of the Iranian Kurdish movements and opposition parties were major factors behind their decision to seek asylum in Europe. Many of my interviewees, from both Iran and Iraq, also indicated that, after several years in the mountains, personal reasons influenced their decisions. Often their children's future was the ultimate reason why they decided to leave their mountain hideouts.

Turkey has ratified the 1951 United Nations Refugee Convention and acceded to the 1967 Protocol, but has kept the geographical limitation of the convention. This means that Turkey, from a legal point of view, only accepts as a refugee a person who has fled from his or her country as a result of events that occurred in Europe (Kirisci, 1996; United Nations, 1995). Consequently, refugees from neither Iran nor Iraq are recognized as refugees in Turkey and are not allowed to stay in the country. Instead, there is an informal agreement between the UNHCR and Turkey that the UNHCR can take care of and determine the refugee status of persons from non-European countries and, if necessary, organize their resettlement in a third country. Despite this cooperation, there are frequent reports that the Turkish authorities deport refugees back to the countries they came from, and that even persons awaiting resettlement are under the constant threat of being sent back. There are several reports of refugees who have been forcibly returned to Iran where they are reported to have been executed or imprisoned (Amnesty International, 1994). The UNHCR is therefore trying to resettle people as fast as possible. Unfortunately, this is a complicated process. Even in the fastest cases it seems to take at least one year, and two years is not uncommon, to determine the status of a person and find a country for resettlement.[9]

Finland has accepted Iranian refugees within its yearly quota since 1989, and a large number of the Iranian refugees in the country are Kurds who have arrived as quota refugees since 1990. All Iranian Kurds in my sample in Finland had arrived as quota refugees. As in the case of the refugees from Iraq, none of the persons I interviewed had originally planned to move to Finland. Some of them told me that they had wished to move to a country where they had relatives or friends, but since their lives were in immediate danger they accepted any country the UNHCR suggested.

Iranian refugees regard themselves as being under a continued threat from Iranian agents in Turkey. In fact, several Iranian opposition politicians have been killed in Turkey (Amnesty International, 1994). Iranian refugees are housed near Ankara by the UNHCR in certain cities which they are not allowed to leave and where they are monitored by the local police. This arrangement might be resorted to in order to protect the refugees from assassination attempts, but it also allows the Turkish authorities to isolate Iranian Kurds from the local Kurdish population.

Because of the above-mentioned factors, many Iranian refugees in Turkey fear for their lives and wish to leave as soon as possible. Since Iranian refugees, for obvious reasons, have seldom been in a position to obtain valid travel documents, those who wish to leave Turkey immediately have to buy expensive documents on the black market. This was the case for all Iranian refugees whom I met in Britain. Only one person told me that she had planned to go to the UK from the beginning because she had relatives in the country. The other interviewees did not have any plans and travelled to the first place for which they could get valid tickets, since they did not dare to stay in Turkey. A young woman from Iran told me about her escape:

ÖW: Did you actually plan to go to Britain from the beginning, or, did you choose the country?
R: First let me say, I did not want to go anywhere, honestly, and I had to make decision in just a few days, in about three days, and I did not mind where I was going, just I wanted to

leave Iran, I had a plan to go to Germany because of some friends
I had there. Many times I was taken to the Airport in Istanbul,
but I could not, they could not manage, and after a while I decided to come here and they took me.

ÖW: It was more like a coincidence that you came here?

R: When I left, in that particular situation I did not care very much
where I was going to, I was just going to leave Iran and I was in
a very bad condition of everything, mentally and whatever. When
you are forced to leave you do not mind where you are going to.

KURDS IN EXILE

The conflicts in Kurdistan have grown more serious over the years.
During the earlier local conflicts, refugees were able to flee to another
part of Kurdistan and return when the conflict was resolved. During the more intensive conflicts between the governments and the
Kurds in recent years the refugees have been forced on a massive
scale to flee to neighbouring countries or to become displaced persons
within the country. However, the complicated political situation in
the region and the simultaneous conflicts between the Kurds and
the governments in Turkey, Iraq and Iran have made it increasingly hard to find refuge in the neighbouring states. At the same
time the size of the conflicts and the devastation in the region have
made repatriation more difficult. The need for asylum outside the
region has consequently increased.

Although the Kurds are oppressed by the governments in Turkey,
Iraq and Iran, and this oppression is a major reason for the flight
from these countries, there are also other reasons for the flight
from Kurdistan. The reasons are often a complex combination of
the various political, economic and social problems which I have
outlined above. For example, Bruinessen (1992b) points out that
the reason for flight is often a combination of state persecution
and various local conflicts, and that furthermore there are also
religious and sectarian conflicts in the region which can create
refugees. It is also important to remember that many persons have
not been personally involved in politics, but are merely victims of
violent conflicts or forcible deportations. In terms of the typologies
of refugee migration mentioned in Chapter 1, it is difficult to classify
the Kurdish refugees. None of the typologies is totally suitable for

the Kurdish case because of the complexity of the political situation and the variety of reasons for flight.

Most of the Kurdish refugees and displaced persons are found in the Middle East. For example, ERNK (1995) estimates that the number of Kurds forced to move because of the conflict in Turkey alone is 3.5 million. Furthermore, the conflicts in Iraq and Iran have uprooted large population groups. The refugees who leave the Middle East are of course not representative of the whole Kurdish population. It is only certain persons who can and will flee abroad. First, politically active persons are of course more likely to become refugees than others. Secondly, not all persons have the economic resources to pay for the travel expenses that a flight to Europe entails. Usually the money is collected by and borrowed from relatives, but still the opportunity to seek asylum outside the Middle East is not open to all refugees. However, the refugees resettled by the UNHCR are often made up of large families and other persons who have not had the necessary economic resources.

Outside the Middle East, most of the Kurds are found in European countries. Although Kurdish refugees can be found all over the world, the numbers outside Europe have been relatively small. Sheikhmous (1994) estimates that the Kurdish diaspora outside the Middle East and the CIS numbers at least 500 000. Of these, at least 300 000 can be found in Germany, where the labour migration from Turkey included many Kurds. Since the labour migration to Europe was stopped in the early 1970s, most Kurds have arrived in Europe as refugees. In the early 1990s, the following countries were also estimated to have large Kurdish populations: France (approximately 60 000 persons), the Netherlands (30 000 – 40 000), Austria (20 000 – 30 000), the UK (20 000), Switzerland (15 000 – 20 000), Sweden (16 000 – 18 000), Denmark (12 000 – 13 000) and Belgium (10 000) (Blaschke, 1991b; Sheikhmous, 1990, 1994).

Already the first Kurds who settled in Europe established cultural and political associations (Sheikhmous, 1989) and today there is a great variety of organizations and activities among the Kurds in exile (*Kurden im Exil,* 1991). The Kurds in exile have been referred to as a diaspora. This is the case, for example, in *An Atlas of International Migration* (Segal, 1993). The Kurds living in Germany are called a diaspora by Blaschke (1991a), although he does not define the concept. The term is also occasionally used among the Kurds themselves. Just to give one example: in a recent interview Abdullah Öcalan, the chairperson of the PKK, comments on the Kurdish asylum problem and declares that 'the Kurds are living in a vast Diaspora like the Jewish Diaspora of the past' (Laizer, 1996b: 47).

CONCLUSION

This chapter shows that at least one of Safran's characteristics of a diaspora is fulfilled in the case of the Kurds in exile. Kurdish refugees have experienced a forced dispersal, since 'they, or their ancestors, have been dispersed from a specific original "center" to two or more "peripheral," or foreign, regions' (Safran, 1991: 83). In Iran, Iraq and Turkey the conflicts between the governments and the Kurds became worse during the 1980s and early 1990s. The conflict in Kurdistan is a complex one where international, national and local conflicts overlap in a situation where ethnic identities, economic inequality, political ideologies and religious divisions all play a role. The oppression the Kurds face has taken different forms and there are differences in the political situations in the Kurdish parts of Turkey, Iraq and Iran. There are also considerable differences between the prospects for the Kurdish political parties and the Kurdish national projects in the three countries. Serious disagreements and violent conflicts between different political parties have also divided the Kurdish population. There is, however, still a common Kurdish nationalism which unites Kurds from different countries.

At the same time as the situation in Kurdistan has deteriorated, it has become increasingly difficult for refugees to seek refuge within another part of Kurdistan or in the neighbouring countries. Consequently, there is an increased need for asylum outside the Middle East. The protection, or lack of protection, that two countries in the European Union, the United Kingdom and Finland, have been able to offer to persecuted Kurds will be discussed in the next chapter.

3 Resettlement Policies: Two Different Models

It can be assumed that the receiving society and its resettlement policies play a fundamental role in the process of integration among refugees. In this study, England and Finland were chosen as locations for the fieldwork. These two countries provide examples of two different models of resettlement policies. The UK (or more specifically, England) is a relatively large country with a sizeable ethnic minority population and a long tradition of communitarian and multicultural policies. Finland is a small country with few immigrants and can be characterized as an egalitarian welfare state with a large public sector. In terms of the dichotomy of state and civil society, England is an example of a society that emphasizes the importance of civil society, while Finland exemplifies a society where the state plays a large role. When it comes to asylum policies, the United Kingdom and Finland have relatively similar restrictive policies. Both England and Finland also have recently arrived Kurdish refugee populations coming from identical backgrounds in Kurdistan. However, in most other respects relating to refugee resettlement the two countries are different. A comparison between these two different societies makes it possible to study the impact of different social structures on refugee communities. The consequences of these differences are discussed in the following chapters, while this chapter concentrates on identifying the differences and similarities in the two receiving societies. It can be expected that the different social structures in England and Finland have different consequences for the process of integration and for the social organization of their Kurdish refugee communities. A comparative perspective also provides an opportunity to highlight some general features in the way refugees are integrated. Despite all the differences between the two cases, a number of features remain the same.

UNITED KINGDOM

The well-known political history of Britain, including the country's history as a dominant colonial and political power, still gives the

United Kingdom a world-wide cultural and political influence. This also has consequences for the migration flows to and from the country, as well as for British immigration and refugee policies. In fact, both immigration to Britain and emigration from Britain have been relatively extensive for a long time. Although there has been a large immigration into Britain, emigration from Britain has actually been larger than immigration during most of the years since 1964 when statistics started to be collected through the International Passenger Survey (OPCS, 1994).

The colonial history and the experiences of the British Empire still have a profound influence on ethnic relations in Britain. The United Kingdom has well-established 'ethnic minorities', largely originating from post-war migration movements from the so-called New Commonwealth. Until the 1990s, refugees constituted only a very small part of the migration to Britain. Because of the long history of 'ethnic minorities' and 'race relations' in Britain, the whole question of refugee admission in Britain is connected to the constantly important political issues of immigration and 'race' (Miles and Cleary, 1993).

In the 1991 National Census of Population 5.5 per cent of the population indicated that they belonged to some of the ethnic minority groups in the UK, which is just over three million out of a total population of 55 million. The biggest category was 'South Asian', including Indians, Pakistanis and Bangladeshis, and comprising 2.7 per cent of the UK population. 'Black' ethnic groups accounted for a further 1.6 per cent followed by 'Chinese and other ethnic groups' with 1.3 per cent (Owen, 1994). In Britain there is an awareness and a large public discussion of issues related to what is often called 'race relations'. Britain has, for example, a comprehensive 'race relations' legislation enforced by the Commission for Racial Equality.

Refugees in the UK

Britain is often seen as having a tradition of offering hospitality to refugees, beginning with the French Huguenots in the seventeenth century. Later, a small number of German revolutionaries, among them Karl Marx, lived as refugees in London in the mid-nineteenth century. However, the number of refugees did not become significant before the end of the nineteenth century and the arrival of Jews from eastern Europe. This also coincides with the first efforts to control the influx of refugees. Later, in the 1930s, many persons fled from Nazi Germany to Britain. The United Kingdom was among the initial signatories to the UN Refugee Convention in 1951 and acceded to the Protocol in 1968 (United Nations, 1995). However, until recently the number of asylum applicants has been relatively small by international comparison.

In the 1990s, however, there is no longer any reason to talk about a hospitality towards refugees in Britain. Despite the relatively small numbers of asylum seekers coming to the UK, the British government has adapted a range of measures designed to keep the figures as low as possible. These measures include the introduction of visa restrictions for certain countries and new laws like the 1987 Immigration Act, which made airlines and shipping companies liable to a charge of £1000 for each improperly documented passenger they bring to the UK. This sum was later increased to £2000. Furthermore, various measures discouraging asylum seekers from coming to Britain have been introduced, including the removal of social welfare benefits from certain groups of asylum seekers. In 1996 the new Asylum Bill sought to cut the welfare benefits for asylum seekers who had not applied for asylum immediately upon arrival in Britain. There have also been changes in the appeals procedure and, as described later, a radical increase in the number of negative decisions on asylum applications. Finally, there is also an extensive use of the inhumane practice of detention (Cohen, 1994). In Britain immigration authorities can detain an asylum seeker while his/her case is being considered despite the fact that the person has not broken any law. The Refugee Council (1994) estimates that immigration detention in the early 1990s annually affected about 10 000 persons, although most of these were detained for less than two weeks.

In the light of the changes mentioned above, the British official refugee policy has clearly lost many of the humanitarian values on which it was originally based. Today Britain is certainly not a country offering hospitality to refugees, and, according to Amnesty International (1996), recent developments have largely demolished the right to asylum in the UK. Most of the recent changes have obviously been introduced in order to discourage people from applying for asylum in Britain. This was explicitly stated by the British government in the following news item published in the *Financial Times* (8 March 1996):

Bogus asylum seekers are being attracted to the UK in increasing numbers because of the lure of its welfare system, the High Court was told yesterday. Many applicants had no proper claim to asylum and were "economic migrants", two judges heard. New regulations had been introduced "to make the UK less attractive and therefore reduce the burden on the taxpayers and the social security fund", said Mr Stephen Richards, appearing for the government. Mr Richards was defending Mr Peter Lilley, the social security secretary, against accusations by the Joint Council for the Welfare of Immigrants that the refugees are unlawfully being deterred from seeking sanctuary in the UK by the regulations, introduced last month. ('Benefits lure fraudsters', 1996)

Until the 1990s the number of persons applying for asylum had been low in comparison to other major European countries such as Germany or France. Counted in terms of asylum seekers per inhabitants, the UK received fewer refugees than most other Western European countries in the 1980s (Cohen and Joly, 1989). There was, however, a remarkable increase in the number of asylum seekers in the late 1980s and early 1990s (see Figure 3.1).

During the early 1980s more than half of the applicants received full refugee status. However, in recent years the British asylum policy has become increasingly restrictive. Already during the 1980s the percentage of persons receiving refugee status decreased radically. This was initially compensated by an increase in the percentage of persons receiving the British 'B-status' called Exceptional Leave to

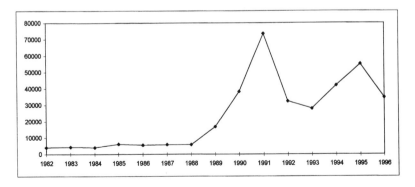

Figure 3.1 Asylum seekers in the United Kingdom, 1982–96, including dependants. (*Sources:* Home Office, various years)

Kurdish Diasporas

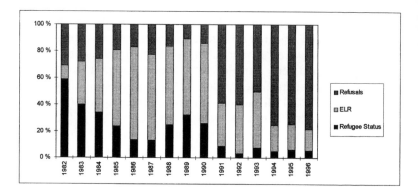

Figure 3.2 Decisions on asylum applications made in the United Kingdom, 1982–96, including dependants. ELR = Exceptional leave to remain. (*Sources:* Home Office, various years)

Remain (ELR). The ELR does not, however, entitle a person to the same rights and services associated with full refugee status. For example, persons with an ELR do not have the right to family reunification. During the 1990s the refugee policy has become even more restrictive, and the proportion of persons receiving ELR has declined while more and more persons have received a totally negative decision on their asylum applications. This development is shown in Figure 3.2. The reason for the introduction of even more restrictive policies is undoubtedly the increased numbers of asylum seekers.

It is possible to apply for British citizenship after five years of residence and settlement in Britain. The applicant needs to have indefinite leave to remain, and not exceptional leave to remain, at the date of application. In addition, naturalization requires sufficient knowledge of English, Welsh or Scottish Gaelic, a good character and the intention to live in the UK (JCWI, 1995).

Reception and Resettlement Policies in the UK

The British system of refugee resettlement can be seen as connected to more fundamental perceptions of the roles of, and relations between, the state and civil society. One interesting feature of British society is the emphasis on the 'local community', which is understood to be a part of civil society rather than of the state. Traditionally, voluntary organizations working within the 'local community' have played a major role in the British social welfare system. It can be argued that in the UK the state has not taken over functions from civil society and the voluntary organizations to the same extent as in many other European countries. Furthermore, one has to remember that British society is still strongly ordered along class lines. As Rex (Rex and Tomlinson, 1979; Rex, 1986b) argues in his early writings on this subject, the immigrants have largely been integrated into the underclass of British society, and are disadvantaged in comparison with working-class whites.

The whole immigration and minority policy in Britain is often described as a communitarian policy in contrast to the French citizenship model which emphasizes assimilation (Lloyd, 1993, 1994; Melotti, 1997). The notion of 'communities' is clearly related to the multicultural discourse in Britain. As discussed in Chapter 1, there are some dilemmas connected with a multicultural discourse. According to Anthias and Yuval-Davis (1992), there is a multiculturalist discourse in Britain in which people are seen as belonging to specific, usually culturally defined, communities which are distinct from each other and which also have clear boundaries. It can be argued that the British multicultural project has not only involved a positive recognition of ethnic minority communities, it has also led to a new culturalist and racist construction of exclusionary boundaries in society. The problem is that the preoccupation with communities has created new divisive lines between people. The 'community' is a label put on a complex reality. For example, community centres or their leaders are never fully representative or democratically chosen by the people they are seen as representing (Anthias and Yuval-Davis, 1992). Different political goals within ethnic groups have also been described by Werbner (1991), who argues that it is the wider society which encapsulates and marginalizes ethnic groups by insisting on community-wide policies. Goulbourne (1991a, 1991b) sees a danger in what he calls the British 'communal option', which has prevented the full inclusion of ethnic minorities into the British national community.

Briefly, the communal option presumes that humanity can be legitimately and properly divided into easily recognisable ethnic or racial categories, and that members of these categories wish to enjoy security within specified enclaves which are exclusively their own. These enclaves are further presumed to constitute the proper boundaries within which individuals should be encouraged to conduct their daily lives. (Goulbourne, 1991b: 297)

At least since the 1980s, the multiculturalist discourse has been more dominant than assimilationist policies within social policy in Britain. In social work with ethnic minorities, cultural differences and the importance of consulting with communities became fully acknowledged. Likewise, there was an emphasis on 'self-help' and support to associations working within specific communities (Candappa and Joly, 1994).

In Britain, refugee reception is in practice largely organized by non-governmental organizations and not by the British authorities. The National Health Service and the Department of Social Security provide their specific services, but more general advice and services are offered by a wide variety of non-governmental service providers. Although funding for refugee resettlement is to a large extent organized from public sources, the practical work is mainly carried out by various charities and voluntary organizations. In the mid-1990s, the British refugee resettlement policy was described in the following way:

> Central government responsibility for oversight of arrangements for the settlement of refugees rests with the Voluntary Services Unit (VSU), located within the Home Office. VSU's general policy is to provide the help and support needed by refugees through voluntary organizations and community groups, through local authorities, or through special programmes within existing statutory agencies. Compared to national statutory provision, such arrangements are intended to allow greater flexibility and sensitivity to local needs and consumers' voices. (Carey-Wood et al., 1995: 1)

In addition to the Home Office, public funding is available from the local councils and the London Boroughs Grants Unit.[1] There are also other public programmes and private trusts that support organizations working with refugees. Nevertheless, a lack of funding remains a serious problem for many voluntary organizations. In practice the British authorities have largely handed over the responsibility for the reception of refugees to organizations in the voluntary sector and to the 'local community'. The refugees can thus 'choose' between a number of 'competing' service providers, although in practice different groups come under the care of particular bodies. It is possible to argue that the various organizations form an 'extremely dynamic, determined, and innovative set of actors' (Majka, 1991: 273). However, this plurality also means that there are many organizations whose activities overlap and there is often a lack of professionalism among those within the voluntary sector.

There have been specific resettlement programmes for quota refugees in Britain, including the Chilean, Vietnamese and Bosnian quota refugees. Most other refugee groups, including the Kurds, have not been part of any special resettlement programme. These groups largely have to rely on the support and advice given by charities and local community centres. The first voluntary organization that Kurdish refugees encounter is often the Refugee Arrivals Project (RAP). After arrival at Heathrow most refugees are handed over from the Immigration Service to the RAP. The organization is funded by the Home Office to provide the necessary service to refugees immediately after arrival in Britain, and it is expected to be able to move people into the community within a day or two of their arrival.[2] Obviously, this task is almost impossible. For example, housing is very scarce in London and the local councils can only provide housing to those with special needs. Single refugees must largely fend for themselves and usually face acute housing problems. The RAP writes in its 1993 Annual Report that 'the task we face has become more complex and demanding and the project is stretched to breaking point by the additional pressures on us all' (RAP, 1994: 7). Clearly, in this situation many refugees need help and advice from other sources. Perhaps the most important provider of practical help, after refugees have stayed in Britain for a few days, is the Refugee Council. This is a large organization mainly funded by the Home Office. It has a wide variety of services, programmes and activities aimed at giving practical help to refugees and at promoting refugees' rights both in Britain and abroad.

In addition to the Refugee Council there are many smaller British organizations which give valuable support to refugees. For example, many of my interviewees were grateful for the help they had received from the Medical Foundation for the Care of Victims of Torture. However, in the case of Kurdish refugees the various Kurdish community centres and organizations in London are of special importance and these are the primary object of interest in this book. These Kurdish associations will be examined more closely in Chapter 6.

Kurds in Britain

Britain has received Kurdish refugees from all parts of Kurdistan. Since the 1970s the UK has been a significant host for Kurdish students, and later refugees, from Iraq. Kurds from Iraq constituted the first large group of Kurds in the UK, probably because of the historical ties between Iraq and the UK (cf. al-Rasheed, 1994). Since many Kurds from Iraq arrived as university students, today they are often well educated, and many male refugees possess doctorates. Consequently, some Kurdish men from Iraq at present have well-established positions in universities and private companies. In this respect the Kurds from Iraq living in Britain are clearly different from the quota refugees in Finland. There has been a continuous flow of Kurdish refugees from Iraq arriving in Britain and the number of asylum applications from Iraq has been higher in the 1990s than in the 1980s (see Figure 3.3).

In Britain, the Kurds from Iraq have recently been outnumbered by Kurdish refugees from Turkey, who since 1989 have arrived in significant numbers and moved into the Turkish community in north London. A total of 4650 Turkish citizens (including dependants) applied for asylum in the UK in 1989 (Home Office, 1990), of whom a large number arrived in May and June. The British authorities introduced a number of different measures to stop this major influx of refugees from Turkey (Collinson, 1990). Visa requirements were imposed on 23 June 1989 for all Turkish citizens wanting to enter the UK. The Home Secretary, Douglas Hurd, explained the decision in the following way: 'These developments have placed strain on immigration control, creating long delays and inconvenience for the main body of passengers.' According to him, many of the asylum seekers were 'young men who have admitted to making their claim because of employment difficulties in Turkey' (Crisp, 1989: 18). The sudden influx of a large number of Kurdish asylum seekers during the spring of 1989 created a dramatic situation in the Kurdish community in north London. The authorities did not have the necessary facilities nor the ability to take care of this large group of people. Local authorities, voluntary organizations and churches in north London had to do whatever they could to help the newly arrived Kurdish refugees. The Kurdish associations in London had to shoulder a particularly heavy burden during this period. The areas in London where the asylum seekers arrived, principally the boroughs of Haringey and Hackney, were largely deprived inner-

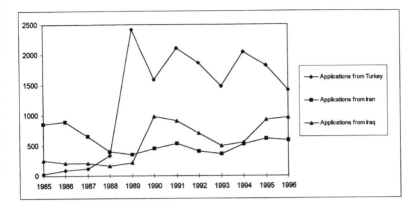

Figure 3.3 Asylum applications from Turkey, Iran and Iraq made in the United Kingdom, 1985–96, excluding dependants.
(*Sources:* Home Office, various years)

city areas. Among other problems, it was difficult to find proper accommodation for all asylum seekers (Crisp, 1989; Collinson, 1990; Reilly, 1991).

The Turkish community in north London was initially established by Turkish Cypriots who migrated to Britain from the 1950s onwards. There has also been a labour migration from Turkey, but by comparison with other European countries this has not been significant. In any case, many of the migrants now regard themselves as refugees. The Kurdish refugees from Turkey today constitute a large part of the Kurdish and Turkish community in north London. The Kurdish refugee migration from Turkey has largely been a chain migration. As explained in Chapter 2, many of the Kurds who have moved to north London during recent years are from the areas of Marash and Sivas in Turkey and belong to the Alevi religious minority.

Since the revolution in Iran in 1979, Iranian Kurds, together with a large number of other Iranians, have arrived as refugees in Britain. It is difficult to estimate the number of Iranian Kurds in the UK. It is possible that many of the Kurds from Iran identify themselves primarily as Iranians and that they cannot therefore be regarded as part of the Kurdish community. A rough estimation is that there were between 20 000 and 30 000 Kurds from Turkey, Iraq and Iran living in the UK in the mid-1990s. The number is

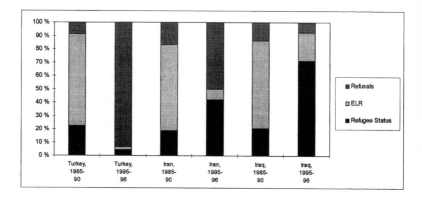

Figure 3.4 Decisions on asylum applications from Turkey, Iran and Iraq in the United Kingdom, 1985–90 and in 1995–96, excluding dependants. (*Sources:* Home Office, various years)

constantly growing and about two-thirds of the Kurds are from Turkey. At least 90 per cent of the Kurds in the UK live in London.

In Figure 3.3 the numbers of asylum seekers from Turkey, Iraq and Iran are presented. The number of asylum seekers from Iran reached a peak immediately after the revolution in 1979 but the number of refugees has only slowly declined since then. In contrast, the number of refugees from Turkey has increased dramatically since the 1980s. In the late 1980s asylum seekers from all three countries had the same statistical chance of obtaining full refugee status. The policy has dramatically changed in recent years. The number of negative decisions concerning asylum applicants from Turkey has recently increased radically, although the human rights situation in Turkey has not improved in the 1990s. This change in the asylum policy is described in Figure 3.4.

FINLAND

Finland has never experienced any large scale immigration of labour migrants. On the contrary, until the early 1980s it remained a country of emigration. The number of refugees arriving in the country has also until the 1990s been very small. Although the changes have been slow, Finland has changed during recent years from a country of emigration to one of immigration (Korkiasaari and Söderling,

1998). When looking at the reception of refugees in Finland, and ethnic relations in general, one has to remember this historical context.

Finnish history includes comparable situations to the present patterns of immigration. The country was a part of Sweden until 1809 and a part of the Russian empire between 1809 and 1917. Finland has been a meeting place between East and West, and can already be regarded as a multicultural society upon gaining independence in 1917. The Swedish-speaking minority (of approximately 300 000 persons) has a relatively secure legal position since Swedish is one of the two official languages of the country (cf. McRae, 1997). Also, the relations between the majority and the smaller cultural minorities (in order of estimated size: Gypsies, Samis, Jews and Muslim Tartars) have in an international comparison often worked relatively well in Finland (cf. Pentikäinen and Hiltunen, 1995). Until recently, ethnic relations in Finland mainly related to these old and well-established minorities. Still, migration is certainly not an uncommon phenomenon in the history of Finland. The total number of persons who emigrated from Finland between 1860 and 1992 is estimated to be slightly more than 1.1 million (Korkiasaari, 1993), which can be compared to the fact that the population of Finland today is 5.1 million. At the turn of the century the emigration from Finland was mainly directed towards North America, but later, after the Second World War, it was mainly directed to Sweden. In addition, there is reason to mention the 420 000 displaced persons, from the areas in eastern Finland that were occupied by the Soviet Union, who after the Second World War had to be resettled in other parts of Finland.

After the Second World War Finland managed to keep its independence, but the country found itself in a rather remote and isolated geographical location in a post-war Europe that was divided between East and West. Despite the special relationship with the Soviet Union, the border between the countries was in many ways a closed one. During the post-war years the successful Swedish economy experienced a shortage of labour at the same time as there was a relatively high level of unemployment in Finland. These circumstances produced a situation with minimal immigration to Finland accompanied by a large emigration to Sweden. This combination of factors meant that the formerly relatively pluralistic society during the post-war years became a country which can be regarded as ethnically homogenous. For example, as late as 1980 foreign citizens living permanently in Finland numbered only 13 000 persons.

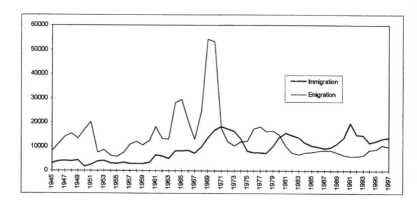

Figure 3.5　Immigration and emigration in Finland, 1945–97.
(*Sources:* Korkiasaari (1993), Nieminen (1994) and Statistics Finland (1995, 1996, 1997)

Until the 1980s, the migration movements described in Figure 3.5 consisted mainly of labour migration to Sweden and a return migration from Sweden. The total number of Finns who officially moved to Sweden in 1945–92 is 520 000 persons, but about half of them later moved back to Finland. Since 1980 the number of people moving to Sweden has been low, and more Finns have moved from Sweden to Finland than vice versa (Korkiasaari, 1993).

During the 1980s the post-war pattern of migration changed greatly in Finland; immigration became larger than emigration. The available statistics clearly indicate that the immigrants in the 1980s and 1990s are no longer only former Finnish emigrants who are returning to Finland (Korkiasaari, 1993). By 1997 the number of foreign citizens in the country had increased to 80 000 persons. Immigration is now largely made up of persons from the CIS and the Baltic states, but other nationalities are also found among the immigrants. Since 1990, persons from the former Soviet Union who can prove Finnish ancestry are treated as repatriates and have a right to move to Finland. In practice this right of repatriation has been applied to the Ingrians, who since the seventeenth century have lived in the area around St Petersburg. Some of the older Ingrians speak Finnish, but most of the young people have no knowledge of the language. No exact numbers are available, but there were probably around 13 000 Ingrians living in Finland in 1995 (Pitkänen and Jaakkola, 1997).

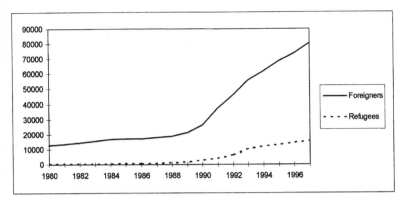

Figure 3.6 Foreign citizens and refugees living in Finland, 1980–97. (*Sources:* Korkiasaari (1993), Nieminen (1994), *Monitori* and *Pakolasinfo*. The number of refugees is an estimate made at the Ministry of Health and Social Affairs based on the number of refugees arrived in Finland)

Figure 3.6 outlines the number of foreign citizens living permanently in Finland. Although the increase in the number of foreigners looks quite spectacular, one has to remember that this increase in a comparative European perspective only represents a return to a more 'normal' proportion of foreigners within the country. In fact, the number of foreigners living in the country remains relatively small. One can identify three reasons for the increase in the immigration to Finland during the 1980s. First, the positive economic development in Finland during the 1980s was an enabling effect (although the country later in the 1990s went into a severe economic recession). Secondly, the collapse of the Soviet Union created a situation where some migration from the east became possible. However, the border remains heavily guarded by Russia and the migration has perhaps not been as significant as expected. The third reason, although quite marginal, is refugee migration. As Figure 3.6 shows, only a small part of the foreign population in Finland is made up of refugees.

Refugees in Finland

The first main influx of refugees into Finland happened after the Russian Revolution in 1917. Finland was mainly a transit country, but there were still 33 500 Russian refugees in Finland in 1922 (Jaakkola, 1989). After this, the country did not experience any larger flows of refugees until the 1980s. One aim of Finnish foreign policy has been to strengthen the role of the United Nations and to be actively involved in its work. A logical outgrowth of this is Finnish participation in the work of the UNHCR. In 1968 Finland acceded to both the Refugee Convention and the Protocol. In the late 1980s, Finland was among the ten biggest contributors to the budget of the UNHCR. Another aspect of this international coop- eration has been the introduction of an annual quota for refugees. In comparison with some other Nordic countries the quota has been rather small, but there has been a significant increase in recent years. The selection of the refugees has been made on humanitarian grounds and Finland has tried to compensate for its small quota by accepting refugees whom the UNHCR has found it difficult to resettle elsewhere. The first group to arrive within a quota were 300 Chilean refugees, who arrived from 1973 onwards. Vietnamese refugees have arrived as quota refugees since the late 1970s. In recent years the quota has included refugees from the Middle East and from former Yugoslavia.

The number of asylum seekers, who, of course, arrive outside of any quota, has been relatively small. At least in part the small number can be explained by the geographically remote location of the country. Another issue which previously affected the number of asylum seekers, especially from socialist countries, was the sensitive political rela- tions between Finland and the Soviet Union during the period of the Cold War. For example, even if a Soviet citizen did manage to cross the heavily guarded border to Finland, it was possible, at least until the 1970s, that he or she would be immediately returned by the Finnish authorities. In the 1990s, the persistently restrictive implementation of the Refugee Convention has probably also in- fluenced the number of asylum seekers arriving in Finland. Only around 1 per cent of the asylum seekers have managed to gain full refugee status and this percentage has been remarkably constant during recent years. Finland, together with Norway, has recently had the lowest recognition rates in Europe. However, the various 'B-statutes' in Finland have been granted relatively frequently. During the last ten years around half of the decisions have been negative and half of the decisions have granted the asylum seeker a resi- dence permit. In practice those who have 'B-statuses' have the same rights (including the right to family reunification) and receive the

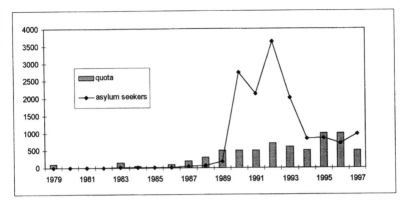

Figure 3.7 Asylum seekers and the refugee quota in Finland, 1979–97. (*Sources: Monitori* and *Pakolasinfo*. The annual quota does not correspond fully with the actual number of quota refugees arrived during the year)

same services as those who have full refugee status. Despite some positive changes in recent years, the Finnish asylum policy can still not be described as anything other than restrictive. The number of asylum seekers and the size of the annual quota are presented in Figure 3.7.

The Ministry of Health and Social Affairs estimated that there were almost 12 000 refugees living in Finland in 1994, mainly from Somalia, Vietnam and former Yugoslavia. The exact number was not known since some refugees might have become naturalized Finns, and thus would no longer be refugees.[3] A foreigner, including a refugee, who has been living permanently in Finland for five years may apply for Finnish citizenship. In addition, an applicant often has to wait for several years before a decision is given. 'Naturalisation is conditional upon the alien being fluent in either Finnish or Swedish and being considered "an honourable member of society", i.e. s/he should not have a criminal record or have incurred large debts' (ECRE, 1994: 135).

Finland has followed a clear policy designed to keep the number of refugees as small as possible and to discourage asylum seekers from spontaneously arriving in the country. Strong evidence of a strict refugee policy can be seen in the introduction of visa regulations for 'refugee producing' countries. Furthermore, the legal procedure has been changed with the introduction of the notions of 'safe countries' of origin and transit, whereby a negative decision in certain cases can be made through a fast procedure. On the other hand there has been support for a humanitarian resettlement of refugees in an orderly and controlled way. The future policies of the country are guided by the fact that Finland joined the European Union in 1995 and has to harmonize its refugee policy and immigration rules. Since other European countries today are closing their borders (Joly, 1992, 1996; Amnesty International, 1997) we might end up in a situation where Finland is closing its borders without ever really having had them open.

Reception Policies in Finland

Finnish society is largely based on the model of the Nordic welfare state, with an extensive public sector and a tradition of actively striving to remove social inequalities and differences. In the Nordic welfare states the state and civil society are often regarded as rather intertwined since the state has largely taken over functions from civil society and the voluntary sector (Allardt, 1994). These features of Finnish society also have an impact on the refugee reception policies (cf. Söderling, 1993). Refugees in Finland are provided with health services, social benefits and, if necessary, housing from the public sector in the same way as other residents. In addition, there are extensive public sector resettlement programmes for refugees. Most refugees take part in orientation courses consisting of language training and occupational training for about one year. These extensive programmes are supposed to encourage a positive integration of the refugees into society. One major aim of the programmes is to find employment for the refugees. The introductory courses for immigrants include practical experience in various jobs and guidance about career opportunities. In Finland, as elsewhere, employment is seen as a key factor in the integration of refugees. Although the resettlement of refugees is an object of special consideration by the authorities, this all happens within the framework of the normal structures of social welfare and public support. In practice, the reception and resettlement of refugees are decentralized to the local municipalities since the Ministry of Social Affairs and Health disperse the refugees to municipalities all over the country.

Cultural pluralism has not usually been regarded as a political issue in Finland, and there is a kind of multicultural ethos embedded in the official resettlement policies. However, as Matinheikki-Kokko (1997) points out, the Finnish policy of refugee resettlement is contradictory. Government papers on the subject of refugee resettlement are based on liberal pluralist ideas, but the policy recommendations are still universalist. In other words, the Finnish authorities do not take into account cultural differences or communities in their practical work although the official policies are supposed to be multicultural.

It can be argued that in practice Finnish resettlement policy is often based on rather unrealistic expectations of a quick integration or even assimilation of refugees. Finland, compared to Britain, is a relatively homogenous society with relatively small income differences and blurred boundaries between social classes. The egalitarian ideals which have traditionally been a part of Finnish society also support an assimilationist policy towards refugees. The notion of ethnic minorities living in their own insular communities within the larger society cannot easily be fitted into the traditional ideal of an egalitarian society. In addition, the resettlement of refugees has been profoundly influenced by humanitarian considerations. Refugees are regarded as disadvantaged persons who, like other weak groups such as children, disabled people and alcoholics, need special support in order to be integrated into society. Refugees are often seen as persons who have lost everything in terms of material, social and cultural capital. Furthermore, they are often understood as persons who must undergo a kind of re-socialization into Finnish society. Consequently, they might even be treated in the same way as small children. As Valtonen (1998) points out, the disempowerment of refugees is a problem in the Finnish resettlement process. It can be argued that there is a risk that the official welfare system transforms active adult refugees into passive clients.

There is also a policy of dispersal, according to which refugees are resettled in small groups all over the country. This practice does not support the creation of cultural communities among the refugees; nor does it seek to take into account the resources which exist within the refugees' own social networks. Furthermore, Liebkind (1993) has argued that the lack of cultural communities is a detrimental factor affecting the psychological well-being of refugees in Finland. Refugees are usually regarded as persons who have arrived in Finland to be permanently resettled, since they no longer have a home country. Accordingly, the Finnish resettlement system has not taken into account the transnational networks and the diasporic nature of refugees' experiences. Instead the resettlement system has been dominated by the Finnish authorities' preoccupation with 'integration'. Hence, this study argues that the Finnish resettlement policy, in practice, is relatively assimilationist and less multicultural than the resettlement policy in the United Kingdom.

Public Opinion

The question of refugee admission has been a highly debated issue in Finland, despite the fact that the number of refugees is relatively small. Refugees, rather than immigrants in general, seem to be especially likely to face hostility among the general public. In the late 1980s, when the number of refugees arriving in the country started to grow, newspaper reports usually portrayed refugees as 'problems'. In addition, the attitude of some politicians and the authorities' official policies towards refugees might have further fuelled the xenophobic and exclusionary discourse.

Finnish attitudes to refugees and immigration have been studied in two surveys undertaken by Magdalena Jaakkola (1989, 1995). In 1987, only 16 per cent of the respondents wanted Finland to receive fewer refugees, and the overall picture was perhaps less xenophobic than was expected (Jaakkola, 1989). In 1993, the survey was repeated and it seemed that the Finns had become less willing to accept immigrants and refugees: the percentage of respondents who wanted Finland to receive fewer refugees had risen to 44 per cent (Jaakkola, 1995).[4] Jaakkola (1995) argues that one major reason for the change in attitudes was the deepening economic recession in Finland. The rate of unemployment rose to almost 20 per cent in the early 1990s. Immigrants and refugees easily became scapegoats for economic problems, while immigration was widely perceived as a socio-economic threat. Consequently, in terms of public opinion, the situation has in recent years deteriorated for refugees and foreigners in Finland. A later study carried out in 1995 by Söderling (1997) has largely confirmed this shift in attitudes. Bearing in mind this change in attitudes, it is easy to understand the increase in xenophobic and racist attitudes as a consequence of increased immigration. However, this would be a crude oversimplification of the problem. It is obvious that there is no clear causal relation between the actual number of foreigners living in the country and the attitudes towards particular groups of immigrants. When discussing the racist and xenophobic discourse, one has to remember that not all immigrants are defined as 'foreigners' or 'problems'. Although only a small part of the present immigration to Finland consists of refugees, the whole discussion about immigration control has been centred on the question of refugee admission. Refugee issues have been much more widely debated than issues related to the present immigration from the former Soviet Union. The number of Ingrian immigrants from Russia and Estonia has been at least as large as the immigration of refugees, but still the refugee migration is perceived as a far bigger problem.

In Finland, the discourse on asylum policies seems largely to have been based on a social construction in which refugees have generally been defined, first of all, as people who do not belong in the country, and secondly, as a social problem. In this discourse there is no room for alternative interpretations which would see the similarities between the present refugee immigration and other, both historical and contemporary, migration movements to and from Finland. Despite the fact that the refugees are few in number, the public discourse on immigration has defined refugees as a 'problem'. On the other hand, there is of course at the same time also a humanitarian discourse that advocates a more inclusionary refugee and asylum policy. These competing arguments and discourses have been described, for example, by Laari (1998) and Wahlbeck (1992).

Kurds in Finland

It is impossible to know the exact number of Kurds in Finland since the available data indicate citizenship and mother tongue, but not ethnic identification. However, by comparing different sources it is possible to estimate their number. A conservative estimate of the number of Kurds living in Finland by the end of 1994 is 1250–2000 persons (see Table 3.1). Of these persons, 300–550 were from Turkey, 550–800 from Iraq and 400–650 from Iran.[5]

Probably the first Kurdish refugees who arrived in Finland were three Iraqi students who through various coincidences came there in the late 1970s. In the 1980s a few Kurds from Iraq also arrived as asylum seekers in Finland. However, most of the Kurds have arrived in Finland in the 1990s. Most of the Kurds from Iran and Iraq have arrived as quota refugees through the UNHCR since 1990. Consequently, a majority of the Kurds in Finland have full

Table 3.1 The estimated number of Kurds and citizens from Turkey, Iraq, and Iran living in Finland

Country of origin	Estimate of Kurds 1.1.1995	Citizens 1.1.1995	Citizens 1.1.1998
Turkey	300–550	1166	1663
Iraq	550–800	989	2433
Iran	400–650	1114	1669
Total:	1250–2000	3269	5765

Sources: The number of citizens is based on figures published in *Monitori*.

refugee status in accordance with the UN convention, but there are also large numbers with other legal statuses. Most of the quota refugees have lived under the protection of the UNHCR in Turkey, but some refugees have lived in other refugee camps in the Middle East. The refugees are selected for resettlement by the Finnish authorities in cooperation with the UNHCR.

In addition to the quota refugees, the number of Kurdish asylum seekers in Finland has increased in the 1990s. In 1990–4 there were 233 asylum seekers from Iran and 403 from Iraq. In the same period 377 persons from Turkey applied for asylum. In the case of Turkey it can be assumed that most of the applications were made by Kurds, but in the case of Iraq and Iran the applicants included other ethnic groups as well. In 1991, especially, many Kurdish asylum seekers from Turkey arrived in Finland. However, in contrast to the applicants from Iran and Iraq, a majority of the asylum seekers from Turkey have experienced difficulties in getting protection from the Finnish state. In 1991–4, a total of 188 Turkish citizens received a negative decision on their asylum applications.[6]

None of the Kurds in Finland, neither the quota refugees nor the asylum seekers, have arrived in a pattern of chain migration. The quota refugees have often arrived in groups whose members did not previously know each other. Those who have arrived as asylum seekers have usually done so individually without any initial intention of going to Finland. Most of my interviewees had hardly heard of Finland before they entered the country. Since most Kurds from Iran and Iraq have arrived as quota refugees, this gives a special character to the Kurdish community in Finland. The quota refugees were selected from persons who were under the protection of the UNHCR in the Middle East. Therefore the quota refugees include persons who did not have the possibility and the economic resources to continue their flight on their own to Europe. The Finnish authorities furthermore use humanitarian criteria to select from among those who are accepted as refugees by the UNHCR. This means that the quota refugees include many families and children. Those who arrive as asylum seekers generally comprise a different group of people. In particular, almost all asylum seekers from Turkey have been single young men. The official statistics support this observation, showing that 83 per cent of the Turkish citizens living in Finland in 1992 were men (Nieminen, 1994).[7]

Due to the resettlement practice in Finland, the Kurds are dispersed in small groups around the country. There is a tendency for the Kurds to later move either to the Helsinki capital area or to some of the regional centres. The Kurds from Turkey, in particular, tend to live in the capital area. According to the official population statistics from 31 December 1995, published in *Monitori,* 58 per cent of the Turkish-speaking population and 45 per cent of the Kurdish-speaking population lived in the administrative province Uusimaa. Only 26 per cent of the total population lived in this province, which includes the capital area and the south coast.

Although the Finnish government is successfully trying to prevent asylum seekers from reaching Finland, it can be expected that the number of Kurdish refugees will grow. At the time of writing, Kurdish refugees continued to be part of the annual quota. In addition, Kurdish refugees also arrive in Finland as family reunification cases. By the end of 1997 the number of Kurds living in Finland was probably close to 3000 persons.

CONCLUSION

International comparative studies always face problems concerning the comparability of the phenomena under study. Different historical developments, different conceptual definitions, different political systems and different social structures often mean that the validity of observed similarities or differences between countries can be disputed (cf. Lloyd, 1993, 1994; Weiner, 1996). In the case of England and Finland, however, there are some indisputable differences. For example, the historical contexts in which ethnic relations have developed in Britain and in Finland could hardly be more different.

Britain has a history as a major political power, being the centre of a world empire. In present-day Britain, where migration to and from other parts of the Commonwealth has been common for a long time, multiculturalism is an intrinsic feature of life in cosmopolitan cities like London. In addition, British society has traditionally been a class society and a society where local communities are regarded as fundamental units of society. In these social structures of plurality and diversity it is relatively easy to implement various communitarian and multicultural policies. Not surprisingly, refugee reception policies largely revolve around the refugees' own communities. The arrival of refugees in Britain is also commonly misunderstood as a continuation of previous immigration to the country.

The fact that social networks and associations are important for refugees has largely been acknowledged in Britain. However, this acknowledgement seems to assume that associations have to be based on clearly defined homogenous ethnic communities. The multicultural discourse in Britain has included a tendency to impose artificial ethnic boundaries on a diverse and complex social reality. Because of the communitarian policies towards ethnic minorities, there is a tendency to regard refugees as 'ethnic minorities' in a multicultural society. However, many refugee communities in Britain, including the Kurds, have specific experiences which are very different from those of the British ethnic minorities, whose long history of settlement in the UK often has to be seen within a colonial context. Therefore, there is a danger that the British authorities' policies towards refugees are not always sensitive to refugees' specific social situations and problems.

Finland, by contrast, is a country with a small population and a remote geographical location. Finnish society is characterized by the model of the 'Nordic welfare state' with its extensive public sector and blurred borders between civil society and the state. This type of society actively strives to integrate and equalize all its members. As argued in Chapter 1, however, the model of a multicultural society is largely based on the acceptance of difference. Thus, although Finnish policies are often officially described as multicultural, the policies are in practice relatively assimilationist by comparison with British policies. The Finnish approach seldom takes into account the diasporic nature of the refugees' social relations in the country of settlement. In addition, during the post-war period Finland has experienced very low levels of immigration. The sudden increase in immigration, which furthermore has largely occurred during an economic recession, has led to a xenophobic reaction among parts of the general public. This reaction has been fuelled by racism and biased mass-media reports, and has largely become focused on the refugees in the country. Thus, although the official reception policies support an inclusion of the refugees into society at large, there are parts of the population who actively strive to exclude the refugees.

Consequently, when one talks about solving problems connected with migration and multiculturalism, it would be easy to regard Finland as lagging behind other countries. As Lloyd (1993) points out, Britain is often wrongly seen as being ahead of other European countries in this respect. In reality, this kind of comparison of countries is not possible. Strictly speaking, countries are different and cannot be understood as being 'ahead' of each other. Lloyd (1993) argues that different European countries have developed differently and that one cannot use an evolutionary perspective where countries are seen as going through a set procedure of developments. Furthermore, one has to remember that because of the differences, any theories and policies which are adopted in one country are not necessarily transferable to another.

Thus, any sweeping normative comparisons are avoided in this chapter and it is only established that the two countries are different. The refugee resettlement policies are heavily dependent on general social policies and are connected to more fundamental conceptions of the state, local communities and the civil society. The UK adopts a traditional communitarian and multicultural approach, while in practice Finland has a more assimilationist resettlement policy. It can also be argued that although they approach the issue from different perspectives, neither country has fully understood the specific nature of refugee migration. Chapters 4, 5 and 6 describe the consequences that these different approaches have had for the Kurdish refugees and how the different policies have influenced the social organization of the Kurdish communities.

4 Towards a Wider Understanding of the Refugee Experience

The following three chapters present results from the fieldwork in England and Finland. This chapter is focused on the experiences of Kurdish refugees in these two countries. Obviously, the Kurdish refugees have encountered a whole range of problems, and this book cannot deal with all of them. The aim is to indicate and discuss the main problems experienced by refugees, and thereby to present the framework in which the social relations of the refugees were constructed in the two countries of reception. The research findings outlined in this chapter form a basis for the discussion in the following two chapters concerning the process of integration and the social organization of the refugee communities.

ARRIVAL

Refugees who arrive in a new country experience a variety of problems. For those who arrive as asylum seekers, the arrival can be a very traumatic experience. A widow from Iraq described her arrival at Heathrow Airport in London:

> It was horrible, really horrible – I cried so much and did not know what to do and I did not speak the language. I tried to explain that here I am with my two children and we do not know what to do. It was all really horrible.

The first obstacle refugees face is often the asylum application. Many interviewees explained that when they first arrived as asylum seekers they did not properly understand what the status of a refugee was. The problems upon arrival were complicated by the fact that few of the refugees had been able to plan their flight in advance. Most had only a very superficial knowledge of the country they had travelled to, and only a few had even a basic knowledge of English. Since many persons had been forced to obtain falsified travel documents in order to travel to Europe, there was the additional fear of how the authorities would react to this.

Many Kurds have great expectations of democracy in Europe when they arrive and they think that the European countries will welcome them warmly. They are not prepared for the bureaucratic procedures and all the other difficulties refugees encounter in Europe. Two young men from Turkey described their arrivals:

> I planned all the time to go to England, tried to get here all the time. Because I trusted this country's democracy much more than any other European country, but after staying two years without decision and with the problem with family reunion, I understood what kind of democracy it was. I did not expect that these things would happen.

> When I came to Finland it was between twelve and one o'clock in the night. I was really tired . . . I did not know what I was doing here and what a refugee was. . . . Then I just thought that I am a Kurd and I have problems in my own country, and there are human rights in Finland and a democracy, and so on. I thought that perhaps there is a possibility that I can stay in Finland. But then, when I myself saw what the real situation was like, it was completely different from what I had expected. [t]

The real attitude towards refugees in Europe often came as a total surprise to the refugees. A woman from Iraq who had been active in the Kurdish resistance movement told me the following about her expectations before arrival:

> We really valued ourselves and our political struggle very highly when we arrived and thought that we would be warmly welcomed. We were surprised that this was not the case and that people did not care who we were. In Kurdistan, the United Nations and its refugee status is well known and people speak about it, so we thought that refugees were welcomed in Europe and that our fight for human rights would be highly appreciated.

Because of the situation in their countries of origin, many Kurds are suspicious of authorities and afraid of the police. This leads to problems when asylum seekers are interviewed by the authorities in order to determine their legal status. Many refugees are afraid of telling the truth since they believe that what they tell will ultimately end up with the authorities in their homeland. The refugees are afraid of what might happen to them if they have to return, and if they do not return, they have to be afraid of what might happen to their relatives. This understandable reluctance to tell the authorities the real reasons for their flight can seriously damage the refugees' chances of obtaining asylum. These problems were emphasized by many informants. For example, an Iranian man who subsequently gained full refugee status said:

> You know, it is difficult to describe the feelings that you have when you arrive. . . . You are scared of what will happen. Maybe they will deport me. People from Kurdistan and from the third world in general have a different view of the police and the state. They are not seen as somebody who can help you in any way. You have to be scared of them, you see them as an enemy and not as somebody doing something for you.

In Britain many refugees do not apply for asylum at the border, and instead prefer to seek help first of all from people they trust. This is one reason why many applications for asylum are made when the applicant is already in the country and not at the border. Another reason for in-country applications is that many students and other visitors might find that it is impossible to return home because of political changes in their country of origin during their stay in Britain. According to statistics from the Home Office (1994), around half of the applications from Turkish, Iraqi and Iranian citizens in 1990–3 were made in-country. Comparable statistics are not available in the case of Finland.

Unfortunately, the refugees' fear of the authorities in the country of reception did not seem to be totally without reason. During this research I heard several stories of how the authorities often showed a surprising lack of confidentiality, which might even have endangered the safety of the refugees themselves and their relatives back home. Furthermore, the interpreters used by the authorities were not always persons whom the refugees felt confident with.[1]

Among the refugees from Turkey there was a common belief that there was cooperation between Turkish and European governments and police forces, a cooperation which was nurtured through contacts in NATO, the European Union and other international organizations. Once an application for asylum was made in Western Europe, it was assumed that sooner or later this would be known by the authorities in Turkey. In fact, refugees from both Turkey and Iran told me about problems and threats experienced by their relatives back home after the refugees had left the country.

ANXIETIES AND PSYCHOLOGICAL PROBLEMS

Several respondents described traumatic memories from Kurdistan. It can be assumed that most of the Kurdish refugees have close relatives or friends who have been executed or killed in combat, have disappeared or have been imprisoned. Many Kurdish refugees have themselves experienced imprisonment and torture. These kinds of experience often leave refugees with serious mental health problems. This is obviously a sensitive issue and the interviewees were not directly asked about these experiences. Still, the traumatic memories were often mentioned incidentally in the interviews.

Because of the political and economic situation in Kurdistan many refugees in exile are inevitably worried about their relatives living in Kurdistan. Sometimes the whereabouts of the relatives is not known, or there is no possibility of getting in touch with them. A man from Turkey, who lived alone in London, told me about his tragedy:

> I have not been in contact with my family since 1992. I am too scared of what will happen to them if I call. I have not been able to be in contact with my home village, and I do not know if it even exists any more. I am very worried for my family. [t]

Waiting for a decision in the country of exile often becomes an additional problem. The quota refugees in Finland avoid this problem since they have had their refugee status defined by the UNHCR before arrival, and thus they know that they can stay in the country and will get help from the authorities. The asylum seekers, however, have to live in uncertainty for a long time until they get a decision on their applications. It was not uncommon for the refugees in this study to wait up to three years for a decision; this was the case both in the UK and in Finland. This long uncertainty aggravated all the practical and psychological problems experienced by refugees.

As long as the asylum seekers were waiting for a final decision, the uncertainty over their future made it difficult for them to make any plans or to start a new life in the country of settlement. A young man from Turkey, who despite being almost four years in Finland had still not got any decision on his asylum application, described the help he had received from the authorities:

> Personally I can say that Finland was like a prison to me; it really went badly for me here. . . . Several times I have decided that I will leave this country, because of the authorities. Some of them, they do not know what they are doing. And when you complain about the situation, the person just tells you that they do not know, everything is a mess. . . . When I look back I hate that three and a half years, almost four years has gone by and what have I seen? My youth has passed by, I have not studied, I did not get a decision, I did not understand anything. All this time it has been so hard. Many times I went to the doctor, but that did not help either. It has been difficult, so difficult. [t]

Obviously asylum seekers are living under much psychological stress which is directly related to their flight and refugee experiences. Yet, it is also obvious that the reception policies have a great impact on the kinds of difficulty that occur. Stress and uncertainty are difficulties that all asylum seekers and refugees, regardless of their country of settlement or country of origin, have to face to some extent. However, the practical problems that refugees face in the receiving country might aggravate the psychological stress they experience. As described in Chapter 3, the reception and resettlement of refugees are organized in different ways in England and Finland. Because of this, there are many practical problems that are specific to the country of reception. These different experiences will be discussed in more detail later.

Those who are probably in the worst situation in Britain are those who are imprisoned in the detention centres for asylum seekers. As previously mentioned, detention is used relatively frequently in Britain. In recent years, several Kurdish asylum seekers have organized hunger strikes and made suicide attempts in the detention centres. On 5 October 1989 two Kurds who were in detention set fire to their room after hearing that they would be sent back to Turkey. One of the men, Siho Iyiguven, subsequently died in hospital while the other suffered severe burns (Collinson, 1990; Crisp,

1989). Among the interviewees in this research there were, however, only two persons who had been kept in detention for around two weeks. In Finland there is an organized system whereby asylum seekers are accommodated in official reception centres while they wait for the outcome of their applications. Although these open institutions cannot be compared to British detention centres, they are still depressing places. The long stays in these centres were often a traumatic experience. All of the six interviewees who had arrived as asylum seekers in Finland told me about negative experiences during their stay at different reception centres.

Because of all their various problems and anxieties, the asylum seekers can easily get off to a very bad start to their stay in the country of resettlement. Furthermore, the very long processing times for asylum applications in both England and Finland aggravate all the problems that the refugees experience.

SAFETY AND GRATITUDE

The experiences of the asylum seekers who are waiting for a decision are completely different from the initial experiences of the quota refugees in Finland. When the latter arrive in the country they are usually welcomed by the authorities at the airport and they can normally move into their new homes at once. The reception is usually well organized and the resettlement is prepared before their arrival. Of course, the quota refugees also experience difficulties, but their smooth arrival in their new country of settlement has a positive impact on their experiences. An emotional attachment to the place where they first arrived and to Finland was described by many of the quota refugees. Although he had moved to Helsinki, a young man from Iran still showed a great affection for the town where he arrived and where he lived for one and a half years:

> In Smalltown [fictitious name], there I have known people, and it is the people and nature [that make a difference], Smalltown was the first place in Finland that I saw. I do like Smalltown more than Helsinki, it feels like it really was my home town, this kind of notion I got of the town. [t]

Despite all the problems refugees experience upon arrival, there is reason to emphasize the sense of relief and security refugees feel after they have been allowed to stay in the country. There is also a huge gratitude felt towards the country that has accepted them as refugees. Not surprisingly, this is especially evident among those who arrive as quota refugees.

The interviewees were asked to mention things that they regarded as positive in the country of asylum compared to their situation in Kurdistan. All refugees mentioned issues like security, the fact that they no longer experienced war, and the democratic institutions which meant that they no longer had to fear for their lives. A large family from Iraq summarized the differences between Finland and Kurdistan as follows:

> Father: One important difference is that there [in Kurdistan] you did not know what could happen in the next one hour for example: insecurity. Mother did not know when the children went out in the morning if they would return home and what would happen to them.
> Son: Our life there was not a normal life for a normal person, we did not know what our future was.
> ÖW: Is your life here in Finland more secure?
> Whole family: Yes!
> Daughter: Your stomach was full [in Kurdistan], but life was insecure. . . .
> Father: I was always afraid and upset for my children while we lived in Kurdistan; I was afraid for my own sake as well, but most afraid for my children. In economic terms life was OK in Kurdistan, we had our own house and owned land. If it had not been for the regime, it would have been good for us, but they destroyed everything. [t]

For those refugees from Iraq or Iran who have spent several years as displaced persons within Kurdistan, the ultimate reason for their flight has often been the safety of their children. A woman from Iraq had lived in refugee camps within Kurdistan for several years until her large family fled to Turkey, from where the UNHCR re-settled them in Finland:

> ÖW: In what way do you think that your life has changed since you moved to Finland?
> R: It is a little bit easier now, not war and problems here in Finland. In Iraq we have many problems and much war. I think

we really had a lot of problems. Here now my children can live and my children can attend school, this is why I came here.... In Iraq there is war, but I was not hungry and did not come here because I was hungry. Sometimes Finnish people perhaps, not all but some, are angry or say that many refugees get much money and buy many things. But I also had a house in Iraq and I had a car, I had many things. It was only because I wanted to live that I came here. And I did not come here on my own, Finnish people came and talked to us and after that we came here.

ÖW: So, it was largely for the sake of the children that you made the decision to come here?

R: Yes, my husband wants to go back to Iraq. It was only for the sake of the children that we came here, so the children could live and attend school.

ÖW: So if you did not have children you would perhaps never have moved?

R: In that case I would not mind going back. [t]

EDUCATION AND LANGUAGE SKILLS

Refugees generally tend to come from the affluent and well-educated parts of the population of their countries of origin. Since refugees are often well educated, they can become an important asset for the receiving society. In Britain, for example, this has been revealed by Carey-Wood et al. (1995). The educational background among the Kurdish refugees is very heterogeneous. Those male refugees from Iraq who arrived in Europe in the 1970s and 1980s were often well educated. There are also highly educated Kurds from Turkey and Iran, but an interest in studying and a high level of formal education seems to be especially evident among the male Kurds from Iraq living in Britain. Clear differences also exist between different cohorts of refugees from Kurdistan. The more recent refugees from Iraq and Turkey often come from a more humble background and often have a poorer school education than earlier refugees from Iraq.

Regardless of their level of formal education, Kurds generally have extensive language skills, with the possible exception of Kurds from Turkey who seem to master fewer languages. It is not uncommon for a man from southern Kurdistan to speak four or five languages, usually some combination of Kurdish, Arabic, Turkish, Azerbaijani and Farsi. Unfortunately, none of the languages used in Kurdistan is very useful in Europe, and only those who have attended secondary school or university have any knowledge of English. However, the extensive language skills many Kurdish refugees possess might make it easier for them to learn additional languages.

Results from the fieldwork indicated that Kurds from Turkey living in London had particularly weak linguistic skills. This observation was supported by the Kurdistan Workers' Association (KWA) in London, which estimated that only 7 per cent of the newly arrived Kurds in north London had a fair or good knowledge of English while 92 per cent knew very little English or none at all (Refugee Council, 1993). In Britain, refugees from Iran and Iraq generally seemed to have a better knowledge of English than the Kurds from Turkey. The level of education and language skills were also clearly connected to gender. Kurdish women have usually received less formal education and tend not to speak as many languages as Kurdish men. It is common in all parts of Kurdistan for women to be illiterate, and among recent refugees from Kurdistan there are many women who have never attended school.

A clear majority of the informants felt that in the beginning language was their biggest problem. Of those who did not mention language, several persons both in Britain and Finland emphasized problems associated with their asylum application; one asylum seeker in Britain mentioned that he had not been able to find a doctor for his son; and one family in Finland complained about the isolated location of their flat. A good knowledge of the receiving country's language was regarded by the refugees as a resource that could solve many of their other problems. A woman from Iran living in London gave a typical answer to the question about her first major problems:

Unfamiliarity with the society – everything was strange at that time – and language. Language was the biggest problem, because when you know the language, getting contact is easier, and you can discover anything by yourself. You know how to contact. Language really suffered a long ... time I am not such a person sitting asking others to do everything for me. I can cope with myself anywhere, but if you do not have language, how can you help yourself?

My results indicated that the refugees, somewhat surprisingly, experienced worse language problems in England than they did in Finland. However, there were also very big individual differences within the communities. The Kurds in London, especially in the Turkish community, often had very little knowledge of English. The language tuition given to refugees in Britain often seemed to be inadequate, sporadic and inefficient, largely because of a lack of funding (cf. WUS, 1991; Ali, 1990). Furthermore, there was often no interpretation service available during contacts with the authorities. For example, the refugees usually had to organize interpretation themselves during visits to the Department of Social Security (DSS). In contrast, the language tuition given to refugees in Finland was relatively efficient and successful. The Kurds in Finland generally seemed to have a better knowledge of the majority language than the Kurds in England. In addition, the availability of interpretation services during contacts with the authorities was in general well organized in Finland.

PRACTICAL PROBLEMS

The flight from Kurdistan is usually financed through contributions and loans from relatives. Even those who are resettled by the UNHCR have usually been forced to borrow money from relatives. Kurdish refugees, with few exceptions, are penniless when they arrive in the country of asylum, and therefore refugees usually have to rely on social benefits. Although the situations in the two countries are not totally comparable, one can say that the social benefits are generally more generous in Finland, while refugees in Britain often face huge problems making ends meet. An additional burden is that refugees are supposed to pay back the money they have borrowed from their relatives when they have established themselves in Europe. Furthermore, they often feel that they have an obligation to send contributions to needy relatives in Kurdistan.

Since many Kurdish refugees have belonged to the more affluent parts of the Kurdish population, they often experience a downward economic mobility in exile. One thing which has improved is the range of public services available in European countries, but in other respects refugees tend to face far bigger economic problems in exile than they did in Kurdistan. An older man in London told me about his property in Turkey:

In Kurdistan I owned a lot of land, I was rich and lived comfortably. This was a good thing in Turkey. All the rest was bad because
Kurds do not have any rights in Turkey. You can never imagine
how big my land was. I had so much land that you could not see
the end of it. But there was no safety, so we had to flee. [t]

The downward economic mobility of many refugees questions the
popular misconception of refugees as economic migrants. Many
refugees would in fact have had a more secure economic future in
the country of origin. Closely connected to the economic problems
were a number of other practical problems experienced by refugees. Although most refugees experienced a downward social and
economic mobility, the interviewees still had widely different experiences in the two countries of settlement. The differences in the
reception and resettlement policies become very evident when looking
at the practical problems experienced by the refugees.

England

Since, in Britain, there were no structured official resettlement
programmes for Kurdish refugees, their life situation was initially
very chaotic. These issues were discussed with a woman from Iran:

ÖW: Do you think that you got the help you needed? Or I mean,
if you could now decide yourself, how refugees in this country
should be taken care of –
R: I would change everything. It is a very strong bureaucracy
system here. If you speak English, maybe it is better, maybe you
can face it much better, but if you do not speak English it is
horrible. I had horrible days, unforgettable, but with the situation we had – I was ill, and then no English, no house, no money,
no work – everything was complicated when we arrived.

The housing situation in London is dreadful. The local councils
and charities do not have enough accommodation for all homeless
refugees, and the prices on the private market are very high. The
houses and flats that are available are generally of a low standard
and are usually smaller than those the families have been used to
in Kurdistan. Furthermore, the refugee associations have only very
limited resources to alleviate these problems (cf. HACT, 1994).
Many refugees are forced to live with relatives for a long time

until they manage to find a place of their own. Some single persons live at hostels provided by charities, like the Refugee Council, for example, until they manage to rent a place from a private landlord. To find enough money for the rent is a serious problem for many refugees, since the housing benefit does not cover the prices they have to pay for privately rented flats. However, families with children normally manage to get a roof over their heads through the local council or a housing association.

One issue that aggravated the practical problems in Britain was that there was no system to ensure refugees automatically got the benefits to which they were entitled. The refugees had to apply for the benefits themselves. If you are totally unfamiliar with the language and how the society works, this is not very easy. A man from Iraq who had lived in Britain for nine years reflected on this problem:

My experience of the UK is that you have to fight your way in, find your way by yourself. If you do not find it by yourself, you will not be granted any help. For example, housing benefits, people get neglected if they do not find their way on their own: you have to do it yourself.

Finland

In Finland, refugees generally found that the social benefits and other support they received from the authorities were sufficient. Similarly, housing was not perceived as a big problem. The local municipalities were usually able to provide all refugees with flats. Housing in Finland is generally of a good standard, although the flats which the refugees rent are sometimes smaller than the homes the families have been used to in Kurdistan. Some refugees also felt that their flats were poorly situated. Most respondents were very pleased with the social services they received from the Finnish authorities but, of course, other problems and conflicts still occurred in their relations with the authorities. In the words of a man from Iran:

Oh yes, [the authorities have helped me] during the first months after we came to the country, and in a very positive way, except for some things that we did not understand. It was because of culture, and living here – how to behave. Because we did not know very much about the system here and you had to quickly transfer [your former] life into this life. It was very hard. We almost got a kind of – mental problem, not totally mad but that is perhaps what it is anyway, and tired and angry all the time because everything is new. [t]

In any event, none of the interviewees in Finland felt that they had been discriminated against by the authorities in the area of social services and benefits. A refugee from Turkey, who had also helped other Kurdish refugees with their practical problems, told me about the variety of difficulties asylum seekers experienced in Finland, but still found that things had worked well in one respect:

> In the social sector the Kurds have received everything they need in Finland. Kurds and Finns have been treated in the same way, and you cannot say that one has got a better service than the other. The rights of the Kurds have been the same as those of Finnish people. [t]

However, the public support offered to refugees is not always wholly positive. It includes a power relationship which supports a 'clientelization' of the refugees, so that they are regarded as more helpless than they actually are. The outcome can be a kind of declaration of incapacity of the refugees. According to a man from Iran, there is a hidden racism which can even be part of actions that have the best intentions:

> For example, there are people who want to help you more, but that is not good either. They think that you are disabled, you do not have this or that. Usually we are disabled since we do not know the language, but we can learn the language. But some people want to help you so much like you do not know anything and cannot learn anything, which is bad. [t]

The supportive and active resettlement policies in Finland are supposed to provide a good basis for a positive integration of the refugees into Finnish society. The refugees have generally been pleased with these policies and the resettlement programmes have undoubtedly led to some positive results. However, as is shown in other parts of this book, positive integration has not taken place. Nevertheless, the shortcomings in the integration of refugees should not be blamed solely on the resettlement policies. Rather, the major reasons for the shortcomings in the resettlement of refugees are to be found in the more general structures in Finnish society. As discussed in the next chapter, issues like unemployment and racism have played a crucial role.

It is difficult to make any normative comparisons of the different resettlement policies in England and Finland. However, there were some informants with experience of both the British system and the system in some of the Nordic countries (which tend to have fairly similar policies). The sample includes one refugee who had two sisters in Sweden with whom he had close contact. This is how he compared the Swedish and British policies:

ÖW: Now, when you look back at the time when you arrived and the problems you had, how would you organize the reception of refugees, if you could decide exactly how things should be done?
R: I think that the system that they have in Sweden, as you probably know, seems to be better. The Swedish system is more relaxed, while here you have to be worried when you arrive. But on the other hand, the English system helps you more to manage yourself, to be able to do things on your own. There are advantages and disadvantages in both systems. But some people need more help. For example, when people come from a small village in Kurdistan they have problems. For those people the Swedish system is better. But I do not want to put the systems side by side and say that this is better than that. Some people do, but I do not want to compare. But still, some people do need help and this is why I think that perhaps the Swedish system is better.

The Swedish resettlement system is similar to the Finnish system. Obviously, as indicated in the above quotation, one advantage with the resettlement policies in these Nordic countries is the equal treatment they also guarantee to refugees with fewer skills and resources to find their way on their own. It appears that the British resettlement policies do not fully recognize the refugees' specific problems and experiences. In the words of a man from Iraq:

When looking back at my own experiences, generally speaking, I think that the authorities to a greater extent have to take into account that they are dealing with political refugees and not usual

migrants. Refugees have a lot of problems on arrival that have
to do with their connections back home, and they are in a very
difficult situation upon arrival in the UK. There should be some
provision to help refugees psychologically; now there is nothing.
Genuine political refugees may have experienced a very difficult
time before arrival. Treating them as ordinary migrants and giving them no relaxation time is a big mistake. I think that refugees
might need something like a couple of months relaxation time.

The British authorities have not fully recognized the specific nature
of refugee migration, and they seem to deal with it in the same
way as they dealt with earlier immigration to the country. As pointed
out in Chapter 3, the British government's view has been that many
asylum seekers are illegal immigrants who arrive in Britain in order to use British welfare benefits. On the contrary, however, my
research findings indicate that refugees and other legal immigrants
faced huge problems even in getting the limited public services to
which they were legally entitled.

To summarize, the resettlement policies in the country of settlement have a decisive influence on the practical problems refugees
experience. The Kurdish refugees in Finland experience relatively
few practical problems connected to housing, income support,
education, interpretation services and other aspects of the social
services. This is in contrast to the Kurds in England, who often
experience a number of practical problems in their contacts with
the authorities. Yet, the strong local communities in Britain can
provide refugees with many advantages. The Kurdish associations
and ethnic networks are able to play a far greater and more positive role in Britain than they do in Finland. The functions and
importance of the Kurdish associations and of informal networks
are discussed in more detail in the next chapters.

THE EXPERIENCE OF DISPLACEMENT

In addition to the practical problems that refugees experience upon
arrival, there are other problems which, in practice, cannot be solved
and thus simply have to be lived with. In particular, there is a sense
of displacement, alienation and uprootedness which is common for
all refugees. To be a refugee means that you have been forced to
flee from your home and that you are living in a country to which

you never wanted to move. The experience of exile is best described in the refugees' own words. For example, a woman from Turkey recalled her experiences upon arrival in Britain:

Because you do not even know what it means to be a refugee, you know, what does it mean? You feel, you come, it is kind of a shock. You feel like you will never go back again to your country, the feeling is so bad, because it makes you more vulnerable, if you like, in terms of going back home and seeing family and all that, so that is quite serious. . . . I think it is the same for everybody, but it is just so bad, that you cannot go back.

The experience of exile and loss was expressed in different words by all the interviewees. It is also clear that nothing in the new country of settlement can compensate for the social relations one has lost. In the words of a young woman from Iraq who had lived in Finland for two years: 'I feel safe here and it is a convenient place here, and I live in peace and tranquillity here, but still I am all the time longing for my relatives in Kurdistan. [t]' To be a refugee not only means being forced to leave one's home, but since a refugee never had the original intention to move to the country of exile, there is an additional feeling of alienation. This sense of alienation in the country of exile was clearly evident in most interviews. A woman from Turkey stated:

I definitely do not consider this country as my country, and I do not really feel like [I am at] home, but I do not sort of allow myself to be a guest either. I try to be involved as much as I can, within the community and with the people that I – I feel that I have to be involved with British people, with the public, but I also know the fact that this is not my country. I am a refugee. The word refugee is itself – something. And I still have the ultimate goal of going back.

For political refugees the sense of loss is also closely connected to the political struggle in Kurdistan. This has previously taken up a large part of their lives, and in exile it is no longer possible to be active in the same way. Thus many refugees feel that they have lost the meaning and sense of purpose in life. A woman from Iran described the differences between her life in the Kurdish mountains and her life in London:

A lot of things [have changed in my life since I left Kurdistan]. I used to have a very hard life, always bombardments, fighting, these things. But I was very active, I was in other ways very happy, I had many many friends. I do not know, I was happy, I was really happy, I thought that I was doing in that community, something useful. But when I came here, things changed a lot, I did not do anything, I did not have any work, I just had to stay at home. This studying helped me a little bit. I lost all my activities, there was nothing to do in this country, I could not get involved in their society, it was so difficult to be accepted by them, language difference, culture difference, and so on. It is not the same, everything has changed.

It can also be argued that refugees do not relate to the country of settlement in the same way as labour migrants. Many refugees wanted to stress the specific refugee experience. A young man who had lived in Finland for almost three years explained:

The biggest problem here is how to mentally or ideologically relate to this. If my country were free, if my people were a free people, I would not have to be worried, about anything. Instead I would be very satisfied with wherever I am and whatever I do, I would not notice that at all. But because Iran is very different, and I have been fighting for freedom, and I still feel like I am part of that, so I still feel I have an obligation to myself, I should go back there again. You would not expect this to be the case because, for example, the things I am doing today are different from what I did before, but still it is the case ... Every day I live with it, because, for example, in the night when I sleep, perhaps five, six times I see dreams about it, about my own people, my own life and other things. [t]

The experience of being a political refugee clearly has a profound psychological significance for all refugees. This experience distinguishes the refugee from the ordinary migrant. Another Iranian man who had lived in Finland for more than three years tried to explain more clearly the difference between himself and labour migrants:

Really I am speaking about political refugees, not about migrants or others, it is only because of politics that they have left their country. Because they cannot live in that country and they do not want to die. ... They are waiting for something, ... [refugees] do not want to become, for example, Finnish, they want to go back to their country some day, to their own land. ... I did not think that I would stay in Finland or in the UK or in whatever country, I did not think anything else than that I would like to continue my fight against that government, if necessary from here. ... Because if I am here I want to live, and I have a right to live, and the political life is part of my life. I should have the possibility to live for politics, ... I am a political person, I am not labour, there is so often this misunderstanding. Somebody should tell the people why we are here. [t]

The continuous political orientation towards the 'homeland' seems to be characteristic for refugees. However, the alienation refugees feel is not only related to the political struggle in which they have been involved. Ultimately, this alienation is also related to the fact that although they have moved to a new place, they will still carry with them their old identity and culture for the rest of their life. A man from Iraq pointed out that he thought he could never become truly assimilated.

ÖW: What do you think about Finnish people, do you think that they want you to become as Finnish as possible, or do you think that they want you to preserve your own culture?
R: It depends actually from person to person. What I would say is that some Finnish people would not accept that I, in any way, would become a member. Some others, they have something to do with these cultural issues and foreigner's affairs, in many instances they unfortunately are trying to force you to become Finnish, and that I have rejected and rejected continuously, because I cannot become Finnish when somebody wants me to. I will never become Finnish because I have lived 24 years in another country, and I have grown up in another culture and now I have arrived here and it is true that I can learn a lot of things and behave like a Finnish person, but I am not thinking like one. Because I know a lot of things that Finnish people do not know; because I have knowledge of, in addition to the Finnish culture, also my own, which the Finnish people do not have any knowledge of. [t]

The refugees' relation to their societies of origin was not only a matter of memories; it was an ongoing and continuous relationship. All interviewees continued to be influenced by contemporary developments in Kurdistan. In particular, the political developments played a large role for the refugees. A woman from Turkey said:

> I think all Kurdish refugees have the problems in Kurdistan still inside them although they are away from there. They still think about Kurdistan and have it with them here, they have relatives still living there and hear news from Kurdistan. When they hear that villages have been destroyed it affects them directly although they are living here.

These quotations exemplify how all interviewees continued to relate to, and identify themselves with, Kurdistan. After several years in exile the refugees continued to feel alienated from the receiving society. This section has thus indicated that the refugees felt partly alienated and insulated from the country of settlement. Instead, they continued to relate to their countries of origin in several different ways. However, the connection with Kurdistan did not only have a psychological aspect; there were also quite tangible flows of information, ideas, capital and people between the countries of origin and the countries of settlement. These transnational networks are described in more detail in later parts of the book.

THE WISH TO RETURN

Related to refugees' sense of displacement and alienation is a feeling that their stay in the countries of reception is only temporary. The refugees look forward to the day when they can return home and everything will become 'normal again'. All respondents, with only two exceptions, stated that they wanted to move back to Kurdistan as soon as possible.[2] A man from Turkey living in London and a man from Iraq living in Finland expressed typical opinions about their wish to return:

> It is not just me. All of the Kurdish people, all over the world, not just in England or Britain or Europe, all over the world, they all want to go back to their country. [t]

I would like to return to Kurdistan, I think that I am the first family that will move back when Kurdistan becomes free. If there was a democratic leader, and peace and safety, after that I would go back. That is why I am now here, because there is no security. I think that some day I will go back; it is impossible for me to imagine that I would stay here. If that happens it is not my fault but because of life. Now we live in Finland but we do not know what will happen in the future. [t]

The circumstances that most respondents mentioned as necessary for a return included a change of government in the country of origin, the introduction of democracy and human rights and some kind of autonomy or independence for Kurdistan. Despite their wish to return to Kurdistan, all interviewees told me that they found it very hard to plan anything for the future. The political future of Kurdistan was regarded as very unclear and some refugees pointed out that they did not know if it would ever be possible for them to return. Many of the refugees from Iran and Iraq thought that, although they would like to return, this was very unlikely to happen within the near future. However, the refugees from Turkey were more likely to regard their stay as temporary and were more optimistic about the possibility of political change. The following quotation is typical of the optimism and hope that many refugees from Turkey expressed in 1994 and 1995:

I do not really hope [to stay in Britain]. Only while we are waiting for a free Kurdistan. But for me personally I do not think that we are going to stay in England for the rest of our lives. My personal feeling is that in a couple of years, two or three years, a kind of solution will be found between the Kurds and the Turks, so that actually we can return and be in our country, in a free environment.

In contrast to the optimism of the Kurds from Turkey a strong sense of alienation from politics was found among many refugees from Iraq. A man living in Finland reflected on the complicated problems in Iraq:

One does not know. Kurdistan lies between Turkey, Iraq, Iran and Syria. You do not know what can happen. I do not believe in Kurdish politics any more, but perhaps the USA or the United

Nations can do something. There are local problems as well between the two parties which have to be solved. I remember 1974,
when the USA did not support the Kurdish revolution. One does
not know, but I do not believe in the future and cannot see how
changes could happen. Perhaps you can ask some of the Kurdish
politicians who live in London what they say about it, they know
better than I do. . . . But I will stay here until the situation gets
better. [t]

In the case of the Iranian refugees, the hopes for a political solution were at least as pessimistic as was the case among the Kurds
from Iraq. A young man from Iran considered it unlikely that he
would be able to return within the near future:

You know, it depends, . . . If Iran becomes a free country, and
Iran lets me study, get a job and live as a human being. But if I
now go there . . . my life will be in danger, and I will end up in
jail and it will be difficult, I will not get a job, I will not have the
right to express my opinion, all these kinds of things. But if I get
what is normal for a human being, the things I can do here in
the Nordic countries. But that will not happen very fast, because
in Iran there is not a very well organized opposition at the
moment. [t]

One has to remember that for some refugees a return is unlikely
even if the political situation in Kurdistan suddenly changes. Many
refugees have lost everything they had in Kurdistan. Their villages
have been destroyed, their land has been confiscated, and their
relatives and friends might have been killed or have disappeared.
This was the case for refugees from all of the three countries concerned. An older couple from Iraq living in Finland described their
situation:

Husband: We cannot move back as long as there is no democratic rule there and human rights are not respected. Personally
I could stay here because I have nothing left in Kurdistan and it
is not so different here.
Wife: Yes, I agree with my husband. [t]

Personal relationships are an additional factor which influences the
plans for the future. In Finland it is relatively common for young

Kurdish men to have relationships with, and eventually marry, Finnish women. This of course has a decisive influence on the future plans of the Kurdish men, especially if the couple has children. As several young men told me, children and marriage would probably mean that they must give up their plans to return to Kurdistan.

To sum up, almost all refugees wish to return to Kurdistan when conditions are appropriate, but when this will be is not yet clear. The Kurds from Turkey were generally more optimistic about the chance of returning and were more inclined to see their stay as temporary. The Kurds from Iran and Iraq, however, did not think that a return would be possible within the near future. Clearly, the different political developments in the countries of origin had a profound influence on the refugees' plans for the future.

FUTURE PLANS IN THE COUNTRY OF SETTLEMENT

Although most refugees would like to return to Kurdistan, it is a fact that they must continue to live in exile for a long time, perhaps for ever. As a man from Iraq who had lived in Britain for five years said: 'Many people say that they are going back, but very few have actually done this. Many people speak about it but nobody goes back.' Thus, all refugees need to make some plans for their future in the country of settlement in case a return migration remains impossible. A woman from Iraq living in Britain and a man from Iran living in Finland described their plans for the future should they not be able to return:

> I would like to go back. But now it is impossible to go back, and if I have to stay here I will do my best and follow British laws and be thankful and live as a Kurd in Britain.

> In the first place I hope that we would have our own country, but if it is not possible to return to Kurdistan we would like to participate in Finnish society and also become citizens. [t]

The refugees want to return, but they also want to establish a life in their new country of settlement. How these conflicting plans for the future can be reconciled is a common dilemma. A young man from Turkey who had lived in Britain for four years described his thoughts:

ÖW: What is bad [in Britain compared to Kurdistan] then?

R: Bad is – in any case, you know you feel yourself, something – that in any case probably you will go back to your country, or you do not think of establishing a life here, a family you know, and in any case it is not your country.

ÖW: So it is still some kind of – some kind of alienation?

R: Yes, yes it is. But I think for much more, for many people they are establishing a community here, or Kurdish or Turkish, you know, a closed community, and they do not feel – to be living in a foreign country. How can I say – statistically if you ask a lot of people they can say: I want to go back actually. But, in fact, actually, the reality is different. But I can say that, in any case, as an example, you want your one leg to be in your country and your other leg to be in this country, if you see what I mean. It is very difficult.

Many refugees wish to take advantage of their lives in exile in order to further political and personal goals that are related to their countries of origin. Lundberg (1989), in his study of Latin American refugees, argues that it is possible to understand the refugees' life in exile as a career during which the refugees are trying to prepare themselves for their ultimate goal, which is a return to the country of origin. For example, many refugees spend their time studying and gaining knowledge which they can utilize after they have returned. A young man from Iran hoped to become a teacher in Kurdistan:

At least now I will study, and when my studies are concluded I would like to study even more, to get knowledge. . . . And if some day it happens that I return, in that case I can work as a teacher for my people. The people who are there surely need it more than the people who are here. And this is my whole future, but I do not know if I shall live so long or not. [t]

A majority of the respondents considered it possible that in the future they would apply for citizenship in the country of settlement. Dual citizenship is possible in both England and Finland. Three of the interviewees in Britain already had British citizenship. Those who did not want to apply for citizenship thought that they would soon return home to Kurdistan, and that they would thus not need a new citizenship. Many refugees indicated that there were largely practical reasons behind their wish for a new citizenship. It was felt that British or Finnish citizenship would make their lives easier, and in particular, it was mentioned that travelling abroad would be facilitated. Although travelling with the Refugee Convention travel document is possible, some interviewees found it embarrassing to use this document while others were afraid of more serious difficulties during trips abroad (if refugees are given full refugee status they are not allowed to keep their original passports, and are instead given the Refugee Convention travel document). As other studies have also shown (Ekholm, 1994; Icduygu, 1996), an application for citizenship is largely a practical question and does not necessarily indicate anything about a person's attachment to the country of settlement or country of origin.

It is also clear that the Kurds, as a persecuted minority, do not necessarily have a strong emotional bond to their original citizenship. This was stressed by some refugees from Iraq who said that since they were Kurds, they did not have any attachment to the Iraqi state, and that they therefore wanted to get rid of their citizenship as soon as possible. A few persons also mentioned that their application for citizenship would be made because of gratitude towards the country that had given them asylum. An Iranian man who had arrived in Finland as a quota refugee felt that he owed a debt of gratitude to Finland:

> I feel that I owe Finland and the Finnish people, Finnish society a lot. Because Finland has given me asylum and security and given me an opportunity to study, and I think I have to pay back a little bit of this debt. That is why I will participate in Finnish society, although in the sense that I can be a Kurd, a Kurd in Finland, or no problem to be a Finnish Kurd. And I think that I can somehow unite these things. [t]

All refugees stressed that they wanted to combine the best parts of the Kurdish culture with the best parts of the culture of the receiving society. The view taken in this book is that it is self-evident that persons can have multiple identities and in multicultural societies it is possible for immigrants to combine different cultures and identities (cf. Rex. 1994, 1996). Although the ultimate goal of the refugees is to return, there is at the same time a clear wish to be integrated into the society of reception. These contradictory future plans are not in conflict with each other since, at present, a return to Kurdistan is not possible, and nor is it very plausible in the near future. The wish to integrate is seen, for example, in the fact that all refugees express a desire to participate in their new society of settlement. Citizenship in the country of settlement was regarded as an instrument which could facilitate integration. For example, many refugees hoped that citizenship would make it easier to find a job and would reduce the discrimination they experienced in the labour market.

However, as some of the quotations in this chapter indicate, some refugees also felt that the process of integration into the receiving society was connected with various psychological problems. It was also often felt that integration was hampered by the attitudes among the majority. Some refugees were afraid that a new citizenship would not lead to any difference in the majority populations' opinions. A man from Iraq was pessimistic about his chances of being accepted as a member of Finnish society:

> I would like to be [a Finnish citizen]. It would make things easier for me, at least officially in this country. But as I told you, not even that would help me mentally in any way, psychologically, as long as I am regarded an outsider in this country.

The process of integration and some factors which have a negative influence on this will also be discussed in the next chapter. In any case, the results indicate that integration is a goal among the Kurdish refugees. Assimilation, on the other hand, is not even regarded as a possible outcome of life in exile, a fact which relates to the question of refugees' ethnic identification.

ETHNIC IDENTIFICATION

This study has not made any attempt to examine the issues of the Kurdish refugees' identity in any detail. However, some questions about the refugees' identification were included in the interviews. For example, all interviewees were asked how they would describe themselves to a person they had not met before, and, depending on the countries of origin and settlement, they were given the following alternatives: British/Finnish, Iranian/Turkish/Iraqi or Kurdish. This question about identification was also asked in order to identify the interview sample, which only included persons who defined themselves as Kurds.

Not surprisingly, none of the interviewees wanted to call themselves British or Finnish. All refugees said that they would present themselves as Kurdish. However, there were still some differences related to the countries of origin. The Kurds from Iraq were most likely to only present themselves as Kurdish, rather than use any other description of themselves. In fact some of them even found my question very strange, if not offensive, and asked me how I could question their Kurdish identity. Many Kurds from Turkey added that they could also use the labels Kurd from Turkey and Turkish Kurd. Most of the Kurds from Iran, however, found that the terms Iranian Kurdish and even Iranian were accurate. This probably reflects the fact that 'Iranian' signifies citizenship in a more ethnically neutral way than, for example, 'Turkish'. Especially those Iranians who had been active in leftist parties seemed to avoid emphasizing a separate Kurdish identification. By contrast, the Kurds from Iraq and Turkey generally wanted to stress their Kurdish identification. A man from Iraq told me that he had always defended his right to a separate Kurdish identity:

No, this has not changed, I have always, always said that I am a Kurd. Wherever I have gone and whoever I have spoken to, I always tell them that I am Kurdish. And this is the reason why I am a refugee today. Because I have fought for my right to be Kurdish, which is why I am a refugee. That is why there are Kurdish refugees, because we are not allowed to be Kurdish and live in Kurdistan. [t]

Most interviewees said that their identification had not changed during the time they had spent in their new countries of settlement. In those cases where the identification had changed, the refugees felt that they had started to feel *more* Kurdish since they moved to Europe. In Turkey, the Kurds have largely been denied the right to exist as a separate ethnic group. Therefore it is not surprising that the refugees from Turkey in exile might feel more 'Kurdish'. An activist in a Kurdish organization told me:

Let me tell you, the Kurds in Turkey have been so discriminated against that they have not even known who they are. They were so discriminated against that they had forgotten that they were Kurdish. Until the PKK came we did not understand this. That is why we have to educate ourselves and learn of our history and tell other people who we are. [t]

The continuous relation to, and flow of information from, Kurdistan also has an influence on the refugees in exile. The news from Kurdistan had greatly affected a man from Iraq who had lived in Britain for nine years:

> I have actually changed the way I am looking at this. Today I am more aware of my identity, because of the things that you hear that have happened in Kurdistan, since the oppression against the Kurds started ten years ago. Before that I was not aware in the same way. So, I have been influenced by the oppression, and there has been a gradual change – I have had both relatives and friends who have been killed and to hear about this has influenced me.

One interesting aspect of Kurdish refugee identity has to do with the widespread practice of ethnic monitoring in Britain. The whole idea of ethnic monitoring was questioned by many of the interviewees. A woman from Iran described her dilemma:

> Oh yes, it is horrible, I do not know, do you ask me do I fill it in? I have to do it – I have to do it, but I think it is very racist. I do not know why they do that, and sometimes I cannot feel myself in any column, because there is no column for me, and I write only 'Other' . . . I do not know why they ask these. I rejected to fill it in last year, and then I spoke with the management of the college, and he told me they do this to make a balance between the students, but I did not accept that.

The terms used in ethnic monitoring (the most common categories are 'White', 'Black', 'Asian' and 'Other') have a rather specific meaning in Britain. A few persons told me that they used to state that they were 'Asians', since Kurdistan lies in Asia, until somebody told them that, in Britain, 'Asian' usually refers to persons originating from the Indian subcontinent. Most had to opt for the 'Other' category and explain on the forms that they were Kurdish. None of the interviewees chose the category 'White'.

'Black', although a controversial and debated term, is often used in Britain as a broad political term referring to all persons experiencing racism, and is widely considered as a relevant category around which resistance to racism can be organized. Of the 28 interviewees in Britain, only two declared that as well as being Kurdish, they could also describe themselves as 'Black'. Both persons had lived in Britain for a relatively long time and had been involved in community work with ethnic minorities, and both considered the term 'Black' to include all ethnic minorities in Britain. This would suggest that the Kurdish communities, over time, might start to feel part of, and be integrated into, the wider category of 'Black' or 'ethnic minorities' in Britain. However, this is a development that is far removed from the present situation, where the Kurdish refugees tend to identify themselves as Kurds rather than anything else.

Actually, many interviewees had problems in understanding the question when asked if they felt that they were an 'ethnic minority' in Britain. Because of the continuing relationship which most refugees have to their countries of origin, they wanted to think of themselves within this framework and not within the framework of British ethnic relations. A refugee from Turkey who had lived for seven years in Britain had a very good understanding of the meaning of the term 'ethnic minority', but still found it incomprehensible to think of the refugee community in these terms:

ÖW: Do you consider yourself to belong to an ethnic minority then, because people in Britain sometimes talk about ethnic minorities?
R: No, I get really angry when they say Kurdish minority. I do not. Kurdish people, Kurdish nation I would say.
ÖW: But I mean in England, an ethnic minority in England?
R: In England?
ÖW: Yes, in England.
R: Hmm – Maybe we are a minority, but I do not know ethnic minority, I do not like the word minority.
ÖW: OK, it has to do with –
R: It is sort of like discrimination, in a way, one way of –
ÖW: Yes. So the reason you do not like the word minority is because it has to do with you not feeling you are a minority in Turkey?
R: How they can call 20 million people a minority is just amazing. There are nations which are smaller than that, what, for example, is the population of Holland or Luxembourg?

This quotation exemplifies that the Kurdish refugees predominantly choose to define themselves as Kurds rather than using any other

ethnic or national label. The strong identification as Kurds therefore makes a rapid assimilation impracticable, since assimilation
into the society of exile would mean that the refugees would give
up their previous identity. Yet, a social and structural integration
is, of course, still possible and is also regarded as a goal by the
refugees.

Because of the orientation towards Kurdistan, it is difficult to
regard the Kurdish refugees as an ethnic minority within the framework of the countries of exile. This supports the argument that
theories of ethnic relations are not easily applied to refugee situations (cf. Bousquet, 1991). However, this does not mean that refugees
do not constitute ethnic groups. As discussed in Chapter 1, ethnicity
is always defined in terms of a relation between social groups. In
the case of Kurdish refugees, the most significant relation is not
within the country of settlement. Instead, the refugees' ethnicity is
primarily defined within the context of social relations in the countries of origin.

THE SPECIFIC EXPERIENCES OF FEMALE REFUGEES

Although many of the problems refugees experience are the same
for both men and women, female refugees are in some respects
especially disadvantaged. In order to discuss the experiences of female
refugees, this section briefly describes some issues pertaining to
gender roles and family values among Kurdish refugees. Differences between the social relations in Kurdistan and in the two
societies of resettlement were in various ways pointed out by all
interviewees. A woman from Iraq described the differences between
Britain and Kurdistan:

> Yes, in Kurdistan there are people around you. When you live
> in Kurdistan all the neighbours, all your family, friends, you do
> not feel that you are on your own in Kurdistan. If you have any
> problem all the friends and families and all the neighbours are
> like your family, they come to help you, and they visit you – it is
> not like here [in England] really.

The differences described in this quotation seem to be connected
to the role which the family plays as a social institution. When
asked to give examples of positive and negative things in the coun-

try of settlement in comparison with the situation in Kurdistan, most people chose to speak about family values. A woman from Iran explained:

> Iranian people are close together, they are very good to each other. If you have some problems you can go to any of your neighbours or friends and they will help you. In England nobody helps you and you cannot get help from, or talk to, your neighbour, you just say hello and that is all. In Iran things are better.... Iranian families are very close together and we look after each other. In England, parents are not responsible for their children, they are not close together and do not take care of each other. Brothers do not help their sisters and men do not help their wives. In Iran we do not know this, this is what I think. You have to be careful with your children, you have to give them advice.... I am responsible for my children. In this country it is different, people are not responsible for each other.

Many of the interviewees, both men and women, had serious doubts about the way the family works in Europe. Divorce and the general breakdown of families in Europe were mentioned by many persons as negative aspects of life in exile. The commitment to the institution of marriage and the family in general seems to be a fundamental part of the Kurdish culture (cf. Songur, 1992), and this was expressed in various ways in most interviews.

Without exaggerating the importance of cultural differences it has to be acknowledged that it is possible to argue that there are cultural differences between contemporary northern European societies (including England and Finland) and the traditional Kurdish society. However, what should be remembered is that these differences do not by themselves lead to problems or conflicts, which are instead determined by other factors. However, it can be argued that because of the cultural differences, the refugees might feel more disoriented and might experience more misunderstandings than they would otherwise do. This in turn might aggravate all the problems refugees experience. As Sheikhmous argues: 'For somebody coming from a social background like Kurdistan (which is mainly agrarian), with its intensive social contacts in the framework of the extended family, neighbours and friends, the experience [of exile] becomes even more dramatic' (Sheikhmous, 1990: 103).

An issue closely related to Kurdish family values is that of gender

roles. In traditional Kurdish society there is a clear division of labour
between men and women, with both having specific roles determined by gender, age and marital status (Songur, 1992). Men are
traditionally dominant in the public sphere of life, while women
are confined to the private sphere. It is sometimes argued that
Kurdish women traditionally have more freedom than women living
in other traditional cultures in the Middle East. Still, whether or
not it is true that the Kurdish women, relatively speaking, are more
emancipated, it is a fact that traditional Kurdish society and public
life are largely dominated by men (cf. Laizer, 1996a). Some of the
interviewees, both male and female, even regarded traditional Kurdish
society as a very sexist society in which women are discriminated
against. However, some other women strongly defended traditional
gender roles and family values and argued that the freedom of
women in Europe is illusory. Some persons even argued that individual freedom in Europe amounted to nothing other than loneliness
and irresponsibility. This section is not able to give a full picture
of gender roles in Kurdistan. The important issue for the purpose
of this book is that although diverse opinions were expressed about
gender roles, all interviewees experienced significant differences
between the gender roles in Kurdistan and those in the societies
of settlement.

Often the two concepts of honour and shame are used to describe
two fundamental virtues in Kurdish culture (cf. Songur, 1992). In
particular, the life of Kurdish women is traditionally ruled by the
importance of honour and shame. Sheri Laizer describes the importance of these traditional customs among the Kurds in Turkey:

> The motivating factor for most Kurds continues to be their sense
> of honour. A family's honour is all-important and is usually seen
> as residing in the purity and fidelity of its women. . . . A woman's
> infidelity to her husband – even when the marriage is an arranged
> and possibly loveless union – brings disgrace to both families.
> (Laizer, 1991: 44)

Some of the female interviewees explained that even in exile the
concept of the family's honour still has a profound influence on
the relations between the sexes in the Kurdish communities. A woman
from Turkey argued that young female refugees in particular experience many problems in England:

Kurdish women's situation is quite difficult here, since they live in a totally different culture. Especially young women, . . . because here the Kurdish community puts a big pressure on women, especially on girls, because they believe English culture is a culture where you can have free sex, and they do not want their children to be like them, especially their daughters. And there are still arranged marriages here, they either get women from Kurdistan, for their boys, or they send their daughters back to Kurdistan for marriage.

ÖW: So, this is done to protect the women –

R: Yes, to protect from the other side.

ÖW: – from the terrible English culture?

R: Yes, to protect their family.

Of all the problems Kurdish refugees experience, some are obviously gender-specific. Therefore a particular effort was made during the fieldwork to gain access to the experiences of women.[3] Kurdish women often have a poorer education and fewer language skills than men. Actually, many of the female informants emphasized that the possibility of studying was one of the positive things about living in Europe. Since Kurdish women have traditionally been confined to the private sphere of life, female refugees often have limited personal contacts with the society of settlement. In the European countries services and resources are mainly available within the public sphere of life, and therefore they are often not as accessible for Kurdish women as they are for men. Consequently, some Kurdish women in Europe have to rely on their men, who have to take care of the whole family's contacts with the authorities and other public institutions. A woman from Turkey gave a description of the problems facing refugee women in London:

Men are more open to the changes, if you like, to the outside world, because of the society back in Kurdistan. Whereas women are more used to a more closed environment, you know, and when you come to a country like this and there is a culture shock, it is more striking for women than it is for men, I would say. Women need a lot of encouragement and confidence because of the treatment of women throughout history, women lost self-confidence and they do not see a role for themselves in the society, they do not see any position and they feel like they cannot really do much in that sense. So the problem for women here, [is that] you get more closed, you know, between four walls at home. For example, you look around you and you do not see many women around you trying to learn the language, but you see more men going to colleges, young or middle-age men trying to learn the language. But women mostly choose to stay at home, and do not get out much. Because they feel like they cannot cope with the changes. It is more difficult for them to understand the society, they just let men do it.

Among the first refugees from Iraq, many women had a good educational and professional background. This has changed in recent years and the women's disadvantaged position has become more evident among the recent arrivals from Iraq and Turkey. Furthermore, the women from Turkey living in London are in a special situation since they are living in a closed Turkish and Kurdish community in north London. Although this has its own advantages, it also means that women tend to become isolated from British society. In addition, some of them work in factories while others work at home taking care of their families. Consequently, many women have limited chances to take part in language courses or to learn English through personal contacts.

Women's issues are not always sufficiently taken into account in the refugee community. Some female interviewees felt that Kurdish associations are not really able to help women enough with their specific problems. The impression given during various discussions was that the emancipation of women was seen by many persons as only a subordinate part of the larger Kurdish national project of liberating Kurdistan from oppression by the states in the region.[4]

To summarize, Kurdish refugee women are in many ways disadvantaged compared with Kurdish men. Since the public sphere of life in Kurdistan is largely reserved for men, women are not used to taking part in public life in a way that is customary in European societies. Female refugees are often also deprived of their traditional support networks in the extended families that exist in Kurdistan. Additional problems are created by a lack of formal education and work experience as well as a high frequency of illiteracy. Kurdish women are also obliged to take care of their traditional duties as housewives and mothers, and are thus often prevented from taking part in educational courses and language training. All these factors contribute to the specific problems that female refugees face in their new countries of settlement. This exemplifies the fact that it is important to take into account a gender perspective in discussing refugees' problems. As Kay (1987) argues, this gender perspective is often forgotten in refugee studies, which tend to concentrate on the public domain and not the private domain of life.

CONCLUSION

This chapter has described the Kurdish refugees' own experiences upon arrival in Britain and Finland. The psychological problems, experiences of displacement and many practical problems are largely the same for all Kurdish refugees, regardless of their country of origin and country of settlement. The experiences of the Kurdish refugees in general are also similar to those of other refugee groups, and this study thus largely confirms results from previous studies discussing refugee resettlement. However, this study seeks to discuss these issues within a slightly different conceptual framework.

The results presented in this chapter indicate that two of Safran's characteristics of a diaspora are evident among the Kurdish refugees. Firstly, there is a wish to return to Kurdistan among the refugees, since 'they regard their ancestral homeland as their true, ideal home and as the place to which they or their descendants would (or should) eventually return – when conditions are appropriate' (Safran, 1991: 83–4). At the moment return is impossible, and, depending on the refugee's country of origin and political convictions, there were different assumptions of when and how the conditions would be appropriate for return. Secondly, the refugees can be seen to have a continuous relationship with their homeland. This means that 'they continue to relate, personally or vicariously, to that homeland in one way or another, and their ethnocommunal consciousness and solidarity are importantly defined by the existence of such a relationship' (Safran, 1991: 84). This is indicated by the feeling of displacement among the refugees. The next chapters will return to this last characteristic and look more closely at the transnational social networks in the Kurdish refugee communities.

The results suggest that the Kurdish refugees have a diasporic consciousness. This indicates that the concept of diaspora might be useful for describing the specific refugee experience. Because of the diasporic consciousness theories of ethnic relations are difficult to apply to the refugee communities. The Kurds do not regard themselves as a minority within the context of the country of exile; instead their ethnicity is defined within social relations in the country of origin. Consequently, any rapid assimilation of the refugees is obviously out of the question. Despite this diasporic consciousness and the impossibility of a rapid assimilation, the refugees actively strive to become integrated into their new society of settlement. The refugees try to combine their Kurdish culture with the culture of the receiving society. Regardless of their plans for the future or their feelings of alienation, all refugees wish to learn the language and, at least temporarily, settle down in the country of settlement.

This dual orientation towards both the country of origin and the country of resettlement is not as contradictory and paradoxical as it seems. In the refugees' own experiences, their country of origin and their country of exile, as well as the time before and the time after migration, constitute a continuous and coherent lived experience. The separation between before and after migration, as well as the separation between the country of origin and country of exile, is largely forced on the refugees' experiences by the outside observer. The concept of diaspora can help the researcher to rethink these issues and to understand the transnational reality in which the refugees are forced to live. The concept can bridge the often artificial duality in which the refugee experience is conceptualized.

All the Kurdish refugees shared the experiences discussed above, but there were also other significant differences between various groups of refugees. For example, there was a gender perspective which has to be taken into account. Among the Kurdish refugees, men and women often had access to very different means and resources to handle their problems. There were also significant differences between the experiences of the refugees in England and in Finland. The refugees in England experienced more practical problems and language difficulties, while the refugees in Finland seemed to suffer more from isolation and various psychological problems.

5 The Process of Integration

The Kurdish refugees' diasporic consciousness and their continuous relations with the country of origin should not divert attention from the fact that refugees do want to integrate into their new countries of settlement. Although refugees do not want to, and feel that they cannot, totally assimilate, there is a clear wish among them to play an active social and economic role in their new societies. Different aspects of the process of integration among Kurdish refugees are described in this chapter. A structural dimension of integration is discussed from the point of view of the refugees' integration into the labour market. Various experiences of racism, xenophobia and discrimination are outlined and their relation to the process of integration into the receiving society is discussed. In the latter parts of the chapter the analysis of integration is developed further through a study of the refugees' interpersonal relations and social networks.

EMPLOYMENT

As argued in the previous chapter, all the interviewees expressed a clear wish to become integrated and participate in their new society of settlement. To find employment was regarded as one of the most important ways to participate in society. A woman from Iran told me:

> I am not working, I am a student, studying English. I would like to work but I cannot find work. I would like to do something with my own hands, not just get help from others all the time. I feel really bad every time I go to the DSS, I think that it is now enough, I have been here five years now and I should be able to do something on my own and not just rely on others.

All refugees would like to find a job or some other meaningful employment in the country of reception. As a man from Iraq said:

'To sit like this, doing nothing, in Kurdistan it would be regarded as a disease.' To have a job is clearly not only an economic issue. Employment also would solve many of the psychological and social problems which the refugees experience. A family from Iran said that their wish was to return to Kurdistan, but if they had to stay in Finland, they did have plans for the future:

> We are trying to be useful persons in any possible way. Our first goal is to establish our own business so we could stand on our own feet, in this way we also would get rid of the psychological pressure and we will secure our future. [t]

The concept of integration is often measured in terms of the migrant's position in the labour market (cf. Ekholm, 1994; Miles, 1993; Phillips, 1989). As the quotations above illustrate, the Kurdish refugees in both countries want to become integrated into the receiving society in this sense of the term. Many refugees are not part of the economically active population since, for example, they are students or housewives; but among those who are a part of the labour market one can find a clear difference between the way they are integrated in the two countries of settlement.

England

The employment situation for refugees in Britain is not good. The national rate of unemployment in Britain was around 8 per cent in 1995. However, among refugees the percentage was probably considerably higher. Carey-Wood et al. (1995) recorded an unemployment rate of 57 per cent among refugees in their sample in 1992. However, as they point out, there are of course other ways of making economic contributions besides having a 'job'. Their research showed, for example, that 36.5 per cent of their respondents had done some kind of voluntary work.

Britain has a comprehensive race relations legislation which, among other things, aims at preventing discrimination in the labour market. Although the efficiency of this legislation can be debated, it can be argued that the British legislation, compared with the situation in Finland, has been relatively efficient in preventing *open* racism and discrimination in employment. Despite this, there is still a clear ethnic segmentation in the labour market. London is a multicultural city including many communities established by persons originating in the Middle East. These communities provided some of the Kurdish refugees with an opportunity to gain employment. Since Britain did not have a statutory minimum wage, these jobs were often very poorly paid. In this study this was particularly clear in the case of the Turkish and Kurdish community in north London. The Kurdish refugees here had an opportunity to be employed in some of the 'sweatshops' in the area.

Estimates of unemployment among the Kurds in London show great variation. The 1993–4 Annual Report of the Kurdistan Workers Association estimated that 95 per cent of the Kurds in north London were unemployed, while many of those in employment were 'exploited by the factory "sweatshops" that run in the area, and perform menial, unrewarding work' (KWA, 1994: 7). A report from Hackney Council (1993) estimated that unemployment in the 'Turkish community' in Hackney was 35–40 per cent, while 20–30 per cent of the Turkish and Kurdish community were self-employed. The report further stated that 'Hackney entertains the greatest amount of "black" economy and the Turkish/Kurdish community appear to rely heavily on this opportunity' (Hackney Council, 1993: 10). There were estimated to be around 800 clothing manufacturing units in Hackney alone. The report criticizes the fact that there are not enough facilities to integrate most members of the community into the national economy, and advocates better incentives and guidance for those active in the garment factories. Other significant economic activities in the Borough's Turkish and Kurdish community were cafés (around 400 establishments), restaurants and various shops (Hackney Council, 1993).

In this research, five respondents have had temporary jobs in Turkish and Kurdish textile 'sweatshops' in north London. These jobs were sometimes part of a 'black' economy where no taxes were paid. The wages in these 'sweatshops' are low and are paid according to results. Needless to say, these jobs provide no social security and give no protection against illness, accidents or unreliable employers. A refugee from Turkey described the working conditions:

Usually you work like 12 hours a day. And you do not have any kind of security. If you are ill that is it, they sack you. They do not care about you at all, and there is a big market here. Most of the Kurdish people, Kurdish refugees, work without a National Insurance Number. I worked in a factory one month ago but it was unbearable for me and I left it. It is again 12 hours, or it is

not 12 hours, you start and you do not know when you are going to finish it. They do not let you, allow you to go out unless the job finishes, and sometimes you work like seven days a week like 20 hours [a day]. . . .
There are so many people, they are on Income Support and Housing Benefit, and they cannot afford to cut it, so they have to find illegal jobs, and since there are so many people looking for jobs, they do not care, if they sack you the next day, or even the same day, they can find somebody else.

As indicated in the quotation above, refugees were often forced to work in the poorly paid 'black' economy because the DSS money was not enough to live on and sufficiently well paid 'legal' jobs were not available. These problems were accentuated by the fact that the Kurds from Turkey seldom speak English upon arrival in the UK and many of them are poorly educated. Thus, many of them face problems in the labour market and have to work in poor conditions in various 'sweatshops' in north London.

This type of employment implies that the Kurdish refugees are integrated into the labour market at the lowest possible level, occasionally working in low-wage jobs and occasionally being unemployed. Even the highly skilled refugees experience a dramatic downward economic mobility (cf. Carey-Wood et al., 1995; Rasheed, 1992; Hackney Council, 1993).

There is, however, some chance that over time the refugees might improve their situation in the labour market. Carey-Wood et al. (1995) regard duration of stay in the UK as one of the factors affecting refugees' career status in Britain. A large number of the Kurdish refugees are actually students who might improve their status in the labour market in the future. In fact, many well-educated men from Iraq can already be found in very good positions in Britain, but these persons are of course only a small minority of the Kurds in Britain.

Finland

The employment situation in Finland was very bad during the period in which the fieldwork was carried out. Ekholm (1994) has used official statistics to calculate the exact unemployment rate for refugees. The rate was 61.4 per cent of the economically active refugees in 1992, when the national average was 13.1 per cent. Since the national average unemployment rate grew to 18.4 per cent in 1994 (Statistics Finland, 1995), one can assume that unemployment among refugees was even worse at the time this research was carried out, during the autumn of 1994.

A few Kurds arrived in Finland before the economic recession, and some of them managed to get jobs. However, among the main group who arrived in the 1990s, the employment situation remained very bad. A few Kurdish refugees have been employed as interpreters and Kurdish language teachers, while others are self-employed in fast-food outlets and shops selling oriental foodstuffs. The 'enterprise allowance' for unemployed persons who establish businesses (a scheme administered by the Employment Offices) has been of great help to many Kurds. Nonetheless, those who have managed to become self-employed are exceptions, and during the fieldwork it became clear that most Kurdish refugees were unemployed.

As described in Chapter 3, the Finnish refugee resettlement programme is clearly oriented towards integrating refugees into the labour market. The programme includes practice in different jobs and guidance about career opportunities. The aim is also to avoid the kind of integration that tends to occur in England, where refugees end up doing the most menial and poorly paid jobs (cf. Steen, 1992). Finland has extensive labour legislation, and also a minimum wage, which to some extent prevents the refugees from being discriminated against in the labour market. However, it has to be stressed that Finnish resettlement policies have not been adjusted for the present employment situation. During the economic recession in the 1990s most refugees have not been able to find any kind of employment. Instead, the integration of refugees has been into the vast army of alienated and marginalized unemployed. Clearly, the relatively high unemployment among refugees can only be seen as a failure of the Finnish resettlement programmes. It also appears that the refugees were not given a fair chance to compete for the few available jobs. A young man from Iran, who spoke rather good Finnish, told me:

Once it happened, in the Employment Office, there was this thought that the worker there had found a job for me as a cleaner. I said that I wanted to have a job, even if it was a job as a cleaner. But then he showed me that it said in the advert that the employer had written that you had to speak Finnish. [t]

This was, however, the only occasion when I heard about somebody even having a remote chance of getting a job through the Employment Offices. Instead, the unemployment situation in Finland has created a situation in which the refugees are so marginalized that they cannot even experience the luxury of being discriminated against in the labour market.

To sum up, there are differences and similarities between the employment situations of Kurds in England and Finland. In both countries the refugees find themselves integrated at the lowest possible level of the labour market. In Finland the Kurds are mostly unemployed, while in Britain they might take poorly paid jobs in various 'sweatshops'. The resettlement programmes in Finland have clearly failed in their goal to achieve a positive integration for refugees, while the lack of resettlement programmes in Britain almost automatically excludes refugees from the better jobs. However, in Britain the Kurds can use their own informal networks to create and find jobs. For example, in north London there is a separate Turkish and Kurdish ethnic labour market in which the Kurdish refugees from Turkey can find employment.

All refugees want to find employment and achieve integration into the labour market. They might not always have the necessary skills for the labour market, but still many of them are highly educated. Taking this into account, the relatively high unemployment rate among refugees suggests that they face serious discrimination. As has repeatedly been proved in Britain, ethnic minorities are disadvantaged and face discrimination in the labour market (cf. Wrench and Solomos, 1993). There is no reason why refugees should not face the same, or even worse, discrimination. In fact, in both countries the refugees experienced many different kinds of discrimination and racism.

RACISM AND DISCRIMINATION

The findings of this study concerning the extent of racism and xenophobia in Finland are rather depressing. A majority of the interviewees had an abundance of experience of various kinds of xenophobia or racism. Most of the single men had experienced racially motivated and vicious, violent attacks. Two young male persons had even been attacked by youth gangs in the middle of the day. The female and older male refugees had mostly experienced vocal expressions of xenophobia and racism. Most interviewees had been insulted by drunken Finns. These experiences had a profound effect on the refugees' relations with Finnish people. An older man from Iraq described how his family's contacts with Finns were influenced by these experiences:

> Yes, all the time when you walk on the street you think that perhaps that person hates me. Because it happens some times, which is why you have it with you all the time. We respect Finland and what they have done for us, but we do not know who is against us here. In Kurdistan we knew who the enemy was. [t]

The tragic incident in the Finnish town of Turku on the night of 29 January 1993 also contributed to the fear of racist attacks. Receb Karagöz, a Kurd from Turkey, spent the night out with his Turkish friend. They became involved in a fight with a group of Finnish youths outside a restaurant. Receb Karagöz was stabbed and he died some days later in hospital. A 17-year-old Finnish boy was arrested by the police after the incident. It was commonly assumed that he had a racist motive, although this was never proven. This tragedy was well known among the Kurds in Finland. The fear of racist attacks led to the fact that some refugees were living a more isolated life than they would otherwise wish to do. Most refugees avoided restaurants, pubs and other places where it was possible that problems might occur. A man from Iraq told me that he usually had no problem apart from encounters with drunken persons:

> On Saturdays and Sundays we do not usually go out very much because they [drunken persons] insult us in the street. For example, we cannot go to any bar, disco or hotel if we want to drink something, because they bother us. That is why we avoid places like that. [t]

Similar experiences of racism in Finland have also been documented by other authors studying refugees (Alitolppa-Niitamo, 1994; Ekholm, 1994), but unfortunately no official statistics of racist attacks were available in the mid-1990s. However, as I will also discuss later, one still has to remember that not all Finns are hostile towards refugees, and that it is only a small minority who create problems. In any event, the extent of racism and xenophobia in Finland came as a surprise to the refugees, especially to the quota refugees who were actually invited to Finland.

Surprisingly, many interviewees in Finland still did not regard racism and xenophobia as a major problem in their lives. Many of the interviewees said that they did not think that the incidents of racism and discrimination which they had experienced were very serious. Taking into account the extent of open racism in Finland, this is rather extraordinary. One reason might be that, compared to the experiences of discrimination and civil war in Kurdistan, these racist attacks were regarded as only minor incidents. Furthermore, the refugees had not experienced any discrimination from the Finnish authorities, only from certain individuals. The refugees' opinions can also be partly explained by the fact that refugees might have seen their stay in Finland as only temporary, since they still hoped to move back to Kurdistan within a few years. Another possible reason why the interviewees did not want to make a big issue out of these incidents might be that they wanted to give me as good a picture as possible about their experiences in Finland. Complaining about racism might be seen as being ungrateful after they had received asylum in the country.

The extent of *open* racism and racist attacks in Finland cannot be described as anything other than alarming. Yet, in some cases, the *hidden* xenophobia and discrimination was experienced as an even worse problem by the refugees. A man from Iran did not regard the overt racist attacks as racism, and argued that the real racism in Finland was a hidden cultural racism towards people from the third world:

Really I cannot say that someone who attacks me is racist. The person is hostile towards foreigners, which is not racism. A person who makes a difference between cultures, this is real racism according to me, because that person wants to say that something is better, and to put people in different classes. . . . It might happen [that Finns have disagreements with each other] but that is person against person. I have this idea, if you meet a foreigner from a different culture. You will blame everything on this person's culture. It is because of your culture that you did this and that. This would not happen between Finns; nobody will tell you that you have a different culture and are a foreigner. This term 'foreigner', it means that the person is different from the rest. But if you have problems with another Finn, will anybody tell you that it is because of your culture? Nobody will tell you this, they will say that it is because of your personality. But if somebody blames your culture, says that it is bad or good . . . This is in my opinion racism. [t]

This Iranian man also argued that the differential treatment which refugees experience arises because refugees are seen to come from inferior and poor countries and cultures. Since the discrimination is based on assumed cultural differences this phenomenon is clearly related to the notion of new racism, as described in Chapter 1. Another refugee in Finland, a man from Iraq, described similar experiences of cultural racism:

R: Towards me personally nothing serious has happened, but the most serious thing for me is the mentality of the Finnish people, I can give you a lot of examples.
ÖW: Yes. That is fine.
R: For example, when you see my face now, I do not look like an African. People believe that I am from Spain or Italy or so on. They have treated me so good, and after that when they notice I am a refugee and from Kurdistan, this is not shown very clearly but I am sensitive about this, and I immediately notice that people treat me differently. This mentality is a problem. Even if he would notice that I am not an Italian or Spanish, he would not start calling me names, but I notice anyway that his voice changes in some way and I know that something has happened inside him.

Finnish xenophobia can take a variety of forms. For example, one refugee living in Helsinki had repeatedly noticed that people avoided sitting next to him on the bus. In addition to the fact that people felt excluded because they were identified as foreigners from the third world, some felt that it was an additional disadvantage to be identified as a refugee. The stigmatization connected to refugee status was common in Finland. A man from Iraq told me:

It is a big misunderstanding here in Finland, but I am not saying that all Finnish people say this or think this way. I do not want to generalize, because I am always talking in a relative way about these things. The big misunderstanding is that about refugees, people think that you have to be poor, you have to be without any knowledge, you have to be this and that. But people do not realize that a real refugee is something different from a person who is here because of starvation.

The quotations above suggest that there are hidden racist ideas at play which are not as obvious as open racism and racist attacks, but which are still serious problems. However, at the same time few of the refugees in Finland experienced actual systematic discrimination. In particular, the authorities were regarded as giving fair and equal treatment to everybody. The conclusion, paradoxically, is that although there existed xenophobia and racism among the general public, actual discrimination was not an intrinsic part of Finnish society. A man from Iraq who had experienced a lot of racism among the general public was still able to tell me:

> The authorities' behaviour is good, I think. At least they do not show their – If they have something against you, they do not show it to us. And all things go without any problems, and on the other hand even sometimes they help us more than they help Finnish people.

In Britain, most Kurdish refugees live in London, which is a cosmopolitan and multicultural city with seven million inhabitants. The human diversity in London seems to contribute to Kurdish refugees feeling more easily at home. A woman who lived in the borough of Kensington and Chelsea described her experiences:

> ÖW: Have you experienced any racism in Britain?
> R: Not myself, no. But, you know, it is different because the area I live in, have you seen it? It is not many English people [who] live in this area. It is all African and Asian people [who] live here, and I really never have seen any [racism]. And I do not feel I live in England, you know. When I go outside [London], it is more like England. But here it is so different, mixed up all peoples and cultures. But I like it, I like it very much, it is more like home.

In a large multicultural city with many persons regarded as 'foreigners', there is also less risk of being personally singled out for racist attacks or insult. Among the interviewees, one male refugee had once experienced a racist attack and some of the female refugees had experienced insulting comments from British persons. Although racist attacks and racism are still a serious problem in London, the extent of this fades in comparison with the situation in Finland. During the fieldwork in England I also had the opportunity to meet a refugee who had stayed in Denmark for some time. He argued that although people in Britain talked about racism all the time, he actually felt that the situation was worse in the Nordic countries. These issues were also discussed with a Kurd who had moved from Finland to England, and who was largely able to confirm my interpretation of the differences between the two countries:

> You know, in Finland I felt like a stranger, I do not feel the same way here. I am of course also a stranger here, but I do not feel it in the same way. You know this street where we live, there are many foreign people here, my next door neighbour is Chinese. In Finland we were the only foreigners, I felt that people thought I was a stranger and looked at me, although everybody was very nice. But actually I liked Finland better than England. Everybody was very nice to me in Finland and I will never forget that and always be grateful for what people did for me, the problem was only that I felt as a stranger there and felt that I cannot live there. I do not feel the same way here. In Finland I did not know what I was doing there and felt as if I was going mad, I feel much better here in London although there are a lot of problems here. But I feel much more comfortable here and do not want to move back.

Obviously, the refugees in Britain do not experience as much *open* racism as in Finland. However, it can be argued that racism in Britain is more hidden and structural. The immigrants in Britain are integrated into the society at the lowest possible socio-economic level. Furthermore, there is often a lack of services for the refugees and they face a lot of obstacles in their contacts with the British authorities. As research has shown (cf. Wrench and Solomos, 1993), the existence of racial discrimination in Britain cannot be denied. However, the discriminatory and racist structures in British society are not always very obvious since they do not necessarily manifest themselves in the personal relations of refugees' daily lives in the multicultural inner city boroughs of London. The situation in Britain is in this respect almost the opposite to the Finnish situation. In Finland, there is an obvious and crude racism and xenophobia which the refugees experience in their daily lives, but nevertheless relatively few of the refugees had experiences of systematic discrimination and none felt that they had been discriminated against by the authorities.

INTEGRATION INTO THE SOCIETY OF RECEPTION

It has already been pointed out in this book that the concept of integration, although frequently used, is problematic. As early as the 1960s, Breton (1964) suggested that the integration of immigrants is possible in at least three different directions: within the majority community, within another ethnic minority group, or within the immigrants' own ethnic group. As was noted in Chapter 1, this framework is clearly an oversimplification of a complex process. Nevertheless, Breton's classification can serve as a useful way to structure the research findings presented in the remainder of this chapter. Thus, the following sections describe the interpersonal relations of the Kurdish refugees with the ethnic majority, with other ethnic groups, and finally with fellow Kurds. Using this description, I will introduce a critical discussion of the concept of integration and suggest a rethinking of the process of refugee resettlement.

This section is thus concentrated on the refugees' social integration into the society of reception. England and Finland are, of course, not unitary and homogenous societies. When studying immigrants' social integration into these complex societies, it is not clear which parts and areas of these societies the immigrants are supposed to integrate into and how this process can be studied. Thus, instead of describing integration in absolute terms, this section outlines the refugees' own experiences of personal relations with the majority. From this point of view the relations with the majority populations are quite different in the two countries under study.

England

In London, the Kurds from Turkey live in a Turkish and Kurdish community which, in many ways, is insulated from English society. The boroughs of Hackney and Haringey, where the Turkish and Kurdish community in north London is situated, are areas with a high proportion of ethnic minority populations. According to the 1991 census, the ethnic minorities accounted for 33.6 per cent of the total population in Hackney and 29.0 per cent in Haringey (Owen, 1994). The situation for Kurds from Iran and Iraq is slightly different, since they are not concentrated to the same extent in particular geographical areas in London. Yet, these groups also tend to live in areas with a high proportion of ethnic minorities, although not necessarily with other Kurds or compatriots. Consequently, the Kurds tend to have relatively few contacts with the ethnic majority in multicultural London.

In the sample in England, 16 out of 28 persons felt that they did not have any English friends at all, although some of the interviewees had friends from other refugee groups and British ethnic minorities. Also, marriage between Kurds and persons from the ethnic majority seemed to be relatively uncommon, although it was not totally exceptional for Kurdish men to have English or British girlfriends. A middle-aged Kurdish man from Turkey described his contacts with the ethnic majority:

I have mostly Kurdish friends, because English people do not have the same culture. If you do not go to pubs you do not meet any. Especially in Hackney and Haringey, there are many Kurds and you do not meet English people. Especially I went outside London once to a small town, and then I realized that I cannot speak English. . . . But in London you can see every kind of race and people. [t]

Since the Kurds from Turkey live in their own community in north London they are relatively insulated from the ethnic majority. Furthermore, the poor linguistic skills and educational background among many Kurds from Turkey is a hindrance to social contacts with British people. Those who had English or British friends often met them through activities in the Kurdish associations or through Kurdish solidarity work. A Kurdish woman explained how she had met her British friends:

I have more Kurdish friends definitely. I know a few English; it is quite difficult to have any relation with English people here. And because of the language, most of the people do not speak English. And the ones who speak English like me, it is quite typical to have some kind of friendship. I had a friend. She was learning Kurdish . . ., so she is quite aware of the Kurdish question. She wants to help, that is why we could get a relation with her. And the other English people I know, they are most of them interested in the Kurdish question. Either they work with the Kurdish community or they are doing research on the Kurdish community. . . . But apart from that, as to kinds of friend, I do not have any, and most of the Kurdish women and men, you know, we have each other actually, as a support group. There are some parties, revolutionary parties, English revolutionary parties, like SWP, Socialist Workers Party, and Anti-Nazi League, and Spartacus, these kinds of organizations, you know, you could have friends from these organizations as well.

Although there might be some contacts with the ethnic majority in England, these contacts can in no way compensate for the close personal contacts the refugees are used to in Kurdistan. A woman from Turkey who had lived in London for seven years described her general impression of English people:

They do not bother, they say it is not their business. Even in Turkey and Kurdistan it is not like that, your next door [neighbours] are like your best and closest family friends. And you know everything, problems or whatever. But here it is not like that. I lived in a place where there were about ten flats in one block, and nobody knew each other, you just smile some time at each other, when you see each other in the corridor.

Finland

In Finland, the integration of refugees into the receiving society displayed quite different features from the English case. The small number of refugees and migrants in Finland, in combination with the official resettlement policy based on refugee dispersal, often creates situations where the refugees have few opportunities to socialize with persons other than Finns. Many Finns also display considerable interest in the few migrants in their country. The refugee resettlement in Finland often engages many persons in the local community where the refugees live. To be the object of curiosity and charitable concern is, of course, not part of normal social relations, but these contacts might later develop into more conventional relations and lasting friendships.

During the semi-structured interviews in Finland, the refugees were asked about their social contacts with the majority population. Most of the interviewees had more Kurdish friends than Finnish friends, but friendships between Kurds and Finns were still surprisingly common in Finland. All interviewees had some – and in many cases they had several – Finnish friends. One way of finding Finnish friends was by being introduced to Finnish 'friend families' by the Finnish Red Cross. All the quota refugees I met had been provided with 'friend families' upon arrival in Finland. This system has functioned relatively well,[1] and several interviewees still had regular contacts with these families or persons. Clearly these relations have been important for many refugees, and I was often told how helpful these families had been. A man from Iraq spoke about his family's Finnish friends:

> Yes, we have a Finnish friend family. They have really helped us a lot. So we have some Finnish friends, although much more Kurdish friends. My wife only has two Finnish friends, but our children have many friends. [t]

The extent of contacts between Kurds and the majority population also became apparent during the *Newroz* celebrations (the Kurdish New Year). Kurds often invite their friends to these parties. In the small parties I attended in Finland it was not uncommon for almost half of those present to be Finns. In Britain, I visited several large parties in London, and no more than 5 per cent of those at the parties appeared to be non-Kurdish. It is of course difficult to compare the small celebrations in Finland with those in London which attract at least ten times more participants. Nevertheless, these figures give an indication of the levels of contact between the majority population and the Kurds in the two countries.

In Finland it was also relatively common for young male Kurdish refugees to have Finnish girlfriends, and some Kurdish men were married to Finnish women. Yet, it was unheard of for a Kurdish woman to marry a Finnish man. One can only speculate about the reasons for this. On the one hand, there were more single men than women among the Kurdish refugees in Finland, especially among the Kurds from Turkey. On the other hand, cultural factors in both the Finnish and the Kurdish cultures may be of significance.

A relatively large number of male Kurds from Turkey had Finnish girlfriends and wives. This is perhaps not surprising since most of the Kurds from Turkey were single young men. Official statistics support this observation: according to the marriage statistics for the years 1990–2 a total of 376 Turkish male citizens married Finnish women, which in fact is more than any other group of male foreigners (Nieminen, 1994).[2] It can be assumed that a major part of the marriages are between persons who have met each other at holiday resorts in Turkey. However, since an asylum seeker can obtain a residence permit when he marries a Finn, this might in a few cases have influenced the decision to get married.

The large extent of social contacts between Finns and Kurds, including marriages, is rather surprising in the light of the previous discussions of Finnish xenophobia and racism. The xenophobia and racism the refugees met might be seen as a detrimental factor in terms of the social integration of refugees into Finnish society. However, it is important not to generalize; not all Finns are xenophobic. Several interviewees explained that it is only a minority who are a problem. This was emphasized by a man from Iraq who had lived in Finland for several years:

> I think that it is obvious that there are different attitudes and behaviour in Finland. Those who behave in a different way, they do not hide their feeling for themselves, but I have not had any experience [of racist attacks]. I have not confronted any such situation.

The relationship between the Kurds and the majority in Finland was thus a rather ambivalent one. On the one hand, there were friendships between Finns and Kurds; but on the other hand, racism and xenophobia were often serious impediments to personal relationships. It is possible that since immigration in Finland is a new experience, there have been two distinct approaches among the majority population; while some Finns are openly hostile towards 'foreigners', others are interested in meeting and befriending them. Since most of the Kurdish refugees do have some Finnish friends, it can be argued that the Finnish resettlement programme has been fairly successful in this particular respect. However, in other respects the policy has been a failure. For example, the extent of open racism in Finland remains a serious hindrance to more spontaneous relationships. Furthermore, the high unemployment rate among the refugees has also diminished the possibilities for social contacts with Finns.[3]

Although there are social contacts with Finns, these relations cannot replace the close social relations which characterize Kurdish society. As in England, the issue of isolation remains a serious problem for the refugees. In Finland this problem has been further accentuated by the official dispersal policy. The refugees in Finland are in this respect in an even worse situation compared to that of the Kurds living in London. A family from Iraq who travelled via Turkey to Finland summarized their problems:

Mother: I am the one who suffers most from living isolated, but I do not want to talk about it, it is so difficult to talk about it.
Son: It is really difficult for old people. It is difficult for young people, for us, for example, but it is twice as bad for old people. It is difficult to be used to this environment.
ÖW: Is the isolation the most difficult thing?
Son: I think the reason is that you cannot make contact. To have contact is for us an important thing. It is the language, and, for example, my mother cannot speak at all.
Mother: It is social questions. In Turkey, although it was very difficult financially for us, the social there, it was much better, in a social sense.
Son: For young people it is better, you can find something to do, to study or to work, but it is difficult for older people.
ÖW: Do you think it would be better for you if there were more Kurds living here?
Mother: What can you do, where are there more Kurds?
Son: We have been talking to the authorities about moving.
Mother: For example, if you are sick you used to get visits, but here, if I get sick nobody will visit me. [t]

To sum up, the Kurds in Finland usually had at least a few friends among the Finnish population, while the Kurds in England were sometimes totally without social contact with British people, although it has to be added that there also were huge individual variations. However, the new friendships could seldom replace the close social relations the refugees had had in Kurdistan. Consequently, isolation remains a major problem for refugees, especially in Finland, where refugees often live far away from other compatriots.

The Kurdish refugees do not wish to be totally insulated from the majority. The existence of some relations between the Kurds and the ethnic majority in the case of Finland suggests that it is possible, at least to some extent, for the Kurds to become integrated into the receiving society. However, how this social integration occurs depends on the receiving society and its social structures rather than on factors within the refugee community. Differences in the integration achieved in the two countries of settlement can clearly be attributed to differences in the resettlement policies and the general social structures in each country respectively.

INTEGRATION INTO ANOTHER MINORITY GROUP

What are the Kurdish refugees' social relations with, and integration into, other ethnic minority groups in the countries of settlement? In the case of the Kurds, one could perhaps expect that they would become integrated into some larger Middle Eastern or Islamic community. In Britain one could even imagine that the Kurds would be part of a larger 'black' ethnic minority. Clearly, none of this has happened. The Kurdish refugees are not part of any new ethnic entity in the countries of settlement. However, there is still reason to discuss the Kurdish refugees' social relations with Turkish, Iranian and Iraqi ethnic groups. When discussing this issue, one must again bear in mind the different situations in Finland and England.

In Finland there are only a few social groups that can be regarded as ethnic minorities (Pentikäinen and Hiltunen, 1995), and the few immigrants in the country do not constitute well-organized communities. The Kurdish refugees in Finland did socialize with other refugees and foreigners whom they had met through resettlement and training courses, but for none of the interviewees were these relationships more extensive than their relationships with either Kurdish or Finnish friends. In England, and especially in London, there are several well-established communities of 'ethnic minorities' and there has been a relatively large immigration from countries in the Middle East. Not surprisingly, compared with the Finnish case, the Kurdish refugees in England had more extensive social contacts with other ethnic minorities. The Kurds in Britain, however, were not a unitary community and the differences between the Kurds from Iran, Iraq and Turkey were very clear when it came to their relations with, and integration into, other ethnic minority groups. The Iranian Kurds in Britain could be seen as largely constituting a part of the broader Iranian community. In the same way the Kurds from Turkey were an almost inseparable part of the Turkish and Kurdish community in north London. The Kurds from Iraq, however, were a different case. Among them only very few persons had any kind of contact with Arabs from Iraq.

The relations between the Turks and the Kurds in the Turkish and Kurdish community in north London presents an interesting issue. Turks and Kurds have lived side by side both in Turkey and in north London, and on a personal level this has usually not been regarded as a problem. However, in London there are also persons and organizations with strong Turkish nationalist sympathies. This can lead to potential conflicts within the community. Thus, some of the Kurdish refugees living in London might continue to fear for their own security. Despite this possibility for conflicts within the community in north London, the interviewees repeatedly emphasized that there was no conflict between Turks and Kurds as such, but only between the Kurds and the Turkish government. For example, during a discussion at one of the Kurdish community centres in north London this was emphasized by a man from Marash in Turkey:

> I want to make a very important point here, we do not have any problem, any contradictions, with the Turkish people, with the Turkish nation. The only problem we have with Turkey is with the system of the Turkish state, with the government of the Turkish state, but we have always been brothers with the Turkish people, and have never had any problem with them. The only problem is the system of the Turkish state. [t]

Nevertheless, it was clear that the ongoing conflicts in eastern Turkey created tensions in the Turkish and Kurdish community in north London. In this way the social integration of that community was related to the situation in the country of origin. Political changes in Turkey can have an immediate effect on the relations between the Kurds and Turks in exile.

In summary, in England the Kurds did have extensive social interaction with other ethnic minorities, mainly with groups from the Kurds' respective countries of origin. In fact the Kurds from Turkey and Iran were largely parts of the wider Turkish and Iranian communities respectively. In Finland, on the other hand, there was not much contact with any other ethnic minority. This difference generally follows Breton's (1964) theory that the institutional completeness of the community largely decides in what direction immigrants will integrate themselves. Nevertheless, it is clear that the Kurds are not integrated into any new ethnic minorities in the countries of settlement. The interpersonal relations that the Kurds maintain are only continuations of the social relations the Kurds have had in their respective countries of origin. In this sense, the Kurdish refugees have not changed their ethnic affiliation upon arrival in the country of settlement.

INTEGRATION WITHIN THE KURDISH COMMUNITY

This section describes the degree of integration among the Kurds themselves through a discussion of the refugees' personal relations with other Kurds. Two important questions are: to what extent is it possible to talk about one Kurdish community, and to what extent do the Kurds from Iran, Iraq and Turkey form their own separate Kurdish communities?

When refugees leave Kurdistan, they do not know where they will finally end up. Therefore it is common for them to bring with them addresses of friends and relatives all over the world. In exile the Kurdish refugees use these social networks from Kurdistan in order to create new social networks. The family and networks of relatives are important social institutions in Kurdish society, and they also continue to be important in exile. A young man from Turkey living in Finland described his Kurdish friends:

> I have more in common with Kurds from Turkey [compared to Kurds from other parts of Kurdistan], because I know persons who have arrived from the same area as I have. And if I do not know them personally, at least I know their family and relatives. [t]

Hence, already upon arrival in the country of settlement the Kurdish refugees were part of a wider Kurdish community which could provide the refugees with help and advice. The social networks that the refugees thus became part of were based on social relations in the country of origin. There is a salience of pre-migration social networks within the Kurdish community. This clearly indicates that, to a large extent, the social relations in the Kurdish refugee communities could be said to be transnational (in accordance with the previously mentioned definition in Basch et al., 1994). These transnational social networks are described in more detail in a later section.

Although the Kurdish refugee communities are largely extensions of communities in the countries of origin, it is still important to remember that there are many factors in the society of settlement which influence the internal integration and social organization of the refugee communities. The social structures in the receiving society, the resettlement policies, and the extent and forms of racism and discrimination all have an impact on the social organization of the

Kurdish communities. For example, in Finland the Kurdish refugees have been resettled in small groups in municipalities all over the country. Therefore it is difficult for the Kurdish refugees to keep in touch and to give help and advice to each other. In Britain, the concentration of the refugees in London, together with other policies, creates a totally different situation where the Kurds can establish their own strong communities. But rather than creating one united Kurdish community in London, the refugees are divided into several smaller communities.

Community Divisions

There were clear differences in the social networks among Kurds from the different countries of origin. These differences were clearly discernible in both England and Finland. In ordinary day-to-day life there was not much contact between refugees from different parts of Kurdistan and it can be argued that a united Kurdish community did not exist. The Kurds from Turkey socialized mainly with other Kurds from Turkey, although some of them might have known some Kurds from Iraq. The Kurds from Iraq mostly had contacts with other Kurds from Iraq, but many of them also had Kurdish friends from both Turkey and Iran. The Iranian Kurds usually knew some Kurds from Iraq, but many of them said that they did not know anybody from Turkey. In the same way, some Kurds from Turkey stated that they had never actually met anybody from Iran. These divisions of the Kurdish community clearly followed the linguistic differences among the Kurds. Furthermore, some Kurds pointed out that the borders between their different countries had been closed, and that there had never been any possibility for Kurds from different countries to meet before they moved to Europe.

Despite the divisions in the Kurdish community, which are very tangible, it must be emphasized that there does exist a feeling of unity among the Kurds, which is based on a common Kurdish ethnicity and nationalism. The Kurdish national project has largely created an 'imagined community' in the same sense as the nationalism described by Anderson (1983). Although, to a large extent, the unity of the Kurds is 'imagined', it still has an impact on interpersonal relations among Kurds. This feeling of belonging together was mentioned in many interviews. A young man from Turkey compared his relationship with Kurds from other parts of Kurdistan to his relationship with Turks in the following way:

Probably we have much more common things with Turkish people in Turkey, but I can say that year by year this is decreasing, as much as the war in Kurdistan is becoming more serious and dangerous. Otherwise – Iranian Kurds are bit different, you know, but if you say Iraqi Kurds, I can see much more common things. . . . This question is a little bit complicated. Maybe you can ask this question as, how do you feel yourself when you are with Iraqi Kurds or with Turkish people from Turkey? I can say that I feel much more comfortable with Iraqi Kurds, I can speak comfortably, I can speak everything easily. But when speaking to a Turkish friend or people you just feel something – not comfortably, something like, you try to keep yourself not to talk a lot of things, or not to talk, for example, about politics, because in any case you will have different views.

It looks as though political divisions are one of the main factors behind the divisions in the Kurdish refugee communities. The allegiances to different political parties in the countries of origin were closely related to the refugees' interpersonal relations. An Iranian man found it hard to establish social relations with other Kurds because of potential political disagreements:

I think I am an exceptional case because of politics. There are no persons from my party here . . . I have problems both with other Iranians and with Kurds. There are Kurds here and Iranians but I am not very close to them. Because I am still afraid of other Iranians, because it can be dangerous. . . . There are some Iranians who were on the side of the Shah and from bourgeoisie parties, and that is difficult because that is different. Because we have very important political opinions and wishes. [t]

In fact, this person was not an exceptional case. Almost all refugees I met had the same feelings about the influence of Kurdish politics on their social relations. This political dimension is perhaps not very surprising since most Kurds in England and Finland are political refugees. A young man from Turkey seemed to avoid the original question but still had an interesting answer:

ÖW: Who do you have more in common with, Kurds from other countries or Turkish people?
R: What I think is interesting, in my opinion it depends on the

political party and not our situation. For example around this party [PKK] we are friends, we know each other and we speak to each other because today the Kurds do not have anything else to speak about than the Kurdish question. [t]

The influence of politics varied according to the refugee's country of origin. The refugees from Iran and Iraq often felt that politics divided their communities. Many felt alienated and isolated from their own communities because of the political disagreements with other Kurds. Among the refugees from Turkey, this feeling was not as common and many persons felt that politics united the Kurds. Undoubtedly, this has to do with the specific political situations in the countries of origin. The Kurdish parties in Iran and Iraq are divided and have not managed to achieve their political goals. In Iraq the Kurdish national movement is torn apart by internal fighting, while in Iran the divided opposition has largely lost its fight against the government. In Turkey, on the contrary, there has been a strong ethnic revival during recent years and the Kurdish refugees seem to be largely united behind one political movement. These political developments clearly influence the social relations among Kurds in exile.

TRANSNATIONAL COMMUNITIES

The previous section's discussion of the Kurdish refugees' social networks clearly shows that the social organization of the refugee communities follows the various patterns from the countries of origin. In addition, it has been emphasized previously in this book that the Kurdish refugees continue to relate to their countries of origin emotionally and psychologically in various ways. However, the Kurds not only keep up a psychological relationship to the country of origin and try to recreate their social networks in the country of exile, but they also quite tangibly continue to keep in touch with their old friends and relatives in Kurdistan and in other countries all over the world. Clearly, the relation to the homeland is not a socio-psychological aspect alone, but is authentically rooted in social and material realities, an argument which previously has been maintained by Schierup (1985) in his discussion of the process of 'migrancy'.

There were various social relations and networks between the diaspora and Kurdistan, as well as between different countries in the diaspora. Personal contacts were maintained through telephone calls, letters and personal visits. In addition, the refugees continued to have a connection with Kurdistan through the mass media, including newspapers, radio and satellite-television. During recent years, fax machines and the Internet have also been used as channels through which Kurds in the diaspora can keep in touch with each other. Modern technology has clearly made it easier to sustain transnational social networks. The advent of new technologies, facilitating communication over vast distances, has a clear influence on social relations in the contemporary world and is related to the processes of transnationalism and globalization. Yet, modern technology is expensive and most Kurdish refugees cannot afford much else besides a radio, letters and occasional phone calls to their relatives. To follow the latest news from Kurdistan sometimes takes up a large part of the day for the refugees. This was the case for a refugee from Iran who lived in a provincial town in Finland:

> I am following news in foreign languages, all the day I am listening. The French radio in the Persian language, Voice of America in Kurdish, and also news from the German radio. It is important to follow what is going on. . . . From France we are also sent the newspaper of Kurdistan Democratic Party, and from Helsinki and from Sweden I get newspapers. Our cultural organization has a newspaper as well. [t]

Besides radio and newspapers, television is also an important source of information. The new satellite channels on television have significantly improved the possibility for migrants to obtain information from their countries of origin. A young man from Iraq living in Finland explained how he obtained news from Kurdistan:

> I follow the Finnish television and radio, but I do not have any Kurdish newspapers. I do listen to Voice of America as well as Arabian radio programmes. However, where we live there are no Kurdish or Arabian newspapers available. My wife's brother has a satellite dish and we follow Arabian programmes on his television. They will start a Kurdish channel in Holland soon and we are thinking about buying a satellite dish ourselves. [t]

It was obvious that satellite dishes were seen as an important investment, although only few could afford them. The television channel mentioned in the quotation above was the Kurdish satellite channel

MED-TV. The interviews in Finland were all made before the broadcasts started in the spring of 1995, but during the fieldwork in England the importance of this satellite channel became clear in many interviews. Besides MED-TV many Kurds, especially from Iraq, followed satellite programmes from various Arabic-speaking countries. Before MED-TV, the only international broadcast in the Kurdish language was the weekly news on short-wave radio sent by Voice of America in both Sorani and Kurmanji. Almost all interviewees said that they had followed these radio programmes.

The Kurds living in exile also keep up personal relations with relatives both in Kurdistan and in other countries all over the world. It is not uncommon for Kurdish refugees to make trips all over Europe in order to keep in touch with friends and relatives. The UK and Finland are situated at the periphery of the European Kurdish diaspora, and are furthermore situated at almost opposite sides of Europe. Despite this, there were a lot of contacts between the Kurdish refugees in these two countries. The same political journals and newspapers (published in Kurdistan, Germany and Sweden) were read by refugees in England and in Finland. Exactly the same posters that the Kurdistan Information Centre in Helsinki had on its walls were found along Stoke Newington Road in north London. There are also a number of semi-professional Kurdish musicians touring all over Europe. For example, I heard the same musicians perform at parties in England and in Finland. The extent of personal contacts between these two countries was amazing. For example, while doing fieldwork in Finland, I was given addresses of persons and organizations to contact in Britain.

To keep in touch with relatives in the Middle East sometimes requires special ingenuity. In the case of Northern Iraq there are no telephone and postal services in operation. A middle-aged man living in Finland explained how this problem was solved:

[Information about] Kurdistan one mostly gets through the radio or Voice of America. This is the main source of information and the fresh information, otherwise you do not get it, unless somebody comes back from Kurdistan, but usually their information is old, but still one is interested. . . . But most of the letters which I have sent at least, and most of the people send it through friends who go there, and just, for instance, last week somebody went there back to visit his family, so I sent a letter with him. This is a normal, more open, way of sending letters.

The Kurds from Iraq have had the opportunity to visit Northern Iraq because of the introduction of the 'safe haven' protected by the United Nations. In November 1994 a woman from Iraq spoke about her future plans:

> R: We have travelled to Kurdistan twice, but it is not enough, we will travel there again next summer.
> ÖW: Will you travel every summer to Kurdistan?
> R: Yes, every summer. If I can afford it I will travel again next summer. [t]

During the summers 1992 to 1994 many Kurds living in exile visited Northern Iraq. However, because of the unstable political situation any permanent return migration was out of the question. At the time of writing, it looks as if it is no longer possible to travel to Northern Iraq because of violent conflicts in the area.

Rethinking Integration

If we return to Breton's (1964) three different directions in which the immigrants can be integrated, it can be concluded that the Kurds are first and foremost integrated into their own ethnic communities which consist of Kurds originating in the same country of origin. In Finland, and to a lesser extent in England, there are also some contacts with the ethnic majority. In England, Kurds might also have contacts with other ethnic minorities. There are also some Kurds who remain isolated and socially 'unintegrated' to any group. This happens especially in Finland and particularly among those who have political disagreements with other Kurds.

However, an additional perspective is suggested by this book. It has repeatedly been demonstrated that the refugees, although they are living in exile, have a continuous relation with Kurdistan and their countries of origin. It can be argued that this is not a case of 'being unintegrated' since the refugees remain 'integrated' within their previous Kurdish social networks. These social relations create a transnational community not bound by the geographical borders of either the countries of origin or the countries of settlement (cf. Basch et al., 1994). This type of transnational social organization is clearly something for which there is no room in most existing theories that discuss integration. The creation of transnational social networks is less difficult today because of various aspects of the process of globalization (Waters, 1995). For example, with the help of modern technology it is now easy to retain personal relationships over vast geographical distances. Undoubtedly, the process of globalization has a profound impact on the social relations of refugees and migrants in the contemporary world.

One form of transnational social organization is the diaspora. However, the whole idea of diasporas challenges conventional ways of understanding integration. Clearly, in a transnational and deterritorialized social reality it is not possible to see 'integration' as something which happens at a specific geographical location. This adds further to the confusion surrounding the concept of integration. Therefore, there is reason to go beyond any simplistic integrationist or assimilationist discourse and rethink the whole process of refugee integration.

It can be suggested that the concept of diaspora provides a tool for an understanding of the transnational social relations found in refugee communities. On the one hand, the social organization of the Kurdish community in exile follows the patterns in Kurdistan, but on the other hand these patterns are influenced by the social structures in the country of settlement. The diaspora concept can relate to both a refugee's country of origin and country of reception, and can bridge the gap between the periods before and after migration. Thus the diaspora concept, with its connection to both the 'homeland' and the countries of settlement, is useful for understanding the duality of the social organization of refugee communities. However, for the refugees themselves there is of course no duality, since the diaspora is one real and lived transnational experience. The findings of the research thus support an understanding of migration as a continuous process. This clearly relates to the concept of 'migrancy', advocated by Schierup and Ålund (1986), which describes the migrants' total 'social field' of experiences, in which emigration, immigration and integration cannot be separated from each other.

CONCLUSION

The results from the fieldwork show that there are both similarities and differences in the process of integration of the Kurdish refugees. The results indicate that the refugees had widely different interpersonal relations in the two different countries. Most refugees experienced various types of racism and xenophobia, as well as discrimination in the labour market. Yet, these experiences were very different in England and in Finland. There was a feeling of alienation among the refugees which was clearly related to the refugees' experiences of racism and discrimination. Thus, the Kurdish community fulfils one more of Safran's characteristics of a diaspora: 'They believe they are not – and perhaps cannot be – fully accepted by their host society and therefore feel partly alienated and insulated from it' (Safran, 1991: 83).

Despite the diasporic consciousness and the impossibility of a rapid assimilation, the refugees strive to become integrated into their new society of settlement. All refugees wish to find employment and aim, in all possible ways, to settle down and establish well-functioning social relations with the majority. Although all refugees largely had the same plans for the future, their employment situations and types of integration into the labour market were not the same in the two countries. The experiences of racism and discrimination were diametrically opposite: in Finland, the authorities and resettlement programmes supported equality but the refugees still confronted an obvious everyday racism, while in the multi-cultural British society, racism and discrimination seemed to be more structural and subtle. These differences between the two countries indicate that the resettlement policies and social structures in the country of settlement have a major impact on how the refugees will be integrated and what kind of problems they will experience. Thus, although the refugees have a diasporic consciousness and remain oriented towards their countries of origin, this should not divert attention from the important role played by the social structures in the countries of settlement. The integration into the wider society seems to be largely dependent on the exclusionary and inclusionary policies of the country of settlement and not on the degree of diasporic feelings amongst the refugees.

The integration into the Kurdish community, the relations with compatriots, and the interpersonal relations with the majority population followed different patterns in the two countries of settlement. The differences between the processes of integration in England and Finland clearly exemplify the major impact of official policies and social structures in the countries of reception. Thus, it can be argued that the main obstacles to a positive integration of the refugees are not their diasporic social relations but the social structures in the receiving society. The diaspora discourse, with its emphasis on the relation to the country of origin, should not ignore the major impact that the exclusionary or inclusionary social structures in the country of settlement have on the social organization of refugee communities.

Thus, although the concept of diaspora is useful, it should not lead to a neglect of the influence of various social structures in the countries of settlement. However, the diaspora concept can take this duality into account. Since the concept describes a transnational social reality it can bridge the gap between the country of origin and the country of reception. This diasporic conceptual framework can embrace an understanding of the influence from both the country of origin and the country of settlement. Furthermore, this suggests a rethinking of simplistic perceptions of the concept of integration. The transnational relations between the 'homeland' and the diaspora are seldom acknowledged in traditional models of integration.

Clearly, there are both advantages and disadvantages in the way the reception and resettlement of refugees is organized in the two countries. The Finnish resettlement policies provide a good base for positive integration, although this is not the actual outcome because of unemployment and racism, among other factors. The British resettlement systems do not provide equal and similar services for all refugees in the same way as the more egalitarian public support systems in Finland do. Nevertheless, the well-established Kurdish communities in London do provide a good base for a positive integration through the support networks and voluntary associations within the communities. Unfortunately, however, integration into British society has largely been into the lowest socio-economic positions. In a perfect world one would of course be able to combine the positive aspects from both countries: public support in combination with strong ethnic communities in both an egalitarian and a truly multicultural society.

6 Kurdish Associations: Community Work and Diasporic Politics[1]

The patterns of social networks and interpersonal relations in the Kurdish community have already been described in this book. These social networks might be expressed in institutionalized forms when specific formal organizations are established. It is usually a well-understood fact that immigrant and ethnic minority associations can perform many important and positive functions for their communities (Rex, Joly and Wilpert, 1987; Salinas, Pritchard and Kibedi, 1987; Jenkins, 1988; Carey-Wood et al., 1995; Joly, 1995b, 1996). However, besides studying formal associations one should also look at the more informal interactions which occur within the group (Rex and Josephides, 1987). John Rex has described in several publications (e.g. Rex, 1996) how migrants in increasingly multicultural western European countries mobilize in order to defend their interests. His publications suggest that it is not only important to describe the social organization of migrant and refugee communities, but also to look at the functions of these social structures for the community in question. Furthermore, in this study the role of associations is viewed within the framework of the diaspora concept. As argued in this book, a diaspora can be understood as a social organization and not only as a consciousness, culture or identity, and consequently it is obvious that what constitutes the diaspora to a great degree are the associations and informal networks within the exile communities.

This chapter describes the Kurdish associations in the refugee communities in England and Finland in 1994 and 1995. The previous chapters have argued that the Kurdish refugees continue to relate to their country of origin in various ways. This chapter discusses the consequences of this relationship for the Kurdish groups. It is argued that the political allegiances and conflicts in Kurdistan, which are briefly described in Chapter 2, have a profound influence on the Kurdish refugee associations. In addition, this chapter outlines how the refugee communities have adapted to the different social situations in the two receiving countries. The Kurdish associations in both countries are presented and the positive roles of associations and informal networks are examined. Finally, attention is given to the diasporic political activities of the refugee communities.

ASSOCIATIONS

This study included all associations in England and Finland which *explicitly* identified themselves as Kurdish and were working with, or for, Kurdish refugees. In England, apart from Kurdish associations, there were many British, Iranian, Turkish and various leftist organizations which gave valuable help to Kurdish refugees. However, this research concentrates on the Kurdish communities, and therefore only the organizations which regarded themselves as Kurdish are included in this overview.

Finland

Although, in Finland, there were only a small number of Kurds originating in Turkey, they were well organized, thanks largely to the activities of the Kurdish Organization in Finland (Suomen Kurdiyhdistys r.y.) and the Kurdistan Information Centre in Helsinki. These organizations were officially founded in 1992 and 1993 respectively and, in practice, they shared the same office in central Helsinki. The organizations had good connections to other Kurdish committees around Europe. The premises also functioned as a meeting-point for many of the Kurds living in the Helsinki area. In early 1995, an official Information Centre of ERNK replaced the previous Information Centre. Because of linguistic and sometimes political differences, the contacts with Kurdish refugees from other parts of Kurdistan were quite limited, but not totally lacking.

In Finland, the Kurds from Iraq and Iran had several loosely organized local groups around the country, and there were also attempts to become better organized. There was a registered nation-wide 'cultural organization' called *Ekgertin* (or *Yekgirtin*, meaning 'unity' in Kurdish). Another organization was the Kurdistan National Peace and Solidarity Committee, which had an intellectual emphasis and international connections. There was also a Kurdish–Finnish solidarity organization (Kurdien ystävyysseura–Suomen Kurdistanyhdistys r.y.) with mainly Finnish members. Since there were so few

Kurdish organizations in Finland, not all refugees could find one that would sympathize with their own political opinions. One Iranian refugee explained that for political reasons he avoided the organizations in Finland, and instead had contacts with organizations in Sweden in order to keep in touch with his political party.

The activities of all the Kurdish organizations in Finland were rather limited. The Information Centre's aim was, of course, to distribute information about Kurdistan, but otherwise the Kurdish associations in Finland concentrated on cultural and social activities for Kurds and their Finnish friends. The *Newroz* celebration was one of the most important of these activities. The Kurdish organizations were usually not involved in giving practical help or advice to newly arrived refugees. Most practical problems were taken care of by the Finnish authorities, and therefore there was no need for the Kurdish organizations to provide this service.

The Kurdish organizations in Finland had to struggle with a number of problems. First, there was the geographical dispersal of the refugees. The Kurdish refugees were resettled in a number of different municipalities across the country. This dispersal made it difficult for the Kurds to sustain nation-wide organizations. Usually, the Kurdish organizations in Finland were small local ones which had more contacts with organizations in other countries than with each other. Consequently, the organizations tended to become both locally and globally based, instead of working on a nation-wide basis.

A second problem was the funding of the organizations. The refugee associations could apply for money for cultural activities (usually *Newroz* parties or publications in Kurdish) from the municipalities and from some of the ministries, but there was no clear structured way of supporting refugee associations and the money available has generally been limited. Furthermore, it seems that neither the refugees nor the authorities always knew what opportunities existed and who was responsible for providing the organizations with support.

An additional problem seemed to exist as a consequence of the Finnish authorities' selection of quota refugees. Kurdish refugees arriving in Turkey have been resettled in a third country after the UNHCR has granted them refugee status. A Finnish delegation has interviewed the prospective candidates for the annual Finnish refugee quota. The selection of refugees has mainly been made on humanitarian grounds, but in addition to this it looks as if Finland has chosen refugees who declare that they will not continue to work politically in Finland. This is, of course, a rather contradictory policy. Finland is willing to resettle refugees who have been politically active but, at the same time, wishes to avoid resettling those who wish to remain so. One quota refugee recalled his experiences from the interview in Turkey:

> R: But it was like, when they asked me why I had left and what I had done, what usually is asked, there was a kind of – you got the feeling that they wanted you to promise that we must not work politically there. Because what they asked was 'do you still work politically, or do you still want to bring up the Kurdish issue there as well?'
> ÖW: You were supposed to answer no to that question?
> R: You should answer no to the question, or you had to roll it around a little bit. [t]

How dominant this selection criterion has been is difficult to say. Among the refugees from Iran and Iraq, the quota refugees in Finland were more likely than the refugees in England to be alienated from the political struggle and their former parties. Although they all still supported a free Kurdistan, there were many who explained that they were no longer active in politics. Some persons even said that they no longer believed in the politics of the Kurdish parties. This often also led to the refugees avoiding the Kurdish organizations in Finland. As explained in Chapter 2, all organizations in Kurdistan tend to be connected to the political parties. Therefore refugees in exile might still associate all organizations with politics. By selecting refugees who do not want to continue to work politically, the Finnish authorities seem indirectly to have chosen persons who are largely sceptical of all attempts to become organized. In addition, there are only a few persons who have any experience of working in organizations. A man from Iran who had been active in various associations in Finland described the refugees' ordeal with organizations:

> The problem is that the Kurds do not have experience of organizations; we do not have this organizational background that is necessary. We have to function on our own background, we simply cannot change. This is one reason why sometimes there are problems with the authorities ... There is a lack of familiarity with democracy in Kurdistan, this is why Kurds associate

organizations with politics, and politics is associated with power and oppression. [t]

Yet, if you are a Kurdish refugee, it is difficult to stay away from politics even if you want to. Even those refugees and organizations who try to be non-political might find it hard to avoid Kurdish politics. This became evident during an interview with a man from Iraq who had been involved in starting a local non-political cultural association:

> ÖW: Your organization has mostly cultural activities for local Kurdish refugees, but has there been any discussion that you also would work as an interest organization in order to improve the situation for refugees?
> R: Yes, this is true. This is difficult with Kurdish issues when you try to do some cultural activities to keep in touch and learn to know each other, to do something for Kurdish culture and language and things like that. But still, when you are a Kurd, you are political, you are active.
> ÖW: So you think that it is difficult to make a distinction then?
> R: It still becomes – our entire life is politics. I do not know how it is in the Nordic countries, how you can separate these. But for us Kurds, we cannot separate these issues when things like these are happening in Kurdistan. [t]

England

The picture is much more diverse and complex in England than in Finland. All in all, there were about 25 Kurdish associations active in London in 1995. Of these, about 10 were community organizations and advice centres which provided advice and services to Kurdish refugees. The community centres often provided a very wide range of services for their members and clients. Their activities included advice on welfare, housing and asylum issues, language and training courses as well as various social and cultural activities. The biggest community centres had bookshops and restaurants on their premises. As explained in Chapter 3, in practice, refugee re-settlement in Britain is largely taken care of by various voluntary organizations working within the 'community'. Funding is available from a variety of sources for the Kurdish community centres and other organizations working with refugees. Therefore many Kurdish associations were able to offer a large number of activities aimed at helping newly arrived refugees.

Usually, newly arrived refugees first came into contact with the organizations through their friends and relatives, but some of the big and established organizations in London were known even in Kurdistan. It should also be noted that some Kurds chose to organize themselves in associations that were not wholly Kurdish. Kurdish refugees from Iran were mostly active in Iranian political groups and community centres and there were numerous organizations in north London visited by both Turks and Kurds.

The oldest Kurdish community centre in London was the Kurdish Cultural Centre (KCC), founded in 1985 and situated in Lambeth. Its members were mainly from Kurdistan in Iraq. Because of the proximity of the Kurdish dialects, some Kurds from Iran visited the centre as well, especially since there was no organization in London specifically for Iranian Kurds. As one of the biggest and oldest Kurdish associations in Britain, the KCC has also tried to be an umbrella organization for other local Kurdish groups in the UK. In recent years the tendency among Kurds from Iraq and Iran has been to establish new local associations (the Greenwich Kurdish Community Association, the Kurdish Community in Ealing, the Kurdish Information Centre in Islington and the West London Kurdish Association in Hammersmith) as well as more specialized organizations (the Kurdish Housing Association, the Kurdish Disability Organization, the Kurdish Scientific and Medical Association and a separate organization for Faili Kurds). This development, together with political disagreements within the Kurdish community, seemed to have led to a decline of the activities of the KCC.

The biggest community centres were found in the Turkish and Kurdish communities in north London. The Kurdistan Workers Association (KWA) in Haringey had between 3000 and 5000 Kurdish members and clients from 'North-West Kurdistan' (Turkey) while the Turkish and Kurdish Community Centre Halkevi in Hackney had about 4500 members, of whom most were Kurds. Halkevi, established in 1984, was initially called a Turkish community centre and it was only during the 1990s that it emphasized its Kurdishness. Both the KWA and Halkevi were very vital organizations with many different activities. During the first half of the 1990s, both centres had elected management committees which were sympathetic to the Kurdish national struggle in 'North-West Kurdistan'. In the early 1990s, the support for the PKK became more evident among the

Kurdish refugees from Turkey. The election of a management committee with sympathies for the PKK happened for the first time in
the KWA in 1990, when candidates sympathetic to the PKK won
an overwhelming victory. The elections had been preceded by conflicts
between different political parties, conflicts which are described in
detail by Reilly (1991). After the election, the activists sympathetic
to the Turkish Kurdistan Socialist Party left the community centre.
Some of these persons later became active in the Kurdish Advice
Centre situated in Tottenham.

In addition to the community and advice centres, which provided
services and advice to refugees, there were several other Kurdish
organizations in London. These were usually oriented more towards
the situation in Kurdistan, and they were engaged in campaigning,
publishing, collecting information, political lobbying and fund-raising
for the Kurdish cause. Both Kurdish and British volunteers could
usually be found in these organizations. The following bodies were
well-established and active during the spring of 1995: the Hawkarani
Kurdistan, the Kurdish Human Rights Committee, the Kurdish
Human Rights Project, the Kurdistan Information Centre and
the Kurdistan Solidarity Committee. A few small, local Kurdish
organizations also exist outside London, but all the major Kurdish
ones in the UK have been concentrated in the capital area. One
problem in identifying the Kurdish organizations arose from the
bewildering speed with which new ones were started and old ones
disappeared.

Among all Kurdish organizations in England there was an often
expressed indirect support for the 'Kurdish cause' and the struggle
of the Kurdish people. A worker in one association in London
explained the political affiliation of Kurdish organizations in the
following way:

> You know, we are not a football team, or some English organ-
> ization like that. We are political refugees. There is a specific
> reason why we came here, and that reason is political and of
> course one still wants to continue with something that earlier
> has taken up your whole life.

The only associations in London not connected with Kurdish political parties were small organizations with a clear and narrow purpose
and a strong desire to keep themselves out of politics. These 'non-
aligned' groups included small local organizations and a few highly

specialized and professional ones. The political character of the Kurdish community in north London is also described by Reilly (1991). Although the Kurdish associations themselves agreed that they were associated with certain political parties, the people interviewed at the organizations usually emphasized strongly that the associations were open for all and that most of their activities had a practical orientation. However, this did not prevent other Kurds from describing organizations according to their political affiliation.

It should be made clear that the politicization of the Kurdish community did not mean that the Kurdish community centres in Britain were directly run by political parties. The connection was more complex than this. The community centres had an elected management committee, and even if persons sympathetic to a certain political party were elected to the management committee, it did not mean that the party ran the community centre. In fact, some of the Kurdish parties, at least the PUK and the KDP, had their own representatives in London. These small party organizations were independent of the community centres and were not involved in practical work with, or for, refugees in Britain.

The Politicization of the Kurdish Associations

What the Kurds in England and Finland have in common is the high politicization of the refugee associations. With few exceptions, the Kurdish associations in both countries were associated with certain political groups in the country of origin. The same political allegiances and boundaries that can be found in Kurdistan were thus recreated in exile. Problems frequently arose in the coordination of activities among competing organizations.

The ongoing support for the liberation of Kurdistan was clearly expressed through different symbols: political posters, pictures of political leaders and the flags of different political parties. These symbols were found in prominent places in the refugees' homes, in the community centres, at demonstrations and at the *Newroz* celebrations. The political allegiances were most clearly expressed by the organizations of the Kurds from Turkey, which often explicitly supported certain Kurdish political parties. The Kurds from Iraq and Iran usually tried, although with little success, to keep their organizations more neutral vis-à-vis the political parties and their disagreements in Kurdistan. This difference undoubtedly has to do with the political situation in the countries of origin.

Upon arrival in the country of exile, Kurdish refugees clearly preferred to join organizations which shared their political views and avoided those which might be associated with conflicting political movements. However, it is important to understand that although refugee associations are strongly influenced by Kurdish politics, they are not necessarily directly connected to the political parties in Kurdistan. The politicization of the Kurdish communities in the diaspora can mainly be understood as a process whereby people who are sympathetic to a certain party want to be together with people they feel comfortable with and who agree with them on political issues.

The Importance of Religion and Kinship

It is interesting to note that neither religion nor kinship was used as a mobilizing force in the same way as politics was. Ethnic mobilization is often based on a common religious tradition. Among the Kurds one would thus assume that Islam could be a powerful force around which social networks and associations are built, or that the Kurds would use existing wider Muslim networks and associations as a resource to solve the problems they experience in their new countries of settlement (cf. Joly, 1995b). However, this has not happened in the Kurdish refugee communities. There was no evidence of Kurdish associations using religion as a mobilizing force. In fact, few of the persons interviewed had any contacts with mosques or religious organizations. However, religiosity is a complex issue and this does not mean that Kurdish refugees are not religious. On the contrary, some interviewees argued that people in Kurdistan in general are deeply religious. In addition, the Kurdish refugees in this study are, of course, not representative of Kurds in general. It is not impossible that the political refugees are less religious than people in general in Kurdistan. Actually, among the interviewees the women often seemed to be more religious than the politically active men. It is also possible that Kurdish religiosity is mainly a private issue which cannot easily be used as a mobilizing force. This conclusion is supported by the fact that, at least until recently, none of the main parties in Kurdistan has been an explicitly religious party.[2]

Another issue which has to be taken into account is that the Kurds from Turkey living in London are mostly Alevis, and therefore do not follow the same religious traditions as Shia or Sunni

Muslims. For example, the Alevis do not have any mosques. This might contribute to the Kurdish community's detachment from Muslim organizations. However, what is surprising is that not even the Alevi belief seemed to be used in the mobilization of the Kurdish community. Taking into account the hostility between Sunnis and Alevis in Turkey (McDowall, 1992) one would assume that this would still have an impact on the social organization of the community in exile. Yet, this distinction was not a very relevant one among the Kurdish associations. My informants in north London repeatedly stressed that the Alevi–Sunni distinction was unimportant for the Kurdish associations. For example, one activist in the KWA interrupted me when I tried to ask him about Alevis with the statement: 'This is not important, what is important is that we all are Kurds here.'

Among the Iranian and Iraqi refugees we might find different reasons for their reluctance to join Muslim organizations or use religion as a resource for mobilization. The Iranians have fled from persecution by a religious government. Not surprisingly, many Iranian refugees remain deeply suspicious of religious organizations and in practice avoid organizations that are mobilized around Islam. The Kurds from Iraq might have a complex relationship with religious institutions since Islam and Arab culture are often associated with each other. The Kurds in Iraq are in conflict with the predominantly Arab government in Baghdad, and therefore religious institutions might also be indirectly associated with the persecution faced by the Kurds in Iraq. An additional factor in all parts of Kurdistan is the influence of Marxist ideologies, which might make some Kurds suspicious of all religions. However, all these suggestions are highly speculative, and within the scope of this research it was not possible fully to investigate the role of religion among Kurdish refugees or in Kurdish society at large.

A further issue which complicates the analysis of the religious influence in the Kurdish community is that deeply religious persons might not identify themselves as Kurds. These persons might regard Kurdish nationalism as something that divides Muslims. A similar issue was that some of the Kurds who had communist or Marxist sympathies also had an ambivalent relationship with Kurdish identification. Kurdish nationalism was seen by some persons as something which potentially divided the working class and its united struggle. Therefore it is possible that persons of Kurdish ancestry who are either religious Muslims or convinced communists prefer not to identify themselves primarily as Kurds.

As mentioned in previous chapters, Kurds consider the family to be a very important social unit within the private sphere of life. Traditionally, the social organization of Kurdistan has largely been based on family allegiances and a 'tribal' structure (Bruinessen, 1992a). Not surprisingly, the social networks of individual refugees were largely based on family allegiances. However, despite this, the traditional 'tribal' networks did not play a prominent role in the refugees' public sphere of life. The research showed that there were no Kurdish associations which would be mobilized on the basis of what could be perceived as 'tribal' networks. Instead, the social organization of the Kurdish refugee communities was dominated by political allegiances. As Bruinessen (1992a) points out, the 'tribal' structure in Kurdistan has given way over time to allegiances based on nationalist and socialist discourses. The latter political allegiances seem to be those which in recent years have also dominated the social organization of the diaspora.[3]

A Politically Divided Community

The results presented in the previous sections indicate that politics has been a far stronger mobilizing force than either religion or kinship. The politicization of the Kurdish refugee associations is a continuation of social networks in Kurdistan. In Kurdistan, the political parties are often important social institutions which also tend to dominate other formal organizations. Thus, when the political refugees in exile recreate their social networks and establish new associations, it would be surprising if these did not continue to be associated with political parties. This high politicization of the Kurdish refugee organizations replicates the political divisions in Kurdistan and divides the Kurds in the diaspora.

One problem connected with the dominance of politics within the Kurdish associations is that social groups that are not politically organized, as well as non-political or anti-political individuals, easily become marginalized in the Kurdish community. This is the case, for example, with Kurdish women, who undoubtedly have a problem in getting their voice heard in the public sphere. In fact, some of the female informants wanted to emphasize that the Kurdish associations are not doing enough to improve the situation of refugee women. Kurdish men who wanted to avoid politics also found that the politicization of the associations was a problem. As a refugee in London told me:

For example, KCC is dominated by a couple of political parties. Other organizations also have their own political background. Exile communities have strong rules, strong rules of how you should behave. The organizations give you help, but they also manipulate refugees, or perhaps not manipulate, but at least influence them in a certain way. You have to take part in their way of thinking and in their activities. A lot of people avoid the organizations because of this.

Clearly, the politicization of the associations divides the community since some persons choose to avoid the associations. This inadvertently leads to the associations not being able to provide equal services to all refugees. Thus, the British policy of giving a large responsibility for the resettlement of refugees to ethnic associations within the community cannot be seen as a good way to provide equal services to all refugees. The problem here is not that the associations are mobilized around politics. Rather, the problem is connected to the community-centred policies in Britain, which will always experience problems in providing equal services to all individuals, regardless of the particular basis of mobilization within the communities.

Thus, it can be argued that the Kurdish refugee associations in both England and Finland have a transnational and diasporic character. The social organization of the refugee communities is not only on an interpersonal level, but also on the formal level, a continuation of social and political allegiances in Kurdistan. In this sense, the Kurdish community is largely a divided community. However, in the same way as politicization divides the communities, it can also be a powerful mobilizing force for smaller groups within the wider community. Although there are no community-wide associations among the refugees, there are several small and well-functioning associations. These smaller social networks and associations constitute important resources for the refugees and can fulfil a number of different functions.

THE ROLE OF SOCIAL NETWORKS AND ASSOCIATIONS

The previous chapters identified a number of different problems that refugees faced upon arrival in their new countries of settlement. This section looks more closely at how the refugees try to solve these problems and discusses the positive functions of social networks and formal associations. Although the refugee communities are divided by the political allegiances of their members, these allegiances can also be a useful resource for the refugees.

Clearly, presenting the opportunity to continue to work politically is one function which the Kurdish organizations and networks can fulfil. Political activism might also serve the function of reinforcing an identity and a sense of order and purpose in the fragmented lives of the refugees. The diasporic political activity alleviated many problems related to isolation and other psychological problems. To fulfil this function it was often enough to engage in political activities which can be described as more symbolic than real. A man from Turkey explained how important it was to have an opportunity to meet people with the same political opinions:

> I am extremely satisfied with the fact that in every place there are supporters of the PKK. And I believe that if this information centre did not exist in Finland, in that case it could happen that the Kurds would all become mentally ill. But with the information centre, and when we are working and we are getting information about our own country, this helps us a lot. It is like morality, our life. For example, without this party I am nothing. With the Kurds, with the PKK, we have contact. This is because of the party, in the name of the party... The PKK is the key, and this key opens the door to all us Kurds. [t][4]

Obviously, for the refugees it is important to continue to have contact with friends, relatives and compatriots. One way of doing this is to become active in the Kurdish associations. A young man from Turkey found that his contacts with other Kurdish refugees and their collective political activities related to their country of origin helped him to overcome his own problems in Finland:

> It was very good [that there were other Kurds in the reception centre in Finland]. And in my opinion, these Kurds, when we were together, it helped me a lot. Because it could have been really very difficult for me. I could have become mad or something. But when I was together with other Kurds, it helped me a lot. I was more interested in the Kurdish issue, and slowly, when I worked together with other Kurds for the independence of Kurdistan, you could say that after a while I totally forgot about

my own problems and application for asylum, because the problems in Kurdistan were more important than my problems in Finland. There was a war, a really terrible war. When I listened to the BBC radio from London and when we called to Kurdistan they told us about the situation. This was all more interesting to us than our own life in Finland, because our family was there and all our relatives and our whole life. Part of our life was there and we ourselves were here. It was really difficult. [t]

The Kurdish associations also performed a wide range of practical functions. In terms of these functions there were significant differences between the two countries. In Finland, the practical problems were largely taken care of by the authorities. Instead, the refugees' worst problems were social and psychological, including issues like exclusion, isolation, alienation and feelings of displacement. For a variety of reasons, the Kurds in Finland had not developed strong communities within the country and there were only a few active Kurdish associations. Not surprisingly, Kurdish associations did not play a decisive role in solving practical problems for the refugees; they had neither the need nor the resources to do this. The refugees tried instead to use their associations and informal networks to solve their social and psychological problems. Thus, the Kurdish associations were mainly active in providing cultural activities and social gatherings, although again only to a relatively limited extent. Nevertheless, these activities indicate that the social networks and formal associations among the Kurds can be used as resources to alleviate the social and psychological problems refugees experience in Finland. However, the associations in Finland could not fulfil the same functions as in England, where the Kurds had strong and efficient organizations.

Associations in England performed a wide range of practical functions and there was also extensive public funding available for these activities. The Kurdish refugees were able to use their associations and their informal networks to overcome many of the practical problems they experienced in their new country of settlement. The difficulties refugees encountered upon arrival and the lack of organized support for refugees in the UK presented the associations with considerable challenges. The Kurdish associations in London had to shoulder a particularly heavy burden during the influx of a large number of Kurds from Turkey in 1989. A man from Turkey who arrived in the spring of 1989 told me:

The Kurdistan Workers Association helped me. The administration office, where they help Kurds who need help and advice and cannot speak English, I came here straight away.... At the airport, somebody was in charge of Kurdish people, and they brought us here straight away. They gathered the Kurdish people together, perhaps 30 persons, and brought us to the Kurdistan Workers Association. [t]

A large number of Kurds interviewed in Britain received most of their initial advice through some of the community centres. The Kurdish community centres often had specific staff who gave advice to refugees. In addition to paid staff, there were usually many volunteers, both Kurdish and British, working in the different organizations. Many refugees experienced the language barrier as their greatest problem upon arrival in the UK. Most Kurdish associations organized interpretation and translation services in order to help recently arrived refugees. Some of the larger community centres arranged extensive language and training courses. Housing is another major problem for refugees in London. The associations tried to alleviate this problem by providing advice and guidance on housing issues. Since newly arrived refugees are not familiar with British society, there is a great need for all sorts of general advice. Some of the bigger associations were even able to provide legal advice with the help of British solicitors. In addition, all Kurdish associations had different types of cultural and social activities which provided an opportunity for newly arrived refugees to establish important social contacts.

The refugee associations and community centres in Britain would be unable to offer the large number of activities and services they do provide without the help of public funding. However, it looks as if the funding available was not always sufficient. For example, the associations often had difficulties in obtaining sufficient funds for the language and training courses they set up. The services provided by the associations were thus often hampered by inadequate funding and a piecemeal structure. Hence, for obvious reasons, the services available in the voluntary sector in Britain were usually not comparable to the more structured and professional resettlement programmes organized within the public sector in Finland.

Friends and relatives also played a major role in helping newly arrived refugees with their problems in England. In fact, the importance of informal networks in giving practical help often seemed to be bigger than that of the associations' role. A woman from Iran who had received most of her help from friends who had arrived some years earlier in Britain explained:

> I do not know if you know, but there is a custom between refugees that those who have been here earlier, they help the newly arrived, and every individual among them works as an association. They were so helpful, they were really so helpful.

Social networks based on social relations in the country of origin are obviously an important source of practical help and advice. In particular, relatives, including distant ones, play an important role for newly arrived Kurdish refugees. Although larger networks and associations based on 'tribal' allegiances are non-existent, the extended family remains very important. A man who had travelled through the Soviet Union and finally ended up in London told me:

> R: My uncle helped me, the first year, just my relative helped me, to do my work, for example, social security or other things, but after that I have done it myself.
> ÖW: What about the local council and social security and these things? Do you think that you have received the help that you needed when you arrived here?
> R: No, because I arrived here without accommodation, I just lived in my uncle's house, so nobody helped me, not the government or something, only the social security. I got income support.

Hospitality is in general highly valued among the Kurds (as I myself frequently experienced). Many refugees explained that if another Kurd asked for a favour, it would be unthinkable not to provide help. Nevertheless, one has to remember that the resources as well as the ability to give help and advice are limited within the Kurdish community. One tangible role of the informal social networks in Britain is that of giving help to refugees looking for a job. Relatives and friends can help each other to find employment and start businesses, especially in the large Turkish and Kurdish community in north London. A refugee who had repeatedly worked in garment factories in north London explained how to find these jobs:

> There is a network; there is a big network. And if you work, people come and ask you about your friends, whether you have

friends who can work in that place with you . . . In factories, you do not have to know English, and most of the refugees work in factories.

These examples indicate that although the Kurdish community is largely a divided one, there are still well-functioning networks and associations. The Kurdish refugees tried to use their associations and networks as a resource to solve the various problems they encountered in their new countries of settlement. Even though the Kurdish refugee associations were based mainly on political allegiances in Kurdistan, these associations and networks served totally new and additional functions in the diaspora.

Many studies of refugees emphasize how the communities are characterized by political divisions (Luciuk, 1986; Kay, 1987; Lundberg, 1989; Bousquet, 1991; Gold, 1992; Steen, 1992; McDowell, 1996; Valtonen, 1997). Although this is generally true, it is not the whole truth. Although a community as a whole may be politically divided, the same politically based networks can unite smaller groups within the community. These smaller groups and associations constitute important resources for the refugees.

In summary, the refugees used their social networks as a resource when they tried to solve the problems they encountered in their new country of settlement. However, the associations and networks in Finland are not as efficient and well organized as the ones in London. Since the situations in England and Finland are different, the networks also worked differently. In England, the refugees used their networks and associations to overcome the practical problems they experienced. In Finland, the refugees used their networks and associations to overcome their social and psychological problems. Thus, although the social networks were based on the distinct patterns in the countries of origin, these networks remain a useful resource for the refugees in their new countries of settlement. In this way the social networks can actually facilitate the refugees' integration into the country of settlement. As this book repeatedly argues, the Kurdish community can be regarded as a diaspora. However, contrary to what one might expect, this does not lead to the absence of integration. The various social networks which constitute the diaspora might be useful resources for the refugees. These networks are used to solve different problems and might facilitate integration into the new country of settlement. The process of integration and the formation of a diaspora do not form a simple causal relationship. Hence, to live in a diaspora is not an obstacle to a positive integration into the society of settlement.

DIASPORIC POLITICS

Since politics plays such an important role in the social organization of the Kurdish exile communities, there is reason to look a bit closer at the political activism of the Kurdish refugees. As Sheffer (1986, 1995) and Shain (1995) point out, the political activism of diasporas is a topical issue within the area of international politics. In various ways diasporas can influence, and be influenced by, the international political relations between the country of settlement and the country of origin.

The three countries of origin in this study have quite different relations with Western Europe. Under their present regimes Iran and Iraq are not regarded as the best friends of the Western world. Turkey, on the other hand, has close relations with the European Union, NATO and the USA (cf. Robins, 1996). These relations also have an impact on the situation of Kurdish refugees in Europe. A refugee from Iran or Iraq might have a less problematic political relationship with the country of asylum, since there is a common adversary in the government of the refugees' country of origin. On the other hand, the close relations between Turkey and Western European countries might have negative consequences for Kurdish refugees from Turkey. The complicated political relations between country of origin, country of settlement, and the diaspora might influence each other in different ways (Sheffer, 1986).

Kurdish Political Activism

As has been repeatedly pointed out, in many ways refugees continue to be oriented towards the country of origin. Politics is one of the areas of life where this is most obvious. As the European representative of ERNK, Kani Yilmaz, puts it: 'Even though we are here, every hour we are living in Kurdistan' (Rugman and Hutchings, 1996: 92). The Kurdish refugees' political activism in exile takes different forms. Although all Kurds tend to be political, the activism of the Kurds from Turkey has been especially evident recently. During the fieldwork, demonstrations were organized by Kurdish refugees in both England and Finland. In most cases the demonstrations are organized by only one or two organizations. However, the Kurds are not always divided. The Turkish army's attacks on Kurdish guerrillas in Northern Iraq in 1995 led, both in Britain and in Finland, to a united condemnation from all the major Kurdish associations. In both Britain and Finland, the Kurdish organizations agreed to sign a common petition demanding an end to the invasion. A demonstration on 9 April 1995 in London against the Turkish invasion was supported by 20 different Kurdish organizations and was attended by Kurds from all parts of Kurdistan. This exemplifies the fact that the diaspora also provides an opportunity for Kurds from different parts of Kurdistan to get together despite their diverse backgrounds. It should be pointed out that political activism is not necessarily oriented towards either the country of origin or the country of settlement. Some interviewees emphasized that the struggle to make other Kurdish refugees aware of the Kurdish national issue is an equally important part of the Kurdish struggle.

The *Newroz* celebration was another way of demonstrating support for the Kurdish cause. This ancient spring celebration among the Kurds and the Persians is now often a political manifestation celebrating Kurdish identity and culture. The largest Kurdish associations in both England and Finland organize their own *Newroz* celebrations. The music, speeches and dances at these parties often have a strong symbolic meaning for the participants. The banners displayed at the parties I visited carried phrases like 'down with Turkish state terrorism' and 'stop genocide in Kurdistan' (I find it illustrative of the political priorities of the associations that these political banners did not carry phrases such as 'fight unemployment among refugees' or 'fight racism in the neighbourhood'). A young man from Turkey who used to visit several parties in London said:

> Actually, *Newroz* celebration nowadays is much more political. It is not something like cultural, maybe much more it is a political thing, or this celebration has been politicized. Because in the *Newroz* celebration, if you have noticed, all these people express political messages. Singers, you know, players or other performers, actors, they all always express political messages: unity, identity, struggle.

Newroz is an important celebration for all Kurds. The parties organized by the Kurdish associations are often very popular. In London, some of the interviewees had visited several different organizations' parties. These gatherings were important occasions during which Kurds from different organizations, backgrounds and countries could meet and enjoy themselves. My own impression is that the emotional and political character of the celebration was most intense at the parties held by Kurds from Turkey. This is perhaps not very surprising since the *Newroz* celebration has officially been banned in Turkey. After years of denial of their ethnicity in Turkey, all Kurdish cultural expressions achieve a greater importance in exile. Ethnicity becomes by necessity a political and not a private issue, because of the oppression experienced by the Kurds in Turkey.

The extent of transnational political activism among the Kurdish communities is indicated by the density of international contacts that the Kurdish organizations have. For example, the Kurds from North-West Kurdistan (Turkey) had a well organized and well established network of contacts through committees and information offices all over the world. The journal *Kurdistan Report*, published jointly by the Kurdistan Solidarity Committee and the Kurdistan Information Centre in London, publishes the addresses of contact organizations in no less than 18 countries. Other recent examples of transnational cooperation include the Kurdistan Parliament in Exile, which held its first meeting in The Hague in the Netherlands in 1995. The Parliament was elected by Kurds in Europe, the former Soviet Union and North America. Although the Parliament aims to represent all Kurds, it is mainly persons from northern Kurdistan who have been involved in its work.

Another interesting form of transnational cooperation with international political repercussions is the Kurdish television station MED-TV, which started its broadcasts in the spring of 1995. This station produces its programmes in different European countries and distributes them all over Europe, the Middle East and northern Africa, thanks to a contract with a British satellite provider using a French satellite. The station is financially supported by private benefactors in the Kurdish communities all over Europe. The economic contributions are mainly collected among Kurds from Turkey. According to a brochure published in London, MED-TV 'evolved in response to calls over recent years, particularly from the Europe-wide Kurdish diaspora, for a television station of its own' (Hassanpour, 1998: 55). The name MED-TV comes from the name of the Medes, who are regarded as ancient ancestors of the Kurds.

Day-to-day programming on MED-TV during the spring of 1995

was mostly in the northern Kurdish dialect Kurmanji or in Turkish, but occasionally other Kurdish dialects were used. The programmes I have seen did not seem to be very political and included children's programmes, documentaries, news and discussions. Despite this, the whole project has enraged the Turkish government, which is perhaps not surprising bearing in mind the Turkish authorities' reaction to any cultural expression of Kurdishness. According to the Turkish government, the station is a PKK organ and they demand that it should be closed down. As Hassanpour (1997, 1998) writes, the Turkish government's actions against the station have been both national and international. In Turkey, there are reports that satellite dishes have been smashed in the Kurdish provinces. In Europe, the Turkish authorities launched intensive diplomatic pressure against MED-TV. A good example of the relations between the Turkish and the British governments is the fact that John Major allegedly promised the Turkish Prime Minister, Tansu Ciller, that his government 'would do "everything within their power" against MED TV' (Imset, 1996: 35). The Turkish diplomatic campaign has been partly successful; there have been serious disruptions in the production of programmes and problems for the station in securing its licence. However, since MED-TV is working legally, the Turkish government, at least at the time of writing, has not been able to close it totally.

The importance of MED-TV for the Kurdish communities can hardly be overestimated. In the interviews during the spring of 1995, it was clear that most interviewees wanted to follow the programmes. Although Kurdish-speaking radio programmes distributed by Voice of America have been popular among Kurds in exile, this is the first Kurdish television station in Europe. Kurds from Turkey were particularly enthusiastic about MED-TV, but Kurds from other parts of Kurdistan also tried to follow it. Watching the programmes also seemed to be a political statement. Even Turkish-speaking Kurds who did not understand Kurdish watched the station's broadcasts.

An even more politically sensitive issue is the fact that the Kurds in exile can play a role in the independence struggle in Kurdistan. In the case of Turkey, a large part of the Kurdish parties' finances allegedly comes from Kurds living in exile in Europe. The ERNK representative Kani Yilmaz acknowledged this in an interview in 1994, when, in response to a question on the role of the Kurds in Europe, he replied: 'They give financial support – the donations are voluntary, continuous and quite high' (Rugman and Hutchings, 1996: 94). There are also examples of persons who have returned to Kurdistan in order to join the armed struggle. *Kurdistan Report* (no. 13 and no. 19) has saluted three PKK guerrillas who lived in London for several years in the 1980s and who died in clashes with Turkish troops in northern Kurdistan.

An interesting issue is that of the differences that exist between the Kurdish refugees from Turkey, Iraq and Iran in terms of the extent and type of their political activism. The Kurds from Turkey often displayed strong emotional support for the Kurdish national movement in northern Kurdistan, while Kurds from Iran and Iraq often were more alienated from Kurdish politics. This was clearly related to the nature of the ongoing struggles in the countries of origin. Joly (1995a) makes a useful observation when she describes how political refugees' forms of organizations and actions can be periodized:

> In the initial period if the conjuncture back home is in turmoil and has not stabilized, exile is envisaged as a very short episode and all energies are tensed towards the goal of overthrowing the regime and returning. As the regime in the homeland stabilizes, this is perceived as a consolidation and an indication that exile will last longer than initially expected. Although one is not here to stay, one is here for a while more. (Joly, 1995a: 22)

Although the refugees' primary aim is to pursue the political project in the homeland, another secondary project pertaining to everyday issues in the society of reception might appear later. When this new project will appear is not determined by time and duration of exile, and even the structure of the receiving society only plays a secondary role. The important factor is the viability of the political project in the homeland which is kept alive by the possibilities of its victory (Joly, 1995a). This periodization was discernible in the Kurdish communities. The Kurds from Turkey were still in the initial period in which their activities were oriented solely towards the liberation of Kurdistan. The Kurds from Iran and Iraq were clearly more disillusioned about their political projects and, although to return was also their ultimate goal, they started to be more oriented towards the country of exile. As Joly (1995a) points out, this is not a consequence of time, but rather connected to the fate of the political projects in which the refugees have been involved. This second project, which comprises orientation towards the country of settlement, can use the social networks and associations which were established during the first period of orientation towards the country of origin. In this way the Kurdish refugees can use their political associations as a resource also in situations which are totally unrelated to the original political struggle. Although the associations are mobilized around a political struggle in the country of origin, they acquire new additional functions related to problems in the country of settlement.

State and Government Political Actions

Clearly, the receiving countries are not happy about political activism among Kurdish refugees, especially since they often have lucrative economic relations (including the export of military equipment) with the governments that are oppressing the Kurds. In Germany, the relations between the German state and the politically active Kurds originating in Turkey have often been problematic. Germany's approach towards its Kurdish minority's cultural rights, the diasporic political activities of the Kurds and Germany's close connections with Turkey have all played a role in the deterioration of relations. The Kurds have had problems in being accepted as a linguistic and ethnic group distinct from the Turkish minority in Germany (Senol, 1992), and a stigmatization of the Kurds as 'less worthy Turks' has been supported by newspaper reports (Blaschke, 1991a, 1991b). This 'institutional racism', largely adopted by the German authorities, has led to an ethnic revival among the second generation German Kurds and antagonism between the German state and the Kurdish community (Blaschke, 1991a, 1991b). In the early 1990s there were frequent petrol-bombings and sabotage of Turkish property and businesses in Germany, carried out by people sympathetic to the Kurdish liberation struggle in eastern Turkey. Attacks on Turkish property have been less frequent in the UK. I am aware of one tragic case involving the petrol-bombing of Turkish banks in London in the summer of 1994, in which a British woman was injured and for which three Kurdish men were subsequently imprisoned. After the wave of political violence, the PKK and the ERNK were declared illegal in Germany and France in 1993. The subsequent closure in several European countries of a large number of organizations associated with Kurds from Turkey has led to all Kurdish communities all over Europe being regarded as potential 'terrorists'. In the case of the Kurds, European integration seems to mean that all Kurds have to be equally persecuted all over Europe.

In England, many Kurds felt that they have been intimidated and suspected of criminal activities by the British authorities. There were also suggestions that the Turkish government and its local supporters were spreading rumours about illegal activities in the Kurdish refugee community. During the fieldwork this criminalization of the community was a topical issue in discussions with Kurds from Turkey living in London. Regardless of whether it is true that there is a systematic criminalization of the Kurdish communities, it is a fact that the British authorities have demonstrated hostile attitudes towards Kurdish refugees from Turkey in quite concrete ways. For example, in Chapter 3 the radical increase in the number of negative decisions on asylum applications from Turkey is described. An incident which has upset many Kurds was the arrest of Kani Yilmaz, the European Representative of the ERNK, during a visit to London on 26 October 1994. When arrested he was on his way to a meeting in the British Parliament to which he was invited as a speaker. Kani Yilmaz was not charged with any crime but was nevertheless indefinitely detained under the National Security Act. His legal case was very complex and he was detained in a British prison until 1997, when he was extradited to Germany. In February 1998 he was sentenced by a German court for coordinating and instigating the arson campaign against Turkish interests in Germany in 1993. Kani Yilmaz was sentenced to seven and a half years in prison, but the court agreed to his release after taking into account the time he had spent in custody in Britain.

In any case, the relationship between the Kurds and the state authorities did not seem to be as bad in Britain as it has been in Germany. In fact, the British general public and many British political organizations have expressed sympathy for the Kurds and their political struggle in the Middle East. Many MPs have showed a genuine interest in the Kurdish question. There are also many small British left-wing organizations who support the Kurds. Bodies like Militant Labour, Socialist Workers Party and other politically marginal left-wing groups often have a visible presence at Kurdish demonstrations. However, in my own opinion, this support from small left-wing groups is rather unhelpful, since firstly, many of these organizations seem to use Kurdish demonstrations mainly as a way of spreading their own political message and literature. Secondly, support from these small marginal political groups can also marginalize the refugees and the whole Kurdish struggle from mainstream politics in Britain.

The contrast with the situation in Germany becomes even greater when we look at the situation in Finland. The small community in Helsinki, consisting of Kurds from Turkey, did not seem to be involved in any conflict with the Finnish authorities regarding the community's political activities. In fact, all interviewees in Finland had largely positive experiences of the few contacts they had had with the police. Since refugees otherwise often had negative experiences of bureaucracy and xenophobia, the positive experiences with the police were perhaps not totally expected. In 1994 a person active in the Kurdistan Information Centre in Helsinki described the organization's relations with the authorities:

> In Finland we have not had any problems with the authorities or the police. And we do not wish that there will be any in the future. The situation here in Finland is different from, for example, Germany where the Kurds do not have the right to free speech. We work democratically as long as we have the right to free speech. But in Germany there is problem, because in a situation where there no longer is democracy then you have to fight. [t]

Obviously, the situation was influenced by the facts that the number of Kurds in Finland was small and, because of the country's geographical location, the Finnish and Turkish governments' political cooperation was not very extensive. Nevertheless, it is also possible that the freedom of expression and the traditional understanding of issues related to minority rights prevented conflicts from arising in Finland. The relationships between the authorities and the Kurdish refugees thus seemed to be quite different in the countries here under study in comparison with the situation in Germany. However, the present attempts to criminalize the Kurdish community in Britain, and Finland joining the European Union in 1995, could have negative consequences for the Kurdish refugees in these countries. These issues indicate that the political actions of the 'host' state are decisive for the forms of political activism the diaspora will adopt.

Although political activism on the part of the Kurds in the diaspora is largely perceived as a problem by the authorities, there is also reason to remember the positive aspects of the refugees' activism. The positive aspects of ethnic associations and social networks among the refugees have previously been presented in this chapter. For the Kurds, who are a persecuted minority in their countries of origin, the diaspora also offers opportunities for forms of political and cultural expression which are not possible in Kurdistan. The diaspora presents an opportunity to develop a common Kurdish ethnic identity among Kurds who have only had limited possibilities for mutual contacts in Kurdistan. The journal *Ronahî*, published by Kurdish students at the School of Oriental and African Studies in London, includes the following anecdote written by a student. Although this quotation deals with the Kurdish national dilemma, it also demonstrates the possibilities for reclaiming a Kurdish identity which the diaspora entails:

> Several months ago, with a friend, I went to the British Library – Oriental Section – to look for a book written by Ahmadi Khani (1650–1706). Fortunately we found it. The manuscript called Nubar (a metrical Arabic–Kurdish dictionary for children) was written in the beginning of the 1700s and while we were looking through the faded pages of it, I was lost in thought.... After almost three hundred years, two students from different parts of Kurdistan were for the first time coming across a book of a leading Kurdish poet and scholar in a library in London. If there is a disgrace for the Kurds, is this not to be enough? (Boz, 1995: 20)

The examples of political activism in the diaspora which are discussed in this section point to the possibilities presented to the Kurds in the diaspora for uniting behind the Kurdish cause. The diaspora also offers opportunities to meet Kurds from other parts of Kurdistan and to freely express their Kurdish identity and culture. This new unity in the diaspora can also serve as a platform allowing the Kurds to get their voice heard and work for the improvement of their situation in their new countries of settlement.

CONCLUSION

This chapter has argued that the social organization of the Kurdish refugee communities is largely a continuation of social relations in Kurdistan. In previous chapters of this book it was shown that the refugees have a continuous relationship to their countries of origin, and this chapter has gone on to describe how this is reflected in the Kurdish associations and in the diasporic political activities of the refugees. The political allegiances that exist in Kurdistan have a profound influence on the social organization of the refugee

community and its associations. As a result of this continuous relationship, one can also find differences in the forms of social
organization and political activism between different parts of the
Kurdish refugee community. The different political developments
in Turkey, Iran and Iraq continue to influence the Kurds from those
countries and can explain differences in the activities and priorities of the Kurdish associations in exile.

Due to the nature of this continuous relationship to the 'homeland' the refugee community can be described as a diaspora in
accordance with Safran's (1991) definition of the term. This chapter,
together with Chapters 4 and 5, has described how the refugees
'continue to relate, personally or vicariously, to that homeland in
one way or another, and their ethnocommunal consciousness and
solidarity are importantly defined by the existence of such a
relationship' (Safran, 1991: 84). Furthermore, this chapter shows
that two more of Safran's characteristics of a diaspora are evident
among the Kurdish refugees. First, although this chapter has only
given a brief picture of diasporic political activities, it still describes
how the refugees 'believe that they should, collectively, be committed to the maintenance or restoration of their original homeland
and to its safety and prosperity' (Safran, 1991: 84). In fact, as Cohen
(1997) points out, this issue can also involve the actual creation of
a homeland. Secondly, it is also evident that the Kurds 'retain a
collective memory, vision, or myth about their original homeland –
its physical location, history, and achievements' (Safran, 1991: 83).
Clearly, the concept of diaspora is useful for an understanding of
the refugees' own definition of their situation.

The Kurdish associations were largely organized and mobilized
according to patterns drawn from Kurdistan, but still these associations were able to play an important role in the receiving country.
Although the community can be regarded as a diaspora, this does
not automatically mean that the community is not integrated into
the society of settlement. On the contrary, these diasporic relations can have a positive influence on the ability to become integrated.
The associations and social networks, which largely constitute the
diaspora, can be useful resources which the refugees can employ
to solve the new problems they face in the country of settlement.
Although diasporic relations might influence the refugees' motiva-
tion to settle down, they can also provide the community with the
means it needs to become integrated.

Conclusions

The fieldwork for this book focused on newly arrived Kurdish refugees from Turkey, Iraq and Iran, who live in exile in England and Finland. The research findings form the basis for a discussion of the concept of 'diaspora' and its relevance for a sociological study of refugees in the country of exile. It is argued that the concept of diaspora, understood as a transnational social organization relating to both the country of origin and the country of exile, can provide a deeper understanding of the social reality in which refugees live. In a way, the concept of diaspora can bridge the gap between pre-migration and post-migration. From a sociological point of view it is not possible to clearly separate these two moments. Refugees do not start their lives from scratch when they arrive in the country of resettlement, as so often seems to be assumed. The concept of diaspora encompasses the refugees' own definition of their situation and provides a tool for understanding the transnational social relations found in refugee communities.

As is repeatedly argued in this book, the Kurdish communities in exile can be regarded as a diaspora. The previous chapters have indicated that even Safran's (1991) precise definition of a diaspora is well suited for describing the Kurdish refugees' situation. All the criteria for a diaspora can be found in the Kurdish refugee communities: forcible expulsion, myths and memories of the homeland, alienation in the host country, the wish to return, ongoing support for the homeland and, finally, a collective identity importantly defined by the relationship to the homeland. Since the Kurds clearly fulfil the requirements of even the strict definition of a diaspora suggested by Safran (1991), it is argued that there are sufficient grounds for speaking of a Kurdish diaspora.

As Marienstras (1989) points out, time is an important factor in defining a diaspora (cf. Chaliand, 1989; Cohen, 1997), and this is a poignant reason why one might hesitate in regarding the Kurds as an established diaspora. All the Kurdish communities in Europe have a relatively short history and all the refugees studied in this research had recently arrived in the country of exile. It might be argued that there is reason to be cautious in using the notion of diaspora before a considerably longer period of time has passed.

179

One cannot rule out the possibility that the diaspora might disappear over time. There is still a theoretical possibility that political changes in the Middle East will make a return migration possible (although as time goes by it can be expected that fewer and fewer actually would choose to return). The future developments of the Kurdish diaspora also depend on the structures and policies of the country of exile. Future generations may, if they are accepted by the host society, be assimilated into the societies in which they live. However, the xenophobia, discrimination and racism directed against all visible ethnic minorities might effectively rule out any assimilation. Thus, although the Kurds in exile today clearly live in a diasporic relation, only time will tell if they will become a permanent diaspora. Despite these cautious remarks, my argument is that a sociological analysis of contemporary Kurdish refugees has much to gain from the concept of diaspora and the diaspora discourse. The point is that regardless of whether the Kurdish refugees of today already can claim to be a 'real diaspora' or not, the concept of diaspora can throw some light on the refugees' specific relationships to their countries of settlement *and* their countries of origin.

The label 'diaspora' is, perhaps, especially appropriate in the case of the Kurdish refugees because of the influence of Kurdish nationalism, which commits many Kurdish refugees to the restoration of their homeland. However, I would suggest that the concept of diaspora can also be a useful analytical tool in the study of other refugee communities. This is because the concept can, at the same time, relate to both the country of settlement and the country of origin. In this way, it can also describe the transnationalism of the social organization of refugee communities in general.

This study highlights the social dimension of a diaspora by looking at the importance of formal and informal associations and social networks. To live in a diaspora not only involves issues of consciousness and identity, it also has a profound influence on the social organization of the community (cf. Cohen, 1995, 1996). A diaspora can be seen as a specific type of social organization which is characterized by transnational social relations. As Lie (1995) and Tölölyan (1991) point out, the study of transnationalism is an important feature of the new diaspora discourse. This transnationalism includes the various social, political, economic and cultural relations which migrants create and develop between country of origin and country of settlement (Basch et al., 1994), as well as between exile communities in different countries. Clearly, this tendency towards transnationalism is related to more general processes of globalization and de-territorialization in contemporary societies. Although globalization, transnationalism and de-territorialization can be regarded as general social processes, the formation of diasporas is a process which is more specific to refugee communities. Obviously, not all diasporas regard themselves as refugee communities, and not all refugee communities become diasporas. Nevertheless, the diaspora concept does highlight some of the typical characteristics of refugee communities. Safran's (1991) strict definition of a diaspora has been used in this book in order to be able to operationalize the concept as an analytical tool. Although some authors propose wider and more inclusive definitions of the concept, these have not been found useful for the subject matter of this study.

This book has examined the situation of Kurdish refugees both in England and in Finland. Despite the large differences between these two host societies, several features remained constant in both cases. Things that all Kurdish refugees had in common included their wish to return, their feeling of displacement and various psychological problems owing to their refugee experiences. All refugees also created and maintained transnational social networks. These networks included contacts with Kurds in Kurdistan and in the world-wide diaspora. These features were found in all Kurdish refugee groups, regardless of the refugees' countries of origin or countries of exile.

However, in some matters this research has also found notable differences between refugee groups depending on the refugees' countries of origin and countries of exile. Clearly, the refugee communities are influenced by both the relationship to Kurdistan and the relationship to the countries of settlement. Thus, it is possible to regard the country of origin and the country of exile as independent variables which affect the social relations of the refugees in various ways.

THE COUNTRY OF ORIGIN AS AN INDEPENDENT VARIABLE

This study indicates that there are specific differences between the refugee communities depending on whether the refugees originated in Turkey, Iraq or Iran. Since similar patterns of difference have been found in both England and Finland, there is reason to believe that these differences can be attributed to factors related to the countries of origin.

Although in some situations the Kurds are united by a common ethnic identity, several factors simultaneously separate them from one another. Today, Kurdistan is divided between a number of different states, each with its own specific political situation and history. There are political as well as ideological disagreements dividing the Kurdish political movements within these countries. The Kurds are also separated by a variety of dialects, many of which are not mutually intelligible, and there are of course gender, class and cultural differences that have to be taken into account. Old 'tribal' allegiances and religious divisions in some parts of Kurdistan make the picture even more complex. This heterogeneity is also found in the Kurdish diaspora, where different patterns of migration from the countries of origin also highlight some of the differences. The Kurds in the diaspora are mainly political refugees and thus the political divisions become especially apparent in the diaspora. There is, nevertheless, a Kurdish nationalism which today has influenced many Kurds. This nationalism can, to some extent, overcome the differences among the Kurds.

The different Kurdish refugee groups showed different patterns of integration within the larger Kurdish community as well as in respect of their degree of integration into other minority groups in the society of settlement. While Kurds from Iraq largely identified themselves only as Kurds and mainly socialized with other Kurds, the Kurds from Iran and Turkey were in practice largely part of a wider Iranian and a wider Kurdish and Turkish community respectively. However, the most important factor explaining the social organization of the Kurdish refugee community was political allegiances based on political parties in Kurdistan. This factor was especially salient among Kurdish refugee associations, which were largely organized and mobilized according to patterns drawn from Kurdistan. The political developments in the countries of origin influenced the diasporic political activities of the refugees. These developments also affected refugees' plans for a return. Refugees from Turkey were relatively optimistic about their chances of being able to return, while refugees from Iran and Iraq largely felt that the political situation in their countries of origin had developed in a negative direction.

Because of the refugees' continuous relation to Kurdistan it is

not easy to understand the Kurdish refugee community as an ethnic group within the context of the countries of exile. In fact, the
refugees' ethnicity continued to be based primarily on relations within
the context set in their countries of origin. The ethnicity of the
Kurdish refugees was not defined through their relationship to the
majority in the country of settlement. Instead, their ethnicity was
mainly based on the experience of being an oppressed group in
the countries of origin. This is something that will probably change
over time, but among the relatively recently arrived refugees in
this study, this feature was very evident. Theories of ethnic relations
can therefore only provide a limited understanding of refugees and
their situation. Instead, the diaspora concept is a more suitable
tool for an understanding of the special relationships that refugees
have with both the society of origin and with the society of settlement. The diasporic conceptual framework sheds some light on the
largely transnational and de-territorialized social reality in which
refugees live.

This continuous relation between developments in the country
of origin and the social organization of the refugee community also
adds a new perspective to theories arguing that there is a connection between the type of migration and the migrant's relation to
their new country of settlement. Kunz (1981) links the processes
of integration and assimilation with classifications of different types
of refugee migration. However, his model seems unable to sufficiently
take into account the refugees' continuous and transnational relations to their countries of origin. The initial reason for flight, or
political activism before flight, is not the only question which has
an influence on the refugee in exile. The relation between the refugee
and the country of origin is also a *continuous relation* where contemporary political developments have a direct influence on refugees
who have lived in exile for a long period of time. Instead of constructing elaborate classifications of various types of refugee
migration, it is enough to say that the refugees' political projects
in the countries of origin continue to influence the refugees and
their communities in the country of exile. The continuous
transnational flow of information, people, capital and ideas creates
a relationship between the diaspora and the homeland which
continues for a long period of time after the initial migration. The
formation of a diaspora is not only dependent on the 'situation
before flight', the refugees' 'background' or their 'cultural luggage'.
Certainly, the formation of a diaspora cannot either be regarded

as a question of the individuals' own free choice, as Sheffer (1995) seems to suggest. Instead, the social reality in which refugees continue to live for a long time is a transnational situation where factors both in the country of origin and in the country of exile play a decisive role.

COUNTRY OF SETTLEMENT AS AN INDEPENDENT VARIABLE

Although the refugees' social reality can largely be understood as de-territorialized and transnational, it is still necessary to remember that in many decisive ways the society of settlement influences the refugees and the social organization of the refugee communities. There is a danger that the new interest in transnational diasporas with its emphasis on globalization, transnationalism and de-territorialization may overlook the local context in which migrants and refugees live. Therefore this book advocates a framework which takes into account the relations with both the country of origin *and* the country of settlement.

This study revealed a number of important differences between the refugees' experiences in England and in Finland. It can be argued that neither country has fully understood the specific nature of refugee migration, although they approach the issue from totally different perspectives. The UK adopts a traditional communitarian and multicultural approach, while in practice Finland has a more assimilationist resettlement policy. Since many of the refugees in England and Finland have identical backgrounds and share similar experiences of Kurdistan, it is possible to argue that the differences which can be observed in the two cases can be attributed to factors related to the society of settlement.

There were notable differences between the two countries in terms of the practical problems experienced by refugees. Not surprisingly, the way the resettlement of refugees was organized largely determined what kinds of difficulties the refugees would experience. In Finland, the official resettlement programmes and the structures of the welfare state greatly diminished the practical problems related to housing, education and income support. The refugees in Finland even experienced fewer problems connected to language than the refugees in England. In London, however, the strong Kurdish communities and the Kurdish social networks were important resources for the refugees. The refugees were more isolated and their associations were less well organized in Finland than in England, which led to a range of difficulties for the refugees in Finland. The ethnic labour market in London was often able to facilitate the refugees' employment. However, the only jobs available in London were poorly paid jobs with bad working conditions. In Finland, the severe unemployment situation in practice excluded refugees from the labour market. Xenophobia and racism were also more visible features of society in Finland than was the case in the multicultural environment of London.

Resettlement policies were widely different in the two countries. The Finnish policy was to resettle refugees in small groups dispersed all over the country, while in Britain almost all Kurds lived in London. Obviously, these differences made it impossible to establish large and well-established communities and associations in Finland on the lines of those found in London. This led to notable differences in the social networks and the types of social integration found in the two countries. Although all Kurdish refugees used their networks and associations to solve problems they faced in the country of settlement, the role played by social networks and associations was completely different in the two countries. In these areas, the official resettlement policies played a decisive role. Kurdish refugees' political activities and their support for a Kurdish homeland are certainly not welcomed by the governments of their host countries. However, if one compares the situation in Finland, England and Germany it seems as though the different policies of the receiving countries have an influence on what forms the refugees' diasporic political activities will take.

All these results suggest that to a large extent the structures and policies of the receiving society determine the process of integration into that society. By stressing the importance of structures this study avoids the danger of using theoretical frameworks where immigrants are mainly seen as choosing whether or not to integrate. Such theoretical frameworks forget the profound importance of various exclusionary structures and discourses within the receiving societies. For example, issues like racism and systematic discrimination have to be taken into account. Yet, it is important to remember that the refugees are independent actors and that there is an interaction between structure and agency. Hence, various inclusionary and exclusionary processes within the receiving society still have a profound importance on the social organization of the refugee communities, despite the refugees' transnational and de-territorialized social relations. This suggests that the new diaspora discourse still needs to take into account earlier sociological research about international migration and ethnic relations.

INTEGRATION INTO THE RECEIVING SOCIETY AND THE DIASPORA

What then is the relation between the process of integration into the receiving society and the process of diaspora formation among Kurdish refugees? The existence of a diaspora may, for example, suggest that refugees do not want to, or are unable to, integrate or assimilate into the receiving society. Thus, the existence of a diaspora could easily be used as an argument for exclusionary policies by anti-immigration political groups. The formation of diasporas could, for example, be used as an argument for more restrictive asylum regulations since 'refugees will anyway never become native inhabitants'.

As described in Chapter 1, assimilation is seldom the outcome of migration, and as has been shown in the following chapters, assimilation was not regarded as a possible outcome by the Kurdish refugees themselves. Assimilation, which here is defined as a question of personal identity, would, of course, also rule out the formation of a diaspora. However, this book argues that integration still is possible and even regarded as a goal by the refugees themselves. As defined in Chapter 1, integration is a structural process by which refugees become part of social groups and institutions in society. I would argue that it is important to understand that to live in a diaspora does not automatically mean that the person is not integrated into the wider society. The process of integration into the society of settlement and the process of diaspora formation are largely unrelated processes, and are certainly not connected in any clear and simple causal relation.

At the risk of over-simplifying, it can be argued that integration into the society of reception mostly depends on factors within that society. In this context, the minority's relation to the society of origin is, of course, not totally without importance, but it does not play as decisive a role as factors in the society of settlement. Likewise, the question as to whether a minority community forms a diaspora or not, depends largely on the type of relationship which exists with the country of origin and only to a lesser extent on the type of relationship to the country of settlement. Yet, in order to gain a full understanding of the social organization of the communities, both dimensions have to be taken into account.

A look at some groups traditionally regarded as diasporas can clarify the relation between diasporas and integration. Regardless of whether you use a wide or a strict definition of diasporas, it is possible to find groups which are well integrated into the societies in which they live. The classic example of a diaspora is, of course, the Jews, but the overseas Chinese are also referred to as a diaspora by some authors. These two groups are often well integrated and might have important socio-economic positions in the societies where they live. Clearly, to live in a diaspora does not automatically entail non-integration. Yet, neither is there any guarantee that a diaspora would automatically be positively well integrated. There are diasporas which experience discrimination and which tend to be only partly integrated into their societies of settlement, the historical experiences of the African diaspora being one example which easily comes to mind.

Nevertheless, diasporas are communities which at least to some degree and in some respects choose to differentiate or separate themselves from the wider society. Is it not possible to argue that this tendency in the case of refugees will hamper their integration into the receiving society? For example, in the case of refugees an isolation from the wider society can contribute to a lack of skills and resources which will hamper an integration into the wider society. This case is exemplified by the refugees living in the largely insulated Turkish and Kurdish community in north London, who have difficulties in finding a job in the mainstream economy because of insufficient language skills. The disadvantages which are connected to living in an insular community are, however, often compensated for by other advantages. For example, in the case of north London there is an ethnic labour market employing Turks and Kurds in so-called 'sweatshops', which, to some extent, compensates for the lack of employment opportunities. However, the most important issue to remember is that disadvantages associated with tendencies towards isolation among the minority communities themselves are often of marginal importance compared to the profound effect on the minority of the social structure of the wider society. In the example from north London, for instance, it is clear that the lack of a minimum wage and other features of the British labour market create a situation with poor salaries and bad working conditions in the 'sweatshops'. A more general problem relating to the social structure of the wider society is the various forms of racism and discrimination that most refugees face. Various exclusionary structures and discourses in the receiving society, for example racism and discrimination, can be regarded as a far more important reason for non-integration into the wider society than the refugees' own diasporic consciousness.

There can also be a relation between integration and diaspora formation in the sense that non-integration might lead to a need for a stronger ethnic community. This may happen as a defence strategy in order to compensate for the discrimination and inferior position in which the minority often finds itself. This defensive community may or may not be a diaspora. It is easy to agree with Clifford (1994) who argues that diasporic consciousness is often a question of making the best of a bad situation. The refugees' exclusion from the wider society is not a product of their own diasporic consciousness; this exclusion can instead be seen as one of many reasons for the formation of a diaspora. In the case of the Kurdish refugees, it seems that to some degree all the groups studied have tried to strengthen their own community in order to solve different problems they experience in the country of settlement. Both informal social networks and formal associations are important resources for a community. For example, the well-organized associations in London today play many different roles for the Kurdish community.

The Kurdish refugee communities are divided largely because the political divisions in Kurdistan have a profound influence on the social organization of the communities in exile. Yet, at the same time as the Kurds are divided politically, similar forces can also unite those refugees who share the same political beliefs and background in Kurdistan. The associations and informal networks growing out of this unity can be used as a resource to solve the problems facing the refugees in their new country of settlement. Minority organizations and networks might actually be important in facilitating integration into the receiving society. Thus, rather than hampering integration, diasporas may in fact facilitate integration. The Kurdish refugees in this study live in a diaspora where their associations and informal networks are largely oriented towards the country of origin. Despite this, the associations and networks can be used as a resource to solve problems that refugees experience in the country of settlement.

Despite the above-mentioned qualities of diasporic communities, the formation of diasporas should not be seen as a totally positive process. Although diasporas are often defined in relation to nation-states, it must be remembered that a diaspora cannot provide its members with the same services and opportunities that the state is able to provide to its citizens. Consequently, although a strong and independent community has its advantages, there is no reason to see diasporas as a positive and sufficient alternative to egalitarian welfare states. For example, the voluntary work and the lack of resources in the Kurdish community centres in London cannot compare with the official reception programmes and the relatively good facilities provided for refugees in Finland.

Both the formation of diasporas and the processes of integration should be seen as complex processes that are difficult to describe by any static models. In this research it has not been possible to identify and measure all the different variables affecting the social organization of the refugee communities. Obviously, there is a need for more research in this area. This study has suggested a number of variables and their relation to one another. Furthermore, an analytical framework in which these issues can be discussed has been presented. It is argued here that the concept of diaspora retains an understanding of refugees' specific experiences and transnational social relations. In any case, the refugees' transnational social reality suggests a rethinking of the concept of integration. This book has sought to show that the concept of diaspora, seen as a transnational social organization, is a useful analytical tool for understanding the special relationships that refugees have with both the country of origin and the country of settlement. The concept of diaspora goes beyond simplistic notions of integration, since the concept of diaspora takes into account this duality of refugees' social relations. For example, within this conceptual framework it makes perfect sense that people wish to return to their countries of origin at the same time as they want to integrate into their new countries of settlement.

The diaspora discourse highlights the refugees' continuous relation to their countries of origin. Despite this, the relation to the country of settlement should not be forgotten. Although the diaspora discourse adds an important transnational dimension, there is still reason to remember older theories relating to inclusion and exclusion within society in more traditional terms. Thus, the diaspora discourse needs to take into account earlier sociological research and theories about ethnic relations and international migration. Understanding a diaspora as a social organization and not only as a psychological relation is one step in the right direction.

In summary, this book argues that the Kurds in exile can be regarded as a diaspora. This concept depicts the transnationalism which characterizes the social organization of the Kurdish refugee communities. In many different ways refugees living in exile have a continuous relation to their societies of origin. Transnational social networks and associations based on this relation can be important resources for refugees. However, there is also reason to remember the importance of social structures and exclusionary policies in the country of settlement, since these continue to have a great impact on how the integration of refugees will happen. Consequently, a study of refugee communities needs to take into account the relationships with both the society of origin and the society of settlement.

Appendix: The Fieldwork

The arguments presented in this book are based on a comparative study of the Kurdish refugee communities in England and Finland. The fieldwork was carried out in 1994 in Finland and in 1995 in England among newly arrived Kurdish refugees from Turkey, Iraq and Iran. The methods utilized in this study were ethnographic field research methods. These allow the researcher to study social phenomena in their own natural settings and support the aim to understand, as far as possible, the social actors' own points of view. This approach is particularly suitable for a study of refugees, which inevitably includes many practical and ethical problems.

Field research enables the researcher to study the *processes* involved in the field of study (Schatzman and Strauss, 1973). By doing so, one can avoid the common problem of regarding 'ethnicity' or 'culture' as stable entities unrelated to the social contexts in which they occur. Field research methods have been elaborated by Glaser and Strauss (1967), among others, who argued that in-depth case studies are efficient for theory generation. Field research methods enable the researcher to look at the persons under study as subjects in their own right, instead of mere dependent variables ruled by the social structure. This is not to say that structures do not exist. In the area of international migration and ethnic relations it is obvious that social structures such as economic inequalities, racist ideologies and migration policies play a very significant role. For anybody studying immigrants it is, of course, especially important not to forget the influence of exclusionary policies and other discriminatory social structures. Any other approach easily leads to a 'blame the victim' situation where immigrants are defined as deviants or as problems. The methodology of this research is described in more detail in my PhD thesis (Wahlbeck, 1997b).

In a study of an oppressed minority like the Kurds ethical questions should be given the highest priority. During my fieldwork I declared who I was and what I was doing as clearly and honestly as possible. Furthermore, confidentiality has been of utmost importance. Since refugees have fled persecution, they or their relatives might still live in danger. Accordingly, the anonymity of the respondents and informants has been protected during the research process and in the book itself. Ethical questions are especially important in the study of vulnerable minorities. Therefore, the research has been planned in cooperation with Kurdish refugees. Prior to carrying out fieldwork, I had discussions with a number of different Kurdish associations and individuals concerning their opinions about this research project. The whole methodology of this research also presupposes that the research process is a continuous interaction between the researcher and the researched, with the researcher trying to understand the latter's own point of view. Through this approach I have been able to develop the research project so as to consider issues which the refugees themselves regard as important. The theoretical perspective of this study also leads to an interest in the relational context in which the Kurdish refugee communities' situation is defined. This means that the study investigates the role of the social structure and the majority society in this process. This relational context guarantees that the refugees are not defined as 'problems'. The chapters presenting the results of the fieldwork also highlight a number of instances where a change of policy could lead to improvements for the refugees. However, at the same time, this study avoids any 'victimization' of the minority by emphasizing that they are also actors in this process.

It should also be noted that I have not been in contact with either the British or Finnish authorities in order to plan this research. Contacts with the authorities could have worked against my attempt to establish a trustful relationship with the informants. In Britain my role as a researcher independent of the British authorities was not difficult to establish since I am from Finland. Actually, I frequently discovered that it was a positive asset to be Finnish and not British. In Finland, my role as an independent researcher was harder to achieve, since I did not hide the fact that I had previously been a social worker. In any case, only a few of my contacts in Finland were with persons who had known me in a professional capacity before I carried out the fieldwork.

Field research covers several different methods and the researcher has to be a methodological pragmatist and must use every possible method which can furnish more knowledge. Among the different kinds of empirical material collected for this research, the most important material consists of 50 semi-structured interviews with a sample of Kurdish refugees from Turkey, Iraq and Iran. Semi-structured interviews were used because this is a method that least restrains the respondents while it still retains a good capacity for later analysis. The aim of the interviews was to give a broad understanding of the refugees' social situation, experiences and problems in their new countries of settlement. The method used to find my sample was a combination of snowballing and quota sampling. The sample was chosen exclusively through contacts with Kurdish individuals and associations. Since I was introduced to my interviewees by fellow Kurdish refugees, I generally experienced fewer problems with access than I had expected. All the persons approached in this way accepted the invitation to take part in the research. The establishment of a trustful relationship was also helped by the fact that the interviews did not include sensitive questions relating to the refugees' activities and background in the country of origin.

The interviews have been conducted only with refugees who fled to Europe as adults and the sample only includes persons who regarded themselves as refugees in the two countries in question. The aim was to achieve a sample with persons who had lived in the country of exile for between two and ten years. The purpose of this time-frame was to provide a sample of refugees who were relatively new arrivals but who had still received a decision on their asylum applications. Since some persons have to wait for up to four years for a decision, the sample still included five interviews with asylum seekers from Turkey. The rest of the sample included persons with full refugee status, persons in Finland with a residence permit given on humanitarian grounds and in the UK persons with Exceptional Leave to Remain or British citizenship. 28 semi-structured interviews were completed in England and 22 in Finland. Out of a total of 50 interviews, 16 were conducted with Kurds from Turkey, 21 with Kurds from Iraq and 13 with Kurds from Iran. 24 of the interviews were conducted with men and 13 with women, while 13 of the interviews were group interviews with the whole family present, varying from two to nine persons. Thus, a total of about 80 participants were involved in the 50 semi-structured interviews. Of the 28 interviews in Britain, 26 took place in London and two in the Birmingham area. In Finland, nine of the 22 interviews were conducted in the capital area of Helsinki, while 13 were made in three smaller cities. This represents relatively well the proportion of Kurds in the capital area in the two countries. The sample represents a fairly wide spectrum of political orientations, comprising both persons who described themselves as non-political and those who were active supporters of political movements in Kurdistan. These political orientations included support for all the main Kurdish parties as well as some smaller left-wing parties. Although the sample is fairly representative according to some variables relating to the whole population, it still cannot be seen as statistically representative of the Kurdish refugee communities in Finland and England. Furthermore, the sample is of course to an even lesser degree representative of the population in Kurdistan. However, the question as to whether this is a representative sample or not is rather beside the point since this study does not use any statistical methods in order to make statements about any wider community. Instead, this book is concerned with the major social processes involved in the refugee communities, and these processes are best studied by comprehensive case studies.

The interviews were mostly carried out in the homes of the interviewees, but some were also conducted in restaurants, in community centres and other public places. The average length of the interviews was two hours. Twenty of the semi-structured interviews were completed with the help of interpreters, since my knowledge of Kurdish is limited to a few words in Sorani, and I cannot speak any Turkish at all. The interviews in England were conducted in English. In Finland most of the interviews were in Finnish, although a few were also conducted in Swedish or English. The interpreters were found in the course of the fieldwork, mainly through contacts with Kurdish associations. In all cases the interpreter and the interviewee knew each other prior to the fieldwork. In fact, it was usually the interpreter who organized the interview. This arrangement secured a trustful relationship between the interviewee and the interpreter. Almost all semi-structured interviews were tape-recorded. The interviews were later transcribed to an electronically readable form and were analysed with the help of a computer programme for qualitative text analysis (Atlas/ti).

In addition to semi-structured interviews of refugees, a large part of the fieldwork was devoted to a study of Kurdish associations. In an attempt to get a clear picture of the Kurdish communities, all Kurdish organizations in both countries were contacted. A 'Kurdish organization' was defined as one which *explicitly* stated that it worked for Kurds and/or Kurdish issues. Separate interviews were undertaken with either the chairperson or some of the employees of the associations (these interviews are not included in the sample of 50 semi-structured interviews). Information was collected about the Kurdish associations' official aims, the extent and nature of their activities, their funding and details of their membership. I was especially interested in the organizations' work with newly arrived refugees and their opinions about the problems experienced by refugees. The associations' publications in English and Finnish were also studied (journals, annual reports and newsletters). These included the following journals in England: *Hawkar, KCC News, Kurdish Observer, Kurdistan Focus, Kurdistan Human Rights Bulletin, Kurdistan Report* and *Ronahî.* In Finland the publications *Denge Kurd – Kurdien Ääni, Dlanpar* and *Kurdistan Review* were studied.

The method of participant observation was also used during a variety of social occasions, including different Kurdish celebrations, public gatherings and private meetings at various locations. Besides the more commonplace visits to Kurdish associations I participated in five different *Newroz* celebrations, two public demonstrations, one gathering remembering the massacre in Halabja, one '15 August party' celebrating the Kurdish insurrection in Turkey, one seminar celebrating International Women's Day and several more private gatherings. These various events enabled me to meet and converse with a great number of Kurds.

Notes

CHAPTER 1   INCLUSION AND EXCLUSION OF REFUGEES:
RETHINKING CONCEPTS AND THEORIES

1. Social organization is here understood as 'any relatively stable pattern or structure within a society, and the process by which such a structure is created or maintained. As such the term is a highly general one overlapping with such terms as social structure, social order, etc.' (Jary and Jary, 1991: 589).
2. Kunz (1981) argued that, depending on the degree of identification with the homeland, one can distinguish three groups of refugees: 'majority-identified', 'events-alienated' and 'self-alienated persons'. These three groups also have a different attitude to the flight from the homeland, the first two groups are 'reactive fate-groups' while the last group is a 'purpose group'. These groups show different patterns of ideological and national orientation in exile. The refugees who are reactive fate groups might show four different patterns of integration: 'integrated accommodation', alienated 'passive hurt' individuals, persons with a 'hyperactive search for assimilation' and finally persons who in exile feel that they have a 'historic responsibility' to work for their cause and speak up for those silenced at home. The purpose group of refugees may become 'revolutionary activists', as may over time some of the events-alienated refugees. A final category consists of the self-fulfilling purpose groups who might leave more or less voluntarily and become 'founders of utopias'. Unfortunately, Kunz never had the opportunity to elaborate upon this model.
3. Miles (1989) argues that there is reason to use the concept of racism solely to refer to an ideology. Miles (1989, 1993), in his discussions of Barker (1981), does not approve of the use of the concept of new racism. Miles (1989) argues that the concept of new racism defines racism in too broad a way since it cannot identify what is distinctive about racism as an ideology. Furthermore, Miles (1993) points out that it is not clear what the supposed differences are between the vaguely defined new and old racisms. Despite this, Miles admits that 'race' and nation can be 'overlapping categories, each functioning to define the parameters of the other' (1993: 59).
4. The origin of this widely used phrase is unknown, but it seems to have been first mentioned by Troyna and Williams (1986).
5. Smith's approach is, however, more elaborate than the characterization of 'primordialist' would suggest. In actual fact, he accepts that nations are largely social constructions. Although nations have ethnic origins and are historical communities, this history is constantly rewritten and manipulated to meet the demands of nationalism. What matters is not the authenticity of the historical record but the poetic, didactic

and integrative purposes which that record is felt to disclose. Smith explicitly rejects an overtly primordialist and fixed notion of nations and ethnic groups. Instead he proposes an intermediate approach, where it is possible to look situationally at ethnicity, but only within certain limits given by history (Smith, 1986). However, this approach is still in conflict with the notion that nations are imagined (Anderson, 1983) and related to the historical process of modernity (Gellner, 1983). A related problem is that Smith's perspective is difficult to combine with the notion of ethnicity as a relation. According to Smith (1986), ethnicity cannot be a wholly dependent tool or boundary marker of other social and economic forces.

6. The studies of social networks made by another 'Manchester school' anthropologist working in Africa, J. Clyde Mitchell (e.g. 1989), has a resemblance to Mayer's approach to migration. Mitchell's network approach to social relations influenced many later studies of immigrants in Britain (Rogers and Vertovec, 1995) and also the later tradition of social network studies in sociology. The network studies in sociology emphasize structures and the researchers in this tradition often develop detailed models of the structure and functions of particular social networks (Mizruchi, 1994). However, this sociological network approach has not been regarded as useful for this study, which examines the processes involved in social relations rather than the structures. Nevertheless, this study uses the term network, but in the more general way used, for example, by Rex and Josephides (1987). These writers, inspired by Radcliffe-Brown (1952), describe networks as the 'relationships which arise between individuals in the course of meaningful action' (Rex and Josephides, 1987: 14).

CHAPTER 2 POLITICS AND FORCED MIGRATION IN KURDISTAN

1. Estimating the size of the Kurdish population is difficult since there are no official figures. Bruinessen (1992a) estimates that in 1975 the Kurds numbered 13.5 to 15 million persons. Sheikhmous (1994) estimates that the total number of Kurds both in Kurdistan and in the diaspora in 1994 had risen to between 28 and 29 millions.

2. Symptomatic of the cultural persecution of the Kurds in the Middle East is the fact that a large part of all literature published in Kurdish during this century has appeared either in the Soviet Union or, more recently, in the diaspora in Europe. The largely state-sponsored literary activities in Sweden deserve to be especially mentioned (Sheikhmous, 1989).

3. There are also Muslim political organizations, including the Islamic Movement in Iraqi Kurdistan. It is also clear that many Kurds in Turkey are active in Islamic organizations. However, the political importance of explicitly religious parties seemed to be relatively marginal in Kurdish politics in the mid-1990s. Therefore they are not included in this short presentation of Kurdish politics.

4. Ismail Besikci has published several articles and books about the Kurdish question. Because of his publications he has repeatedly been sentenced to imprisonment and his books have been banned and confiscated by the Turkish state.

5. In the 1980s Abdul Rahman Ghassemlou worked as the General Secretary of the Iranian Kurdish Democratic Party. He was assassinated in Vienna on 13 July 1989 during negotiations with Iranian emissaries. It is commonly assumed that the Iranian government was behind the assassination.

6. The term genocide is, of course, a serious accusation and it has a defined meaning in international law (Andreapoulos, 1994). The mass murder of Armenians is, however, commonly described as a genocide (for example, Hovannisian, 1994). During the conflict between Christian and Muslims at the end of the Ottoman Empire both Armenians and Muslims were killed, and some Kurds actively participated in the genocide of the Armenians. According to Chaliand (1994), the Kurdish participation in the conflict was largely made in the name of Muslim solidarity in order to re-create the Ottoman Empire.

7. According to McDowall (1992), this is the number of Alevis referred to in the usual Kurdish definition of Alevis. Some Turkish definitions, however, suggest that there are at least 18 million Alevis in several different countries.

8. According to recent publications, there is good reason to believe that the Iraqi *Anfal* campaign fulfils the legal definition of a genocide. After the introduction of the 'safe haven' in northern Iraq the organization Human Rights Watch has had the opportunity to make an investigation of the *Anfal* campaign. In a case study of the destruction of the village of Koreme the organization is still cautious, and while declaring that the report does not prove genocide, it states: 'Research increasingly leads to the conclusion that the Iraqi government's Anfal campaign amounted to the crime of genocide within the meaning of the genocide convention' and 'certainly the campaign was a crime against humanity within the meaning of customary international law' (Human Rights Watch, 1993a: 2). In another report Human Rights Watch explicitly calls the *Anfal* campaign a genocide and declares that the Kurds 'were systematically put to death in large numbers on the orders of the central government' (Human Rights Watch, 1993b: xiv). The intent of the Iraqi government is also described in the eighteen tons of official documents on the *Anfal* Campaign that were seized by the Kurds and later shipped to the USA (Human Rights Watch, 1994).

9. This was the procedure in Turkey when the refugees in this study left Turkey. Turkey has subsequently aimed to determine the status of refugees without involvement by the UNHCR, which, of course, would be the normal procedure. Amnesty International (1994) is concerned about the fact that Turkey still wishes to retain the geographical limitation of the Refugee Convention. Taking into account the Turkish policy towards its own Kurdish minority, this might be disastrous for Kurdish refugees from Iran and Iraq.

CHAPTER 3   RESETTLEMENT POLICIES: TWO DIFFERENT MODELS

1. In 1994, funding from the London Borough Grants Unit was given to the Kurdish Cultural Centre, Kurdistan Workers' Association and the Kurdish Information Centre (in Islington).
2. In practice it is often the RAP that decides where people will live in London. Refugees are in the first instance expected to stay with relatives or friends after arrival. However, if a refugee does not know anybody, the RAP will send him/her to one of the local authorities in London. In practice refugees are often resettled in boroughs where the RAP case worker assumes that other persons who speak the same language live.
3. The Ministry of Social and Health Affairs has information about the exact number of refugees who have arrived in Finland. Information about migration and citizenship is, however, collected by the Registration Offices. According to Finnish law one is not allowed to compare statistics from these different sources on an individual level. Therefore the exact number of refugees cannot be ascertained.
4. Although the question in the survey was the same in 1989 and 1993, the result is not totally comparable because of the notable change in the number of refugees in the country.
5. The estimation of the number of Kurds living in Finland is based on my own fieldwork and a variety of other sources which are described in detail in my PhD thesis (Wahlbeck, 1997b).
6. The figures are from statistics published in *Pakolaisinfo* and *Monitori*.
7. It should be noted, however, that only a small proportion of the Turkish citizens living in Finland in 1990–2 were officially refugees.

CHAPTER 4   TOWARDS A WIDER UNDERSTANDING OF THE REFUGEE EXPERIENCE

1. It is surprising to hear, for example, that in Finland some persons from Turkey, with residence permits granted on humanitarian grounds, were forced to visit the Turkish Embassy to renew their passports. In Britain I was told that the Home Office has allegedly checked personal details of asylum seekers through contacts with Turkish organizations and authorities. Several interviewees told me stories about hostile and non-professional interpreters. In Britain I heard about a case where the Turkish interpreter, during an interview at the Home Office, did not want to interpret the statement that democracy does not exist in Turkey 'since Turkey is a democratic country'. Similar cases of non-professional and hostile interpreters are described by Reilly (1991) and Collinson (1990). According to the Refugee Council (1996), some Kurdish asylum seekers in Britain have even been interviewed with an interpreter from the Turkish Embassy.
2. The only respondents who did not want to return were two women. One was from Iraq and the other from Iran and they had lived in

Britain for ten and six years respectively. Both were afraid that they would have problems in moving back and adjusting to traditional gender roles in Kurdistan. All other respondents indicated that they wanted to return to Kurdistan as soon as possible. The strong wish to return home to Kurdistan as soon as possible is also found by Black (1995) in his study of newly arrived Kurdish refugees from Iraq living in Greece.

3. In order to gain access to the experiences of the women the interviews usually had to be organized without husbands or other men being present. This is because the men often had a tendency to dominate the conversation. Although I am a man, it usually proved to be possible to organize interviews with women. It may be that my status as an outsider, who could not be regarded as following Kurdish social norms, made it easier for me to get access to interviews with Kurdish women than it would have been for a Kurdish man.

4. This is supported by Shahrzad Mojab (1997), who points out that there is a primacy of the nationalist agenda, rather than of gender issues, among the Kurdish women's organizations in exile.

CHAPTER 5   THE PROCESS OF INTEGRATION

1. Often the Finnish Red Cross programme of 'friend families' for refugees is seen to be unsuccessful since many friendships do not appear to last very long. However, taking into account the fact that these friendships are created in a totally artificial way, any of them that stands the test of time should be regarded as a success.

2. In 1990–2 there were 376 marriages between Finnish female citizens and Turkish male citizens, closely followed by 352 marriages with Moroccan males. Finnish men, on the other hand, seem to prefer women from the former Soviet Union, since 1493 such couples were married in 1990–2 (Nieminen, 1994).

3. Alitolppa-Niitamo (1994) describes similar research findings in her study of Somali refugees in Finland. Her informants regarded unemployment among the refugees and negative attitudes among the Finns as significant factors which reduced the personal contacts between the two groups.

CHAPTER 6   KURDISH ASSOCIATIONS: COMMUNITY WORK AND DIASPORIC POLITICS

1. Some of the material presented in this chapter has been published in the article 'Community Work and Exile Politics: Kurdish Refugee Associations in London'. *Journal of Refugee Studies*, vol. 11, no. 3 (September 1998): 215–30.

2. According to some informants, this has to some extent changed in the 1980s and 1990s. Due to the influence of Iran, religious issues have to an increasing extent become political issues, and there is an active Islamic party in Kurdistan in Iraq.

3. One can perhaps argue that the 'tribal' networks continue to influence the diaspora indirectly, since it might be maintained that some of the political parties in Kurdistan are largely based on traditional 'tribal' loyalties. However, to study the extent to which the political parties in Kurdistan are based on 'tribal' allegiances was totally outside the scope of this research.

4. Although this person implies that the information centre in Helsinki was an organization for PKK supporters this was not the official policy of the organization.

References

Ali, Kâzim (1990) *Kurdish Refugees' Employment Training Needs*. London: Haringey Education Service.

Alitolppa-Niitamo, A. (1994) *Somali Refugees in Helsinki: Focus on Social Networks and the Meaning of Clan Membership*. Helsinki: Ministry of Social Affairs and Health.

Allardt, E. (1994) 'Makrosociala förändringar och politik i dagens Europa' (Macro-social changes and policies in contemporary Europe). *Sosiologia* 31, no. 1: 1–10.

Ålund, A. and C. U. Schierup (1991) *Paradoxes of Multiculturalism*. Aldershot: Avebury.

Amnesty International (1993a) *'Disappearances' and Political Killings: Human Rights Crisis of the 1990s*. London: Amnesty International.

Amnesty International (1993b) *Escalation in Human Rights Abuses against Kurdish Villagers* (EUR 44/64/93). London: Amnesty International.

Amnesty International (1994) *Turkey: Selective Protection. Discriminatory Treatment of Non-European Refuges and Asylum Seekers* (EUR 44/16/94). London: Amnesty International.

Amnesty International (1995a) *Human Rights Abuses in Iraqi Kurdistan since 1991* (MDE 14/01/95). London: Amnesty International.

Amnesty International (1995b) *Iran: Official Secrecy Hides Continuing Repression* (MDE 13/02/95). London: Amnesty International.

Amnesty International (1996) *Slamming the Door: the Demolition of the Right to Asylum in the UK*. London: Amnesty International United Kingdom.

Amnesty International (1997) *Refugees: Human Rights Have No Borders*. London: Amnesty International.

Anderson, B. (1983) *Imagined Communities: Reflections on the Origin and Spread of Nationalism*. London: Verso.

Andreapoulos, G. J. (ed.) (1994) *Genocide: Conceptual and Historical Dimensions*. Philadelphia: University of Pennsylvania Press.

Anthias, F. and N. Yuval-Davis (1992) *Racialized Boundaries: Race, Nation, Gender, Colour and Class and the Anti-Racist Struggle*. London: Routledge.

Appadurai, A. (1990) 'Disjuncture and Difference in the Global Cultural Economy'. In *Global Culture: Nationalism, Globalisation and Modernity*, ed. M. Featherstone, 295–310. London: Sage.

Banks, M. (1996) *Ethnicity: Anthropological Constructions*. London: Routledge.

Barker, M. (1981) *The New Racism*. London: Junction Books.

Barkey, H. J. (1993) 'Turkey's Kurdish Dilemma'. *Survival* 35, no. 4: 51–70.

Barth, F. (1969) 'Introduction'. In *Ethnic Groups and Boundaries*, ed. F. Barth, 9–38. Bergen: Universitetsforlaget.

Basch, L., N. Glick Schiller and C. Szanton Blanc (1994) *Nations Unbound: Transnational Projects, Postcolonial Predicaments and Deterritorialized Nation-States*. Basel: Gordon & Breach.

Bell, D. (1975) 'Ethnicity and Social Change'. In *Ethnicity: Theory and Practice*, ed. N. Glazer and D. P. Moynihan, 141–74. Cambridge, Mass.: Harvard University Press.

'Benefits lure fraudsters' (1996) *Financial Times,* 8 March 1996, p. 10.

Berry, J. W. (1988) 'Acculturation and Psychological Adaptation: a Conceptual Overview'. In *Ethnic Psychology*, ed. J. W. Berry and R. C. Annis, 41–52. Lisse: Swets & Zeitlinger.

Besikci, I. (1991) *Selected Writings: Kurdistan and the Kurds*. London: Kurdistan Solidarity Committee and Kurdistan Information Centre.

Black, R. (1995) 'Political Refugees or Economic Migrants? Kurdish and Assyrian Refugees in Greece'. *Migration* 25, no. 4: 79–109.

Blanc-Szanton, C., N. Glick Schiller and L. Basch (1995) 'Transnationalism, Nation-State and Culture'. *Current Anthropology* 36: 683–6.

Blaschke, J. (1991a) 'Die Diaspora der Kurden in der Bundesrepublic Deutschland'. *Österreichische Zeitschrift für Soziologie* 16: 85–93.

Blaschke, J. (1991b) 'Kurdische Communities in Deutschland und Westeuropa'. In *Kurden im Exil*, 2.1 1–16. Berlin: Edition Parabolis.

Bousquet, G. (1991) *Behind the Bamboo Hedge: the Impact of Homeland Politics in the Parisian Vietnamese Community*. Ann Arbor: University of Michigan Press.

Boz, K. (1995) 'Identity, Ethnicity and Nationalism'. *Ronahî* [Published by Kurdistan Society, Student Union of SOAS, London], no. 3 (March–May 1995): 18–20.

Brah, A. (1996) *Cartographies of Diaspora*. London: Routledge.

Breton, R. (1964) 'Institutional Completeness of Ethnic Communities and the Personal Relations of Immigrants'. *American Journal of Sociology* 70, no. 2: 193–205.

Bruinessen, M. van (1988) 'Between Guerrilla War and Political Murder: the Workers' Party of Kurdistan'. *Middle East Report*, no. 153 (July–August 1988): 40–6.

Bruinessen, M. van (1990) 'Kurdish Society and the Modern State: Ethnic Nationalism versus Nation-Building'. In *Kurdistan In Search of Ethnic Identity*, ed. T. Atabaki and M. Dorleijn, 24–51. Utrecht: Houtsma Foundation Publica.

Bruinessen, M. van (1992a) *Agha, Shaikh and State: the Social and Political Structures of Kurdistan*. London: Zed Books.

Bruinessen, M. van (1992b) 'Kurdish Society, Ethnicity, Nationalism and Refugee Problems'. In *The Kurds: a Contemporary Overview*, ed. P. G. Kreyenbroek and S. Sperl, 33–67. London: Routledge.

Bruinessen, M. van (1994) 'Genocide in Kurdistan?: the Suppression of the Dersim Rebellion in Turkey (1937–38) and the Chemical War against the Iraqi Kurds (1988)'. In *Genocide: Conceptual and Historical Dimensions*, ed. G. J. Andreapoulos, 141–70. Philadelphia: University of Pennsylvania Press.

Bruinessen, M. van (1996) 'Kurds, Turks and the Alevi Revival in Turkey'. *Middle East Report*, no. 200 (July–August 1996): 7–10.

Bulloch, J. and H. Morris (1993) *No Friends but the Mountains: the Tragic History of the Kurds*. London: Penguin Books.

Burgess, R. G. (1984) *In The Field: an Introduction to Field Research*. London: Allen & Unwin.

Candappa, M. and D. Joly (1994) *Local Authorities, Ethnic Minorities and 'Pluralist Integration.'* Coventry: Centre for Research in Ethnic Relations, University of Warwick.

Carey-Wood, J., K. Duke, V. Karn, and T. Marshall (1995) *The Settlement of Refugees in Britain* (Home Office Research Study 141). London: HMSO.

Carmon, N. (ed.) (1996) *Immigration and Integration in Post-Industrial Societies.* London: Macmillan.

Castles, S. and M. J. Miller (1993) *The Age of Migration.* London: Macmillan.

Chaliand, G. (ed.) (1989) *Minority Peoples in the Age of Nation-States.* London: Pluto.

Chaliand, G. (ed.) (1993) *A People Without a Country: the Kurds and Kurdistan* (revised and updated edition). London: Zed Books.

Chaliand, G. (1994) *The Kurdish Tragedy.* London: Zed Books.

Chaliand, G. and J. P. Rageau (1991) *Atlas des Diasporas.* Paris: Éditions Odile Jacob.

Clifford, J. (1988) *The Predicament of Culture: Twentieth-Century Ethnography, Literature and Art.* Cambridge, Mass.: Harvard University Press.

Clifford, J. (1992) 'Traveling Cultures'. In *Cultural Studies,* ed. L. Grossberg, C. Nelson and P. A. Treichler, 96–116. New York: Routledge.

Clifford, J. (1994) 'Diasporas'. *Cultural Anthropology* 9, no. 3: 302–38.

Cohen, Abner (1969) *Custom and Politics in Urban Africa.* London: Routledge & Kegan Paul.

Cohen, Robin (1994) *Frontiers of Identity: the British and the Others.* London: Longman.

Cohen, Robin (1995) 'Rethinking "Babylon": Iconoclastic Conceptions of the Diasporic Experience'. *New Community* 21, no. 1: 5–18.

Cohen, Robin (1996) 'Diasporas and the Nation-State: From Victims to Challengers'. *International Affairs* 72, no. 3: 507–20.

Cohen, Robin (1997) *Global Diasporas: an Introduction.* London: UCL Press.

Cohen, R. and D. Joly (1989) 'Introduction: the "New Refugees" of Europe'. In *Reluctant Hosts: Europe and its Refugees,* ed. D. Joly and R. Cohen, 5–18. Aldershot: Gower.

Collinson, S. (1990) 'The Alevi Kurd Asylum-Seekers: "Refugees" or "Migrants"?' Dissertation for MPhil in International Relations, Cambridge University.

Crisp, J. (1989) 'United Kingdom: Fending for Themselves'. *Refugees* 70 (November 1989): p. 18.

Delle Donne, M. (ed.) (1995) *Avenues to Integration: Refugees in Contemporary Europe.* Napoli: Ipermedium.

Denney, D. (1983) 'Some Dominant Perspectives in the Literature Relating to Multi-Racial Social Work'. *British Journal of Social Work* 13: 149–74.

Donald, J. and A. Rattansi (eds) (1992) *'Race', Culture and Difference.* London: Sage.

Durkheim, E. (1938) *The Division of Labour.* Glencoe, Ill.: Free Press.

ECRE [European Council on Refugees and Exiles] (1994) *Asylum in Europe* (4th edition, Vol. II). London: ECRE.

Ekholm, E. (1994) *Syrjäytyä vai selviytyä: Pakolaisten elämää Suomessa*

(Marginalization or survival: the lives of refugees in Finland). Helsinki: Sosiaali- ja terveysministeriö.

Entessar, N. (1992) *Kurdish Ethnonationalism.* London: Lynne Rienner.

Eriksen, T. H. (1993) *Ethnicity and Nationalism: Anthropological Perspectives.* London: Pluto Press.

ERNK (1995) *The Economic and Human Dimensions of Ten Years of War in Kurdistan.* N.p. (Report available at ERNK Information Centre, Helsinki).

Escalona, A. and R. Black (1995) 'Refugees in Western Europe: Bibliographic Review and State of the Art'. *Journal of Refugee Studies* 8, no. 4: 364–89.

Featherstone, M. (ed.) (1990) *Global Culture: Nationalism, Globalization and Modernity.* London: Sage.

Furnivall, J. S. (1939) *Netherlands India.* Cambridge: Cambridge University Press.

Gellner, E. (1983) *Nations and Nationalism.* Oxford: Blackwell.

Gellner, E. (1994) 'Kemalism'. In *Encounters with Nationalism*, 81–91. Oxford: Blackwell.

Ghassemlou, A. R. (1965) *Kurdistan and the Kurds.* Prague: Publishing House of the Czechoslovak Academy of Sciences.

Ghassemlou, A. R. (1993) 'Kurdistan in Iran'. In *A People Without a Country: the Kurds and Kurdistan* (revised and updated edition), ed. G. Chaliand, 95–121. London: Zed Books.

Gilroy, P. (1987) *There Aint't No Black in the Union Jack.* London: Hutchinson.

Gilroy, P. (1992) 'The End of Antiracism'. In *'Race', Culture and Difference*, ed. J. Donald and A. Rattansi, 49–61. London: Sage.

Glaser, B. and A. Strauss (1967) *The Discovery of Grounded Theory.* New York: Aldine.

Glazer, N. and D. P. Moynihan (1963) *Beyond the Melting Pot.* Cambridge, Mass.: MIT Press.

Glazer, N. and D. P. Moynihan (1975) 'Introduction'. In *Ethnicity: Theory and Experience,* ed. N. Glazer and D. P. Moynihan, 1–28. Cambridge: Harvard University Press.

Glick Schiller, N., L. Basch and C. Blanc-Szanton (eds) (1992) *Towards a Transnational Perspective on Migration.* New York: New York Academy of Science.

Gold, S. (1992) *Refugee Communities: a Comparative Field Study.* Newbury Park, Calif.: Sage.

Goldberg, D. T. (1993) *Racist Culture.* Oxford: Blackwell.

Gordon, M. (1964) *Assimilation in American Life.* New York: Oxford University Press.

Gordon, M. (1978) *Human Nature, Class and Ethnicity.* New York: Oxford University Press.

Goulbourne, H. (1991a) *Ethnicity and Nationalism in Post-Imperial Britain.* Cambridge: Cambridge University Press.

Goulbourne, H. (1991b) 'The Offence of the West Indian: Political Leadership and the Communal Option'. In *Black and Ethnic Leadership in Britain,* ed. P. Werbner and M. Anwar, 296–322. London: Routledge.

Gunter, M. (1990) *The Kurds in Turkey: a Political Dilemma*. Oxford: Westview Press.

Gunter, M. (1992) *The Kurds of Iraq: Tragedy and Hope*. New York: St. Martin's Press.

Gunter, M. (1997) *The Kurds and the Future of Turkey*. London: Macmillan.

Gupta, A. and J. Ferguson (1992) 'Beyond "Culture": Space, Identity, and the Politics of Difference'. *Cultural Anthropology* 7: 6–23.

Hackney Council (1993) *Planning for the Turkish/Kurdish Community in Hackney*. London: Hackney Council, Environmental Services.

HACT [The Housing Associations Charitable Trust] (1994) *Housing Issues Facing Refugee Communities in London*. London: HACT.

Hall, S. (1991) 'The Local and the Global: Globalization and Ethnicity'. In *Culture, Globalization and the World-System*, ed. A. D. King, 19–39. London: Macmillan.

Hall, S. (1993) 'Cultural Identity and Diaspora'. In *Colonial Discourse and Post-Colonial Theory*, ed. P. Williams and L. Chrisman, 392–401. New York: Harvester Wheatsheaf.

Hannerz, U. (1996) *Transnational Connections: Culture, People, Places*. London: Routledge.

Hassanpour, A. (1997) 'MED-TV, Großbritannien und der türkische Staat'. In *Ethnizität, Nationalismus, Religion und Politik in Kurdistan*, ed. C. Borck, E. Savelsberg and S. Hajo, 239–78. Münster: Lit Verlag.

Hassanpour, A. (1998) 'Satellite Footprints as National Borders: MED-TV and the Extraterritoriality of State Sovereignty'. *Journal of Muslim Minority Affairs* 18, no. 1: 53–72.

Hein, J. (1993) 'Refugees, Immigrants, and the State'. *Annual Review of Sociology* 19: 43–59.

Hjarnø, J. (1991) *Kurdiske Invandrere* (Kurdish immigrants). Esbjerg: Sydjysk Universitetsforlag.

Home Office (various years) *Home Office Statistical Bulletin: Asylum Statistics*. London: Home Office, Research and Statistics Department.

Hovannisian, R. G. (1994) 'Etiology and Sequelae of the Armenian Genocide'. In *Genocide: Conceptual and Historical Dimensions*, ed. G. J. Andreapoulos, 111–40. Philadelphia: University of Pennsylvania Press.

Human Rights Watch (1993a) *The Anfal Campaign in Iraqi Kurdistan: The Destruction of Koreme*. New York: Human Rights Watch.

Human Rights Watch (1993b) *Genocide in Iraq: the Anfal Campaign against the Kurds*. New York: Human Rights Watch.

Human Rights Watch (1993c) *The Kurds of Turkey: Killings, Disappearances and Torture*. New York: Human Rights Watch.

Human Rights Watch (1994) *Bureaucracy of Repression: the Iraqi Government in Its Own Words*. New York: Human Rights Watch.

Icduygu, A. (1996) 'Becoming a New Citizen in an Immigration Country: Turks in Australia and Sweden and Some Comparative Implications'. *International Migration* 34, no. 2: 257–72.

Imset, I. (1996) 'Technological Sabotage against Peace'. *Kurdistan Report*, no. 23 (March–May 1996): 35–6.

IOM [International Organization for Migration] (1996) *Transit Migrants in Turkey*. Budapest: IOM.

Jaakkola, M. (1989) *Suomalaisten suhtautuminen ulkomaalaisiin ja ulko-maalaispolitiikkaan* (Finnish attitudes towards foreigners and immigration policy). Helsinki: Työministeriö.

Jaakkola, M. (1995) *Suomalaisten kiristyvät ulkomaalaisasenteet* (Polarization of Finns' attitudes to refugees and other immigrants). Helsinki. Työministeriö.

Jafar, M. R. (1976) *Under-Underdevelopment: a Regional Case Study of the Kurdish Areas in Turkey* (Studies of the Social Policy Association in Finland, no. 24). Helsinki: Painoprint.

Jary, D. and J. Jary (1991) *Collins Dictionary of Sociology*. London: HarperCollins.

JCWI [Joint Council for the Welfare of Immigrants] (1995) *Immigration and Nationality Law Handbook: 1995 Edition*. London: JCWI.

Jenkins, S. (ed.) (1988) *Ethnic Associations and the Welfare State*. New York: Columbia University Press.

Joly, D. (1992) *Refugees: Asylum in Europe?* London: Minority Rights Publications.

Joly, D. (1995a) 'Between Exile and Ethnicity'. Paper presented at the Institute for Global Studies in Culture, Power and History, Johns Hopkins University, Baltimore, Md., 28 November 1995.

Joly, D. (1995b) *Britannia's Crescent: Making a Place for Muslims in British Society*. Aldershot: Avebury.

Joly, D. (1996) *Haven or Hell? Asylum Policies and Refugees in Europe*. London: Macmillan.

Kay, D. (1987) *Chileans in Exile: Private Struggles, Public Lives*. London: Macmillan.

Kearney, M. (1995) 'The Local and the Global: the Anthropology of Globalization and Transnationalism'. *Annual Review of Anthropology* 24: 547–65.

Kendal (1993a) 'Kurdistan in Turkey'. In *A People Without a Country: the Kurds and Kurdistan* (revised and updated edition), ed. G. Chaliand, 38–94. London: Zed Books.

Kendal (1993b) 'The Kurds in the Soviet Union'. In *A People Without a Country: the Kurds and Kurdistan* (revised and updated edition), ed. G. Chaliand, 202–10. London: Zed Books.

Kirisci, K. (1996) 'Is Turkey Lifting the "Geographical Limitation"?' *International Journal of Refugee Law* 8, no. 3: 293–318.

Komala (1984) *The Programme of Komala for the Autonomy of Kurdistan: Adopted by the 4th Conference of the Kurdish Organization of the Communist Party of Iran*. N.p. (Available at Resource Centre, Kurdish Cultural Centre, London).

Koohi-Kamali, F. (1992) 'The Development of Nationalism in Iranian Kurdistan'. In *The Kurds: a Contemporary Overview,* ed. P. G. Kreyenbroek and S. Sperl, 171–92. London: Routledge.

Korkiasaari, J. (1993) *Siirtolais- ja ulkomaalaistilastot* (Statistics of migration and foreigners). Helsinki: Tilastokeskus.

Korkiasaari, J. and I. Söderling (1998) 'Finland: From a Country of Emigration into a Country of Immigration'. In *A Changing Pattern of Migration in Finland and Its Surroundings*, ed. I. Söderling, 7–28. Helsinki: Population Research Institute.

Koser, K. (1997a) 'Negotiating Entry into "Fortress Europe": The Migration Strategies of "Spontaneous" Asylum Seekers'. In *Exclusion and Inclusion of Refugees in Contemporary Europe*, ed. P. Muus, 157–70. Utrecht: ERCOMER.

Koser, K. (1997b) 'Social Networks and the Asylum Cycle: the Case of Iranians in the Netherlands'. *International Migration Review* 31: 591–611.

Kreyenbroek, P. G. (1992) 'On the Kurdish Language'. In *The Kurds: a Contemporary Overview*, ed. P. G. Kreyenbroek and S. Sperl, 68–83. London: Routledge.

Kreyenbroek, P. G. and S. Sperl (eds) (1992) *The Kurds: a Contemporary Overview*. London: Routledge.

Kunz, E. F. (1971) 'Political Events "At Home" and the Concept of Catharsis Naturalization among Refugees'. *International Migration* 9, no. 1–2: 55–67.

Kunz, E. F. (1973) 'The Refugee in Flight: Kinetic Models and Forms of Displacement'. *International Migration Review* 7, no. 2: 125–46.

Kunz, E. F. (1981) 'Exile and Resettlement: Refugee Theory'. *International Migration Review* 15, no. 1: 42–51.

Kurden im Exil (1991) Berlin: Edition Parabolis.

Kurdistan Parliament in Exile (1995) *Kurdistan Parliament in Exile*. Brussels: Kurdistan Parliament in Exile.

Kutschera, C. (1994) 'Mad Dreams of Independence: the Kurds of Turkey and the PKK'. *Middle East Report* 24, no. 189 (July–August 1994): 12–15.

KWA [Kurdistan Workers Association] (1994) *Annual Report 1993–4*. London: KWA.

Laari, O. (1998) 'Immigrants in Finland: Finnish-to-be or Foreigners forever'. In *A Changing Pattern of Migration in Finland and Its Surroundings*, ed. I. Söderling, 29–50. Helsinki: Population Research Institute.

Laizer, S. (1991) *Into Kurdistan: Frontiers Under Fire*. London: Zed Books.

Laizer, S. (1996a) *Martyrs, Traitors and Patriots: Kurdistan after the Gulf War*. London: Zed Books.

Laizer, S. (1996b) 'The Opportunity for the Kurds to Live Freely in their Own Country is Greater Now Than Ever Before'. *Kurdistan Report*, no. 23 (March–May 1996): 45–7.

Lie, J. (1995) 'From International Migration to Transnational Diaspora'. *Contemporary Sociology* 24, no. 4: 303–6.

Liebkind, K. (1993) 'Self-Reported Ethnic Identity, Depression and Anxiety among Young Vietnamese Refugees and their Parents'. *Journal of Refugee Studies* 6, no. 1: 25–39.

Lloyd, C. (1993) 'Research and Policy Issues in a European Perspective'. In *Racism and Migration in Western Europe*, ed. J. Wrench and J. Solomos, 251–63. Oxford: Berg.

Lloyd, C. (1994) 'National Approaches to Immigration and Minority Policies'. In *Ethnic Mobilisation in a Multi-cultural Europe*, ed. J. Rex and B. Drury, 69–77. Aldershot: Avebury.

Luciuk, L. Y. (1986) 'Unintended Consequences in Refugee Resettlement: Post-War Ukrainian Refugee Immigration to Canada'. *International Migration Review* 20, no. 2: 467–82.

Lundberg, S. (1989) *Flyktingskap: Latinamerikansk exil i Sverige och*

Västeuropa (Refugeeship: Latin American exile in Sweden and Western Europe). Lund: Studentlitteratur.

Majka, L. (1991) 'Assessing Refugee Assistance Organizations in the United States and the United Kingdom'. *Journal of Refugee Studies* 4, no. 3: 267–83.

Malik, K. (1996) *The Meaning of Race*. London: Macmillan.

Malkki, L. (1995) 'Refugees and Exile: From "Refugee Studies" to the National Order of Things'. *Annual Review of Anthropology* 24: 495–523.

Marienstras, R. (1989) 'On the Notion of Diaspora'. In *Minority Peoples in the Age of Nation-States*, ed. G. Chaliand, 119–25. London: Pluto.

Mason, D. (1986) 'Introduction: Controversies and Continuities in Race and Ethnic Relations Theory'. In *Theories of Race and Ethnic Relations*, ed. J. Rex and D. Mason, 1–19. Cambridge: Cambridge University Press.

Matinheikki-Kokko, K. (1997) *Challenges of Working in a Cross-Cultural Environment: Principles and Practices of Refugee Resettlement in Finland*. Jyväskylä: University of Jyväskylä.

Mayer, P. (1962) 'Migrancy and the Study of Africans in Towns'. *American Anthropologist* 64: 576–92.

McDowall, D. (1992) *The Kurds: a Nation Denied*. London: Minority Rights Publications.

McDowall, D. (1996) *A Modern History of the Kurds*. London: I. B. Tauris.

McDowell, C. (1996) *A Tamil Asylum Diaspora*. Oxford: Berghahn.

McRae, K. D. (1997) *Conflict and Compromise in Multilingual Societies: Finland*. Waterloo, Canada: Wilfrid Laurier Press.

Melotti, U. (1997) 'International Migration in Europe: Social Projects and Political Cultures'. In *The Politics of Multiculturalism in the New Europe*, ed. T. Modood and P. Werbner, 73–92. London: Zed Books.

Miles, R. (1989) *Racism*. London: Routledge.

Miles, R. (1993) *Racism after 'Race Relations'*. London: Routledge.

Miles R. and P. Cleary (1993) 'Migration to Britain: Racism, State Regulation and Employment'. In *The International Refugee Crisis*, ed. V. Robinson, 57–75. London: Macmillan.

Mitchell, J. C. (1989) 'The Causes of Labour Migration'. In *Forced Labour and Migration*, ed. A. Zegeye and S. Ishemo, 28–54. London: Hans Zell.

Mizruchi, M. (1994) 'Social Network Analysis: Recent Achievements and Current Controversies'. *Acta Sociologica* 37, no. 4: 329–43.

Mojab, S. (1997) 'Crossing the Boundaries of Nationalism: the Struggle for a Kurdish Women's Studies'. *Canadian Woman Studies* 17, no. 2: 68–72.

Monitori (various years) (Journal published by the Ministry of Social Affairs and Health, Office for Refugees, Helsinki, Finland).

Morad, M. (1992) 'The Situation of Kurds in Iraq and Turkey: Current Trends and Prospects'. In *The Kurds: a Contemporary Overview*, ed. P. G. Kreyenbroek and S. Sperl, 115–33. London: Routledge.

Nerweyi, F. (1991) *Kurdit* (The Kurds). Helsinki: Sosiaali-ja Terveyshallitus.

Nieminen, M. (1994) *Ulkomaalaiset Suomessa* (Foreigners in Finland). Helsinki: Tilastokeskus.

Öcalan, A. (1992) *Interviews and Speeches*. London: KSC-KIC Publications.

Ofteringer, R. and R. Bäcker (1994) 'A Republic of Statelessness'. *Middle East Report* 24, no. 179 (March–June 1994): 40–5.

Olson, R. (ed.) (1996) *The Kurdish Nationalist Movement in the 1990s: Its Impact on Turkey and the Middle East*. Lexington, Ky.: University Press of Kentucky.

Omi, M. and H. Winant (1994) *Racial Formation in the United States* (2nd edition). New York: Routledge. (First published in 1986.)

Ong, A. and D. Nonini (1997) 'Toward a Cultural Politics of Diaspora and Transnationalism'. In *Ungrounded Empires: the Cultural Politics of Modern Chinese Transnationalism*, ed. A. Ong and D. Nonini, 323–32. London: Routledge.

OPCS [Office of Population Censuses and Surveys] (1994) *International Migration: Migrants Entering or Leaving the United Kingdom and England and Wales 1993*. London: HMSO.

Owen, D. (1994) 'Spatial Variations in Ethnic Minority Group Populations in Great Britain'. *Population Trends* 78 (Winter 1994): 23–33.

Pakolaisinfo (various years) (Journal published by the Ministry of Social Affairs and Health, Office for Refugees, Helsinki, Finland).

Park, R. E. (1950) *Race and Culture*. Glencoe, Ill.: Free Press.

Park, R. E. and E. W. Burgess (1930) *Introduction to the Science of Sociology* (2nd revised edition). Chicago, Ill.: University of Chicago Press. (First published in 1921.)

Parliamentary Human Rights Group (1993) *A Desolation Called Peace*. London: Kurdistan Information Centre.

Pentikäinen, J. and M. Hiltunen (eds) (1995) *Cultural Minorities in Finland*. Helsinki: Finnish National Commission for Unesco.

Phillips, A. (1989) 'Employment as a Key to Settlement'. In *Reluctant Hosts: Europe and its Refugees*, ed. D. Joly and R. Cohen, 133–44. Aldershot: Avebury.

Pitkänen, M. and A. Jaakkola (eds) (1997) *Ingrians in Municipalities*. Helsinki: Association of Finnish Local Authorities.

Radcliffe-Brown, A. R. (1952) *Structure and Function in Primitive Society*. London: Cohen & West.

RAP [Refugee Arrivals Project] (1994) *Annual Report 1993*. Hounslow: Refugee Arrivals Project.

al-Rasheed, M. (1992) 'Political Migration and Downward Socio-Economic Mobility: The Iraqi Community in London'. *New Community* 18: 537–50.

al-Rasheed, M. (1994) 'The Myth of Return: Iraqi Arab and Assyrian Refugees in London'. *Journal of Refugee Studies* 7: 199–219.

Refugee Council (1993) *Kurds: Turkish Kurdish Refugees in the UK/Kurds in Turkey* (Refugee Council factsheet). London: Refugee Council.

Refugee Council (1994) *Detention of Asylum Seekers in the UK* (Refugee Council factsheet). London: Refugee Council.

Refugee Council (1996) 'A Right to be Understood'. *Exile*, January/February 1996: p. 2.

Reilly, R. (1991) 'Political Identity, Protest and Power amongst Kurdish Refugees in Britain'. MA thesis at Churchill College, University of Cambridge, Cambridge.

Rex, J. (1986a) *Race and Ethnicity*. Milton Keynes: Open University Press.

Rex, J. (1986b) 'The Role of Class Analysis in the Study of Race Relations: a Weberian Perspective'. In *Theories of Race and Ethnic Relations* ed. J. Rex and D. Mason, 64–83. Cambridge: Cambridge University Press.

Rex, J. (1994) 'Ethnic Mobilization in Multi-Cultural Societies'. In *Ethnic Mobilization in a Multi-cultural Europe*, ed. J. Rex and B. Drury, 3–12. Aldershot: Avebury.

Rex, J. (1996) *Ethnic Minorities in the Modern Nation State*. London: Macmillan.

Rex, J., D. Joly and C. Wilpert (eds) (1987) *Immigrant Associations in Europe*. Aldershot: Gower.

Rex, J. and S. Josephides (1987) 'Asian and Greek Cypriot Associations and Identity'. In *Immigrant Associations in Europe*, ed. J. Rex, D. Joly and C. Wilpert, 11–41. Aldershot: Gower.

Rex, J. and S. Tomlinson (1979) *Colonial Immigrants in a British City*. London: Routledge & Kegan Paul.

Richmond, A. H. (1988) 'Sociological Theories of International Migration: The Case of Refugees'. *Current Sociology* 36, no. 2: 7–25.

Richmond, A. H. (1993) 'Reactive Migration: Sociological Perspectives on Refugee Movements'. *Journal of Refugee Studies* 6, no. 1: 7–24.

Richmond, A. H. (1994) *Global Apartheid*, Toronto: Oxford University Press.

Robertson, R. (1995) 'Glocalization: Time-Space and Homogeneity-Heterogeneity'. In *Global Modernities*, ed. M. Featherstone, S. Lash and R. Robertson, 25–44. London: Sage.

Robins, P. (1996) 'More Apparent Than Real? The Impact of the Kurdish Issue on Euro-Turkish Relations'. In *The Kurdish Nationalist Movement in the 1990s*, ed. R. Olsen, 114–32. Lexington, Ky: University Press of Kentucky.

Robinson, V. (1993) 'The Nature of the Crisis and the Academic Response'. In *The International Refugee Crisis*, ed. V. Robinson, 3–13. London: Macmillan.

Rogers, A. and S. Vertovec (eds) (1995) *The Urban Context: Ethnicity, Social Networks and Situational Analysis*. Oxford: Berg.

Rugman, J. and R. Hutchings (1996) *Atatürk's Children: Turkey and the Kurds*. London: Cassell.

Rushdie, S. (1991) 'Imaginary Homelands'. In *Imaginary Homelands*, 9–21. New York: Vikas.

Safran, W. (1991) 'Diasporas in Modern Societies: Myths of Homeland and Return'. *Diaspora* 1, no. 1: 83–99.

Said, E. (1990) 'Reflections on Exile'. In *Out There: Marginalization and Contemporary Cultures*, ed. R. Ferguson, et al., 357–66. Cambridge, Mass.: MIT Press.

Salinas, M., D. Pritchard and A. Kibedi (1987) *Refugee-based Organizations: Their Function and Importance for the Refugee in Britain* (Refugee Issues, Working Papers on Refugees, vol. 3, no. 4). Oxford and London: Refugee Studies Programme and British Refugee Council.

Samad, Y. (1997) 'The Plural Guises of Multiculturalism: Conceptualizing a Fragmented Paradigm'. In *The Politics of Multiculturalism in the New Europe*, ed. T. Modood and P. Werbner, 240–60. London: Zed Books.

Schatzman, L. and A. L. Strauss (1973) *Field Research: Strategies for a Natural Sociology*. Englewood Cliffs, NJ: Prentice Hall.

Schierup, C. U. (1985) 'From "Assimilation" to "Pluralism": Perspectives on the Integration of Immigrants'. *Folk* 27: 147–56.

Schierup, C. U. (1987) 'Integration och invandrarpolitiska ideologier' (Integration and ideologies of immigration policies). *Sociologisk Forskning* 24, no. 2: 5–24.

Schierup, C. U. (1992) 'What "Agency" Should we be Multi about? The Multicultural Agenda Reviewed'. *European Journal of Intercultural Studies* 2, no. 3: 5–23.

Schierup, C. U. (1994) 'Multi-Culturalism and Ethnic Mobilization: Some Theoretical Considerations'. In *Ethnic Mobilization in a Multi-cultural Europe*, ed. J. Rex and B. Drury, 38–47. Aldershot: Avebury.

Schierup, C. U. and A. Ålund (1986) *Will They Still be Dancing? Integration and Ethnic Transformation among Yugoslav Immigrants in Scandinavia.* Stockholm: Almqvist & Wiksell.

Segal, A. (1993) *An Atlas of International Migration*. London: Hans Zell.

Senol, S. (1992) *Kurden In Deutschland: Fremde unter Fremden*. Frankfurt am Main: Haag und Herchen.

Shain, Y. (1995) 'Ethnic Diasporas and U.S. Foreign Policy'. *Political Science Quarterly* 109, no. 5: 811–41.

Sheffer, G. (1986) 'A New Field of Study: Modern Diasporas in International Politics'. In *Modern Diasporas in International Politics*, ed. G. Sheffer, 1–15. London: Croom Helm.

Sheffer, G. (1995) 'The Emergence of New Ethno-National Diasporas'. *Migration*, no. 28/95 (1995–2): 5–28.

Sheikhmous, O. (1989) 'Kurdish Cultural and Political Activities Abroad'. Paper presented at the 'Kurdistan Week' arranged by the 'Haus Der Kulturen Der Welt' in West Berlin, 17–22 December 1989.

Sheikhmous, O. (1990) 'The Kurds in Exile'. In *Yearbook of the Kurdish Academy*, ed. K. Fuad, F. Ibrahim and N. Mahvi, 88–114. Ratingen: Kurdish Academy.

Sheikhmous, O. (1994) 'The Estimated Number of Kurds in Kurdistan and in the Diaspora'. (Unpublished document available at CEIFO, Stockholm University, Stockholm).

Sheikhmous, O. (1995) Personal communication. CEIFO, Stockholm University, Stockholm, 12 August 1995.

Sherzad, A. (1992) 'The Kurdish Movement in Iraq: 1975–88'. In *The Kurds: a Contemporary Overview*, ed. P. G. Kreyenbroek and S. Sperl, 134–42. London: Routledge.

Smith, Anthony (1981) *The Ethnic Revival in the Modern World*. Cambridge: Cambridge University Press.

Smith, Anthony (1983) *Theories of Nationalism* (2nd edition). London: Duckworth.

Smith, Anthony (1986) *The Ethnic Origins of Nations*. Oxford: Blackwell.

Smith, M. G. (1965) *The Plural Society in the British West Indies*. Berkeley: University of California Press.

Songur, W. (1992) *Att åldras i främmande land* (To grow old in a foreign country). Stockholm: Stockholms Socialtjänst.

Srinivasan, S. (1995) 'An Overview of Research into Refugee Groups in Britain during the 1900s'. In *Avenues to Integration*, ed. M. Delle Donne, 248–69. Napoli: Ipermedium.

Statistics Finland (various years) *Statistical Yearbook of Finland*. Helsinki: Tilastokeskus.

Steen, A. B. (1992) 'Varieties of the Refugee Experience: Studying Sri Lankan Tamils in Denmark and England'. PhD diss., Institute of Anthropology, University of Copenhagen.

Stein, B. (1981a) 'The Refugee Experience: Defining the Parameters of a Field of Study'. *International Migration Review* 15, no. 1: 320–30.

Stein, B. (1981b) 'Refugee Research Bibliography'. *International Migration Review* 15, no. 1: 331–93.

Söderling, I. (1993) 'Social Work with Refugees in a Nordic Welfare State'. *Migration*, no. 18/93 (1993–2): 171–88.

Söderling, I. (1997) *Maahanmuuttoasenteet ja elämänhallinta* (Attitudes to immigration and life control). Helsinki: Population Research Institute.

Thomas, W. I. and F. Znaniecki (1958) *The Polish Peasant in Europe and America* (2nd revised edition). New York: Dover (first published 1918–20).

Tilly, C. (1990) 'Transplanted Networks'. In *Immigration Reconsidered: History, Sociology and Politics*, ed. V. Yans-McLaughlin, 79–95. New York: Oxford University Press.

Tölölyan, K. (1991) 'The Nation State and its Others: In Lieu of a Preface'. *Diaspora* 1, no. 1: 3–7.

Tölölyan, K. (1996) 'Rethinking *Diaspora*(s): Stateless Power in the Transnational Moment'. *Diaspora* 5, no. 1: 3–36.

Tönnies, F. (1970) *Gemeinschaft und Gesellschaft* (2nd edition). Darmstadt: Wissenschaftliche Buchgesellschaft.

Troyna, B. and J. Williams (1986) *Racism, Education and the State*. London: Croom Helm.

UNHCR (1992) *UNHCR Report on Northern Iraq: April 1991–May 1992*. Geneva: UNHCR.

UNHCR (1993) *The State of the World's Refugees*. New York: Penguin Books.

UNHCR (1997) 'UNHCR and Refugees'. Available from http://www.unhcr.ch/un&ref/un&ref.htm; accessed 16 February 1997.

United Nations (1954) 'Convention Relating to the Status of Refugees'. *Treaty Series* 189: 150–84.

United Nations (1995) *Multilateral Treaties Deposited with the Secretary-General: Status as at 31 December 1994* (E.95.V.5)(ST/LEG/SER.E/13). New York: United Nations.

Valtonen, K. (1997) *The Societal Participation of Refugees and Immigrants*. Turku: Institute of Migration.

Valtonen, K. (1998) 'Resettlement of Middle Eastern Refugees in Finland: the Elusiveness of Integration'. *Journal of Refugee Studies* 11: 38–60.

Vanly, I. S. (1993) 'Kurdistan in Iraq'. In *A People Without a Country: the Kurds and Kurdistan* (revised and updated edition), ed. G. Chaliand, 139–93. London: Zed Books.

Vasquez, A. (1989) 'The Process of Transculturation: Exiles and Institutions in France'. In *Reluctant Hosts: Europe and its Refugees*, ed. D. Joly and R. Cohen, 125–32. Aldershot: Avebury.

Vertovec, S. (1996) 'Multiculturalism, Culturalism and Public Incorporation'. *Ethnic and Racial Studies* 19, no. 1: 49–69.

Wahlbeck, Ö. (1992) *Kvalitativ samhällsforskning om flyktingmottagning* (Qualitative social research on refugee reception). Vasa: Åbo Akademi.

Wahlbeck, Ö. (1996) 'Diasporic Relations and Social Exclusion: the Case of Kurdish Refugees in Finland'. *Siirtolaisuus-Migration* 23, no. 4: 7–15.

Wahlbeck, Ö. (1997a) 'The Kurdish Diaspora and Refugee Associations in Finland and England'. In *Exclusion and Inclusion of Refugees in Contemporary Europe*, ed. P. Muus, 171–86. Utrecht: ERCOMER.

Wahlbeck, Ö. (1997b) 'Kurdish Refugee Communities: the Diaspora in Finland and England'. PhD diss., Centre for Research in Ethnic Relations, University of Warwick.

Wallman, S. (1986) 'Ethnicity and the Boundary Process in Context'. In *Theories of Race and Ethnic Relations*, ed. J. Rex and D. Mason, 226–45. Cambridge: Cambridge University Press.

Waters, M. (1995) *Globalization*. London: Routledge.

Weiner, M. (1996) 'Determinants of Immigrant Integration: an International Comparative Analysis'. In *Immigration and Integration in Post-Industrial Societies*, ed. N. Carmon, 46–62. London: Macmillan.

Werbner, P. (1991) 'The Fiction of Unity in Ethnic Politics'. In *Black and Ethnic Leadership in Britain*, ed. P. Werbner and M. Anwar, 113–45. London: Routledge.

Wrench, J. and J. Solomos (1993) 'The Politics and Processes of Racial Discrimination in Britain'. In *Racism and Migration in Western Europe*, ed. J. Wrench and J. Solomos, 157–76. Oxford: Berg.

WUS [World University Service] (1991) 'Report: Kurdish Refugees in Britain: Language of Freedom'. *WUS NEWS*, November 1991: pp. 5–8.

Yinger, J. M. (1985) 'Ethnicity'. *Annual Review of Sociology* 11: 151–80.

Zolberg, A., A. Suhrke and S. Aguayo (1989) *Escape from Violence*. New York: Oxford University Press.

Index